Social Capital in Eastern Europe

Katarzyna Lasinska

Social Capital in Eastern Europe

Poland an Exception?

Springer VS

Katarzyna Lasinska
Mannheim, Germany

Based on dissertation at University of Mannheim, defended in November 2011.

ISBN 978-3-658-00522-1   ISBN 978-3-658-00523-8 (eBook)
DOI 10.1007/978-3-658-00523-8

The Deutsche Nationalbibliothek lists this publication in the Deutsche Nationalbibliografie; detailed bibliographic data are available in the Internet at http://dnb.d-nb.de.

Library of Congress Control Number: 2012955745

Springer VS
© Springer Fachmedien Wiesbaden 2013
This work is subject to copyright. All rights are reserved by the Publisher, whether the whole or part of the material is concerned, specifically the rights of translation, reprinting, reuse of illustrations, recitation, broadcasting, reproduction on microfilms or in any other physical way, and transmission or information storage and retrieval, electronic adaptation, computer software, or by similar or dissimilar methodology now known or hereafter developed. Exempted from this legal reservation are brief excerpts in connection with reviews or scholarly analysis or material supplied specifically for the purpose of being entered and executed on a computer system, for exclusive use by the purchaser of the work. Duplication of this publication or parts thereof is permitted only under the provisions of the Copyright Law of the Publisher's location, in its current version, and permission for use must always be obtained from Springer. Permissions for use may be obtained through RightsLink at the Copyright Clearance Center. Violations are liable to prosecution under the respective Copyright Law.
The use of general descriptive names, registered names, trademarks, service marks, etc. in this publication does not imply, even in the absence of a specific statement, that such names are exempt from the relevant protective laws and regulations and therefore free for general use. While the advice and information in this book are believed to be true and accurate at the date of publication, neither the authors nor the editors nor the publisher can accept any legal responsibility for any errors or omissions that may be made. The publisher makes no warranty, express or implied, with respect to the material contained herein.

Printed on acid-free paper

Springer VS is a brand of Springer DE.
Springer DE is part of Springer Science+Business Media.
www.springer-vs.de

Preface

The book you have in your hands is a slightly revised version of my dissertation manuscript that was submitted at the University of Mannheim (Germany) in September 2011. The thesis was defended on 9 November 2011 in front of a PhD board including Professors Dr. Jan van Deth, Dr. Rüdiger Schmitt-Beck and Dr. Sigrid Roßteutscher. I would like to thank the board members for an interesting discussion and their critical questions on my project, and the public for the warm moral support.

The general question I ask in this book (What makes Polish society special and why?) is not only of a scientific nature; it is partly a personal question, too. When living in another country you start to perceive your compatriots from a distance, and this perspective highlights the differences between the culture you come from and the one you live in. This is a subjective perspective, of course, and you can never be sure how much of your cultural heritage stays with you when you live abroad. These subjective observations were the starting point for the scientific study presented in this book. During long hours of commuting between Saarbrücken, where I lived, and Mannheim, where I worked at the university, I often caught myself revising my subjective perspective based on the study's objective findings. Since the project is finished, I have a kind of satisfactory "peace of mind." I hope the readers will find the subject intriguing, too, since it revises some of the stereotypes concerning Polish people, post-communist societies in transformation and cultural Catholic heritage.

This book would not have seen daylight without the help of two people in particular. The first is my supervisor and mentor Professor Dr. Jan van Deth. I would like to thank him for his continuing support and patience; he believed in the success of my project from the very beginning, despite the fact that I initially lacked experience in applied research. It was an honour for me to get his undivided attention answering numerous professional questions, structuring the chaotic shower of ideas and encouraging me to go beyond the borders. I would also like to thank a number of colleagues from the Chair for Political Science and International Comparative Social Research in University of Mannheim. In the initial phase of the project, Dr. Julia Rathke helped me obtain the *Schlieben-Lange Programm* scholarship for female PhD students striving to combine family and a scientific career. Thanks to this financial support, I was able to unfold my wings and profit from the department's scientifically fruitful and friendly atmosphere while working on my project. I also thank my colleagues Dr. Martin Elff, Dr. Simone Abendschön and Dr. Marcus Tausendpfund for their critical input when developing my research plan and for the intensive discussions on the preliminary research results during our departmental meetings. I would also like to thank Christian Schnaudt and Dr. Gema García Albacete for their moral and professional support in the final phase of the writing and preparation for the defence; your sense of humour, as well as your encouragement and friendship, helped me accomplish the project. Last but not least, I would like to thank the students working in the department: Sarah Odrakiewicz, for her devoted and enthusiastic engagement in research, and Jasmina Islamovic, for her accuracy and dedication when processing the research data. I am also grateful for backing and understanding from colleagues Andrijana Preuss and Dr. Ellen Quintelier, and many others I met at the European Consortium for Political Research Conference in Lisbon and during my regular work at the University of Mannheim.

The second person who seriously contributed to the appearance of this book is my husband Marcin, who encouraged me to re-enter the scientific career path. Not to mention his emotional and intellectual support over all the years of working on this project, sharing with me periods of frustration and doubt, as well as moments of euphoria and satisfaction. His tolerance of stackes of books, papers and sheets spread throughout a room we converted into an office was quite impressive. I would also like to thank my son Ivo for being understanding not only of my mental absence at times, but also of the closed doors to my office when I was working under time pressure. Last but not least I would like to thank my parents, especially my mother, for keeping my spirits high and for helping whenever it was possible, including financial support for publishing this book. I thank you for believing in me and for all you have given me in life.

Katarzyna Lasinska
Mannheim, October 2012

Table of content

Preface 5
Table of content 7
List of Figures 11
List of Tables 15
1   Exploring social capital in Poland 19
    1.1   Introduction 19
    1.2   Poland – the 'Southern Italy' of Eastern Europe? 20
        1.2.1   Relevance of civic legacies 20
        1.2.2   Lack of civic legacies in Poland; similarities to Southern
                Italy 21
        1.2.3   Contradictions 22
    1.3   Research goal, method and research questions 24
        1.3.1   Communism 25
        1.3.2   Systemic transition 26
        1.3.3   Catholicism 26
    1.4   Study design 27
        1.4.1   Research strategy 27
        1.4.2   Data sources 29
    1.5   Plan of the book 30
2   Social capital – conceptual framework and empirical
    findings 33
    2.1   Introduction 33
    2.2   Social capital: functions and definition 33
        2.2.1   Components of social capital 35
        2.2.2   Double nature of social capital 40
        2.2.3   Social capital as a single construct? 41
    2.3   Why is social capital an important resource for Central
            Eastern Europe? 42
        2.3.1   Social capital and democracy 42
        2.3.2   Social capital destroyed by communism? 43
    2.4   Social capital in Central Eastern Europe: operationalisation
            and distribution 44
        2.4.1   Social networks 45
        2.4.2   Social trust 52

		2.4.3	Norms and values	54
	2.5		Conclusions: is Polish society exceptionally weak endowed with social capital?	60
3	**Communist legacy and systemic transition**			**63**
	3.1		Time perspective	63
	3.2		Before the collapse of communism – similarities across countries	64
		3.2.1	Social networks	64
		3.2.2	Social trust	69
		3.2.3	Norms and values	70
	3.3		Before the collapse of communism – dissimilarities	73
		3.3.1	Frequent protest action in Poland	74
		3.3.2	Relative pluralism and autonomy in Poland	77
		3.3.3	Why was "Solidarność" ephemeral?	79
		3.3.4	The Catholic Church's support of the opposition	80
		3.3.5	Strong family ties and traditional values	81
	3.4		Conclusions – conditions before the collapse of communism	83
	3.5		After the collapse of communism – similarities and dissimilarities	83
		3.5.1	Persistence of behavioural and attitudinal patterns	84
		3.5.2	Negative effects of transition	85
	3.6		Conclusions – is the communist legacy and systemic transition different in Poland?	96
4	**Catholicism and social capital**			**99**
	4.1		Introduction	99
	4.2		Why does religion matter for social capital endowment?	99
		4.2.1	Exploring "denomination effects"	100
		4.2.2	Exploring "affiliation effects"	113
	4.3		Conclusions	118
5	**Catholicism and social capital in Poland in a comparative perspective – empirical evidence**			**121**
	5.1		Introduction	121
	5.2		"Denomination effects" across Catholic societies	122
		5.2.1	The concept of "Religiously Rooted Conservatism"	122
		5.2.2	Religiously Rooted Conservatism and social capital	135
		5.2.3	"Denomination effects" – concluding remarks	152
	5.3		"Affiliation effects" in Central Eastern Europe	152
		5.3.1	Church affiliation and social capital	153
		5.3.2	"Affiliation effects" – concluding remarks	181

	5.4	The impact of religion on social capital in Poland – conclusions	182
6		**Is social capital building different in Poland?**	**187**
	6.1	Introduction	187
	6.2	A comprehensive picture of social capital building in Poland	187
		6.2.1 Reference group	188
		6.2.2 Explaining social capital	188
	6.3	Research strategy	197
	6.4	Exploring determinants of Polish social capital	199
		6.4.1 Social networks	199
		6.4.2 Trust	220
		6.4.3 Norms and values	225
	6.5	Different mechanisms of social capital building in Poland: conclusions	232
7		**Why is Poland an exception among post-communist societies?**	**237**
	7.1	Introduction	237
	7.2	Main findings	237
		7.2.1 Crucial factors	237
		7.2.2 Dissimilar conditions or mechanisms?	241
	7.3	Implications for the future	243
		7.3.1 Future development of social capital in Poland	243
		7.3.2 Implications for further research	247
References			**249**

List of Figures

Figure 1.1	How can Polish exceptionality be explained?	28
Figure 2.1	Membership in European countries (percentages)	47
Figure 2.2	Volunteering in European countries (percentages)	48
Figure 2.3	Informal networks in European countries (percentages)	50
Figure 2.4	Generalised trust across European countries (percentages)	53
Figure 2.5	Norms of civil behaviour in European countries (mean index scores)	56
Figure 2.6	Norms of social behaviour in European countries (mean index scores)	59
Figure 3.1	Infant mortality rates in Europe 1955-1990 (deaths per 1,000 live births; weighted averages for groups of Eastern and Western European countries)	76
Figure 3.2	GDP growth per capita in Europe 1990-2007, PPP (annual growth rates in percentages; weighted averages for groups of Eastern and Western European countries)	87
Figure 3.3	Income inequalities in Europe 1988-2005 (GINI coefficient for income in Eastern European countries; weighted average for groups of Western European countries)	89
Figure 3.4	Unemployment in Europe 1992-2007 (annual unemployment rates in percentage of total labour force; weighted averages for groups of Eastern and Western European countries)	90
Figure 4.1	Membership in religious organisations in European countries (percentages)	106
Figure 5.1	Support for a traditional concept of family (mean factor scores by country; rescaled – TCFI takes values from 0 to 1)	127
Figure 5.2	Relevance of religion (mean factor scores by country; rescaled – RRI takes values from 0 to 1)	129
Figure 5.3	Morality (mean factor scores by country; rescaled – MI takes values from 0 to 1)	131
Figure 5.4	Religiously Rooted Conservatism (mean factor scores by country; rescaled – RRCI takes values from 0 to 1)	133
Figure 5.5	Membership and conservatism (aggregate levels)	136

Figure 5.6	Volunteering and conservatism (aggregate levels)	138
Figure 5.7	Informal networks and conservatism (aggregate levels)	139
Figure 5.8	Membership across the most and the least conservative people (percentages)	140
Figure 5.9	Volunteering among the most and least conservative people (percentages)	142
Figure 5.10	Informal networks among the most and the least conservative people (percentages)	143
Figure 5.11	Trust and conservatism (aggregate levels)	145
Figure 5.12	Trust among the most and least conservative people (percentages)	146
Figure 5.13	Norms of civil behaviour (NCB) and conservatism (aggregate levels)	148
Figure 5.14	Norms of social behaviour (NSB) and conservatism (aggregate levels)	149
Figure 5.15	NCB among the most and least conservative people (mean values)	150
Figure 5.16	NSB among the most and least conservative people (mean values)	151
Figure 5.17	Frequency of church attendance in Central Eastern Europe (percentages)	155
Figure 5.18	Membership and volunteering in religious organisations in Central Eastern Europe (percentages)	156
Figure 5.19	Membership in religious organisations and churchgoing (aggregate levels)	157
Figure 5.20	Volunteering in religious organisations and churchgoing (aggregate levels)	158
Figure 5.21	Membership in religious organisations and church attendance (percentage of members by type of churchgoers)	159
Figure 5.22	Volunteering in religious organisations and church attendance (percentage of volunteers by type of churchgoers)	160
Figure 5.23	Membership in non-religious organisations and churchgoing (aggregate levels)	162
Figure 5.24	Volunteering in non-religious organisations and churchgoing (aggregate levels)	163
Figure 5.25	Membership in non-religious organisations and church attendance (percentage of members in at least one non-religious organisation by type of churchgoers)	164
Figure 5.26	Membership in the four most popular types of organisations in Central Eastern European countries (percentages)	165

Figure 5.27	Non-religious involvement of members and non-members of religious organisations (percent of members in at least one non-religious organisation from two groups – members and non-members of religious organisations)	167
Figure 5.28	Informal networks and churchgoing (aggregate levels)	169
Figure 5.29	Informal networks and church attendance (percentage of people meeting with friends by type of churchgoers)	170
Figure 5.30	Social trust and churchgoing (aggregate levels)	173
Figure 5.31	Social trust by frequency of churchgoing (percentage of trusting people by type of churchgoers)	174
Figure 5.32	Norms of civil behaviour (NCB) and churchgoing (aggregate levels)	176
Figure 5.33	Norms of social behaviour (NSB) and churchgoing (aggregate levels)	177
Figure 5.34	Norms of civil behaviour (NCB) by frequency of churchgoing (mean value of NCB Index by type of churchgoers by country)	178
Figure 5.35	Norms of social behaviour (NSB) by frequency of churchgoing (mean value of NSB-Index by type of churchgoers by country)	180
Figure 6.1	Subjective state of unhappiness (percentage of people reporting being "not very happy" or "not at all happy")	191
Figure 6.2	Concern about the living conditions of the immediate family (percentage of people being "very much," "much," or "to a certain extent" concerned)	192
Figure 6.3	Taking part in protest activities (percentage of people attending a protest action)	193

List of Tables

Table 2.1	Membership by groups of countries (weighted average percentage by country group)	47
Table 2.2	Volunteering by groups of countries (weighted average percentage by country group)	49
Table 2.3	Informal networks by groups of countries (weighted average percentage by country group)	51
Table 2.4	Generalised trust by groups of countries (weighted average percentage by country group)	53
Table 2.5	Extraction of a one-dimensional indicator for "norms of civil behaviour" (factor loadings)	56
Table 2.6	Norms of civil behaviour by groups of countries (weighted average value of NCBI by country group)	57
Table 2.7	Extraction of a one-dimensional indicator for "norms of social behaviour" (factor loadings)	58
Table 2.8	Norms of social behaviour by groups of countries (weighted average value of NSBI by country group)	59
Table 2.9	Indicators for social capital, weighted averages across groups of European countries	61
Table 3.1	Annual inflation rates in 1992-2008 in Bulgaria, Czech Republic, Hungary, Latvia, Lithuania, Poland, Romania, Slovakia and Slovenia; and weighted averages of annual inflation rates for group of Western European countries	91
Table 3.2	Similarities and dissimilarities in conditions for social capital building between Poland and other post-communist countries	97
Table 4.1	Summary of empirical evidence of "denomination effects" at macro and micro levels by components of social capital	102
Table 4.2	Average membership in religious organisations in European countries (weighted averages)	107
Table 4.3	Summary of empirical evidence of "affiliation effects" at macro and micro levels by components of social capital	114
Table 5.1	Extraction of a one-dimensional indicator for "traditional concept of family" (factor loadings)	126

Table 5.2	Extraction of a one-dimensional indicator for "relevance of religion" (factor loadings)	128
Table 5.3	Extraction of a one-dimensional indicator for "morality" (factor loadings)	130
Table 5.4	Extraction of a one-dimensional indicator for "Religiously Rooted Conservatism" (factor loadings)	132
Table 5.5	Relations between membership and conservatism by country (Pearson's correlation coefficient)	141
Table 5.6	Relations between volunteering and conservatism by country (Pearson's correlation coefficient)	142
Table 5.7	Relations between meeting friends and conservatism by country (Pearson's correlation coefficient)	144
Table 5.8	Relations between trust and conservatism by country (Pearson's correlation coefficient)	147
Table 5.9	Relations between support for norms of civil and social behaviour and conservatism by country (Pearson's correlation coefficient)	151
Table 5.10	Correlation between membership in religious organisations and church attendance (Pearson's coefficients)	159
Table 5.11	Correlation between volunteering in religious organisations and church attendance (Pearson's coefficients)	161
Table 5.12	Correlation between membership in non-religious organisations and church attendance (Pearson's and Gamma coefficients)	164
Table 5.13	Spillover effect of religious engagement on secular engagement	167
Table 5.14	Correlation between informal networks and church attendance (Pearson's and Gamma coefficients)	171
Table 5.15	Correlation between trust and church attendance (Pearson's and Gamma coefficients)	175
Table 5.16	Analysis of variances of NCB-Index (Kruskal-Wallis tests and ANOVA)	179
Table 5.17	Analysis of variances of NSB-Index (p-values of Kruskal-Wallis test)	180
Table 5.18	Overview of findings concerning "denomination effects" and "affiliation effects" in all countries and in Poland	183
Table 6.1	Characteristics of the country distributions of the Religiously Rooted Conservatism Index	195

Table 6.2	Logistic regression analyses of membership in at least one organisation (odds ratio Exp (B), R2 Nagelkerke, and N, unweighted)	200
Table 6.3	Logistic regression analysis of volunteering in at least one organisation, excluding Slovakia (odds ratio Exp (B), R2 Nagelkerke, and N, unweighted)	203
Table 6.4	Logistic regression analysis of membership in secular and religious organisations, excluding Slovakia (odds ratio Exp (B), R^2 Nagelkerke, and N, unweighted)	206
Table 6.5	Logistic regression analysis of volunteering in secular and religious organisations, excluding Slovakia (odds ratio Exp (B), R2 Nagelkerke, Hosmer-Lemeshow test and N, unweighted)	211
Table 6.6	Logistic regression analysis of informal networks (odds ratio Exp (B), R2 Nagelkerke, and N, unweighted)	217
Table 6.7	Logistic regression analysis of trust (odds ratio Exp (B), R2 Nagelkerke, and N, unweighted)	223
Table 6.8	Linear regression analysis of norms of civil behaviour (unstandardised regression coefficient B, standard error, R^2 and N, unweighted)	228
Table 6.9	Linear regression analysis of norms of social behaviour (unstandardised regression coefficient B, standard error, R2 and N, unweighted)	230
Table 6.10	Comparative overview of the mechanisms of social capital building in Poland and other Catholic societies	234
Table 7.1	Dissimilarities in conditions and mechanisms of social capital building in Poland	242

1 Exploring social capital in Poland

1.1 Introduction

Poland appears to be "a country in the Moon"[1] in eyes of Michael Moran, an Australian writer who has lived in Poland for several years. In his interview Moran raised the concern that Poland has gotten "tediously normal"[2] since 1992, when he experienced a cultural shock after visiting for the first time. It is not only foreign writers and tourists, whose impressions are based on subjective observations of everyday life, who find several aspects of Polish society exceptional: for instance, the surprisingly high religiosity, the presence of religious symbols in private and public realms and the strong sentiments about Polish history, especially the still vivid memories of resistance against foreign dominance. Social scientists, whose findings are based on empirical comparative social studies (Linz/Stepan 1996, 255 ff.; Barnes 1998, 127; Howard 2003, 58), also think Poland is unique. This study explores one particular aspect of Polish exceptionality, which is especially important for the further development of democracy in that country: Polish society's low endowment of social capital.

The current low stock of social capital in Poland surprises researchers. Looking back to recent Central Eastern European history, Polish society contributed in a special way to the collapse of communist regimes with exceptionally high social mobilisation in the 1980s. In contrast, Poland's level of social participation is now one of the region's lowest (Salamon et al. 2003, 17, 19; van Deth 2004, 305; Fidrmuc/Gërxhani 2007, 27; Pichler/Wallace 2007, 430). Even more astonishing is that participation in religious organisations and trade unions – two major institutional pillars of social mobilisation in the 1980s – is at a very modest level now, compared to other societies in the region (Barnes 1998, 127). Therefore one of the principle objectives of this study is to explain why social participation in Poland is at an exceptionally low level compared to other post-communist societies. The study seeks to answer a number of questions: what happened to the social mobilisation of civil society in the 1980s in Poland? Why did the effective civil society of the 1980s fail to lay a normative and structural foundation for developing social capital after the collapse of communism? What is different about Poland when compared to

---

[1] Moran, Michael. 2009. *Country in the Moon: Travels in Search of the Heart of Poland*. London: Granta UK.
[2] Translation KL. Interview with Michael Moran in Polish Magazine *Polityka* 22.01.2011.

other post-communist societies? Can widespread disappointment after a systemic transition provide the explanation? Can the reasons for low social capital be found in specific aspects of Polish culture?

1.2 Poland – the 'Southern Italy' of Eastern Europe?

Many efforts to understand the origins of social capital across societies resulted in extensive lists of its determinants, whereby country-specific context matters considerably. Robert Putnam (1993), who first introduced the concept of social capital to political science, stresses path dependency as a key factor in understanding why some regions display more social capital than others. Each society is shaped by its unique historical legacy, which noticeably affects current social relations and the level of social capital. Putnam, when exploring differences in the stock of social capital between Southern and Northern Italy, emphasises the importance of the legacy of civic traditions (1993, 157). Can we find similar reasons for the low stock of social capital in Poland today? Can we explain the low social capital in Poland by its historical legacy? In the next three sections I will shed some light on several historical developments and point to similarities between Southern Italy and Poland.

1.2.1 Relevance of civic legacies

Let us return to Putnam's explanation of the persistence of social capital patterns. For Putnam, social capital is a societal resource that remains relatively stable over the long term. He argues that one of the reasons that some regions of Italy cope better with the dilemma of collective action than others lays in differences in social patterns dating back to early medieval times (1993, 121). While in Northern Italy in the Middle Ages a number of self-governing cities such as Florence, Venice, Bologna, Genoa and Milan appeared, in the South the Norman kingdom dominated (Putnam 1993, 122). Both types of political regimes were strikingly distinctive, and both were based on distinctive social orders. In the North, "communal republicanism" dominated, which was for that time "an unprecedented form of self-government" (Putnam 1993, 124). In the South, by contrast, "the regime remained a feudal monarchy" (Putnam 1993, 124). Whereas in the North the basis of social order relied more on horizontal collaboration among considerable sections of urban citizens, in the South of Italy a steep vertical hierarchy characterised the social order; "a landed aristocracy endowed with feudal powers" dominated peasants who "struggled wretchedly close to the limits of physical survival" (Putnam 1993, 124). Furthermore, both regions had distinctive sources of the legitimisation of power:

while in the North the power was delegated to public officials, "legitimate authority in the South was monopolized by the king, who (...) was responsible only to God" (Putnam 1993, 130). These differences in the sources of power legitimisation also mattered for the role of the Church: "In the North, while the religious sentiments remained profound, the Church was only one civil institution among many; in the South, the Church was a powerful and wealthy proprietor in the feudal order" (Putnam 1993, 130). Putnam shows that the patterns of "civic-ness" in distinct regions of Italy today remarkably resemble the patterns of social structures that appeared in the Middle Ages. In Southern Italy societal relations were based on feudal bonds of personal dependence, while in the North citizenship developed promptly: "in the North people were citizens; in the South they were subjects" (Putnam 1993, 130).

When tracing the civic traditions of Polish society, we can find significant similarities to the situation in Southern Italy. Particularly, three relevant factors are common: (1) the development of steep hierarchical social structures with strong interpersonal dependencies; (2) wealth based on land, instead of trade; and (3) the Church as a "powerful and wealthy proprietor in the feudal order" (1993, 130).

1.2.2 *Lack of civic legacies in Poland; similarities to Southern Italy*

1.2.2.1 Legacy one – hierarchical social structures

Steep hierarchical dependencies have been developing since the Middle Ages in Poland. The noble class was extremely large (ten percent of the population) and exceptionally powerful, especially since the extinction of the royal family (Jagiellons) in 1572 and the ensuing elections of kings by the noble estate. The domination of the nobles in the social structure resulted in the development of one of the strongest feudal systems in Europe with the heaviest socage conditions (combined with up to five days a week of compulsory work) and the deprivation of peasants' personal freedom during the 17th and 18th centuries (Emeliantseva et al. 2008, 176, 179, 186-190). Feudal dependencies persisted over centuries within Polish society, and apparently left an endurable impact on its social structures.

1.2.2.2 Legacy two – wealth based on land

Since nobles – the dominant social strata – were mainly landowners, wealth was primarily based on land. Towns, by contrast, were heavily underdeveloped in Poland for at least two reasons: limited social mobility from the villages to the cities and the monopolisation of trade by the noble class (Emeliantseva et al. 2008, 179).

Low social mobility, a consequence of the peasants' lack of personal freedom, limited the growth of urban populations by migration. Additionally, the political dominance of the nobles restricted the rights of city dwellers in trade, a progress-driving activity (Emeliantseva et al. 2008, 179; Schmidt 2000, 112). Nobles monopolised the international trade of cereals, which were the main export goods in the 16th century and the main source of wealth. By the 16th century Eastern Europe was the main source of cereals for the western part of Europe.

1.2.2.3 Legacy three – the Catholic Church's support of the feudal order

The influence of the Catholic Church in Poland grew gradually, especially since the Counter-Reformation (Schmidt 2000). The Church not only legitimised the power of kings (who were crowned by bishops), but also supported and profited from the feudal system in Poland. By the 16th century the Church possessed over 20 percent of the total cultivated land area, which was more than the crown's holdings at that time (Schmidt 2000, 102).

In sum, the historical legacy in Poland is similar to that of Southern Italy in at least three respects – there were vertical social structures, a land-based source of wealth and the Church guaranteed the feudal order. If Putnam points to these legacies as the reasons for weak civic-ness in Southern Italy today, similar conclusions could be drawn in reference to Polish society. In other words, Poles today are reluctant to join social networks and to trust each other, due to a lack of civic traditions in the distant past.

1.2.3   Contradictions

On the one hand, the feudal social order supported vertical social relations in Poland starting in the early 14th century. On the other hand, the political system of Poland, the Nobleman's Republic (established at the end of the 16th century), was one of the most modern political systems in Europe at that time, and was based on egalitarian principles (Emeliantseva et al. 2008, 147). In contrast, at the same time absolutist monarchs dominated other parts of Europe. Are both claims not contradictory? In the Nobleman's Republic, nobles were entitled to elect the king. Irrespective of the differences in their material status, every nobleman had one voice when casting a vote, so they were equal to each other in their electoral rights. One could argue that the way the communal republics were administered in Northern Italy is akin to the way the Nobleman's Republic was governed – based on egalitarian principles. However, there are two principle differences. First, in the Northern towns of Italy almost every citizen was entitled to be involved in the city council.

Putnam gives an example of Siena: "a town with roughly 5000 adult males, had 860 part-time city posts, while in larger towns the city council might have several thousand members" (Putnam 1993, 125). In the Nobleman's Republic, in contrast, a narrow strata (ten percent of citizens) was allowed to be involved in decision-making processes. Second, in the Northern towns of Italy citizens were involved in decisions about everyday regulations, while in the Nobleman's Republic participation was limited to the most crucial issues such as the election of a king or the beginning or continuation of a war. In other words, both the scale of entitlement, in the sense of the percentage of people involved, and the range of topics differed considerably between the Nobleman's Republic and the towns of Northern Italy. The egalitarianism was limited to the narrow social strata – the noble estate. Therefore, despite the fact that some egalitarian principles were incorporated into the political system of the Nobleman's Republic, structures within society as a whole remained dominated by vertical relations between the elite and the majority of the population, and this feature hampered the development of civic-ness in the society.

The next question is whether Poland was an exception among Central Eastern European countries, in regards to lacking civic legacies, or whether weak civic legacies are also characteristic of other countries in the region. The borders of Central Eastern European countries have fluctuated over the centuries, so an analysis of a single society would be very difficult. Nevertheless, we can find different paths of societal development in Poland when compared to regions in Central Europe. For instance Bohemia (Czech Republic today), Moravia (Slovakia) and Hungary experienced different paths in two respects: (1) the development of trade accompanied by progress in urbanisation and, later, industrialisation; and (2) the role of the Church, especially the weaker position of the Roman Catholic Church because of the relative success of the Reformation movements (Cameron 1991, 71; Bahlcke 1997, 77; Johnston Gordon 1997, 222; Emeliantseva et al. 2008, 190). Furthermore, in Southern Europe, several Balkan nations profited from the proximity of the Mediterranean Sea, which resulted in the development of trade (Emeliantseva et al. 2008, 194), in contrast to Poland.

In summary, there are a number of similarities in historical legacies between Poland and Southern Italy. It seems that the historical legacy of Polish society has more in common with Southern Italy than the legacies of other Central European societies. This finding leads to the conclusion that weak civic traditions in Polish society can partly explain the exceptionally low endowment with social capital in Poland. At the same time, other Central European societies are characterised by somewhat different conditions for societal development. So, historical legacies contributed to a greater extent to the lack of civic traditions in Poland, compared to other societies from the region.

Are the historical explanations presented above sufficient to explain the low stock of social capital in Poland today? According to Howard we can find similarities in the levels and nature of social networks within Central Eastern European societies (2003, 90), and the civic legacies in other countries in the region are different from Poland's. This is why historical explanations only partly reveal the truth, so we need to seek **further** reasons for low endowment with social capital – in Poland and in other countries in the region. In particular, we need to focus on exploring the legacies of the recent past.

1.3 Research goal, method and research questions

How can we explore the reasons for the low stock of social capital in Poland? I apply a common method in comparative social sciences: the "Most Similar Systems" design, which is "based on the belief that systems as similar as possible with respect to as many features as possible constitute the optimal samples for comparative inquiry" (Przeworski/Teune 1970, 32). The "Most Similar Systems" designs have following logic: "systems constitute the original level of analysis, and within-system variations are explained in terms of systemic factors (...) Common systemic characteristics are conceived of as 'control for,' whereas intersystemic differences are viewed as explanatory variables" (Przeworski/Teune 1970, 33, quotation mark in original). Therefore we need to compare Polish society with similar systems and seek dissimilarities between Poland and the remaining systems. Common systemic characteristics within this group will be irrelevant in determining the reasons for the low level of social capital, while dissimilar features are the explanatory factors we are searching for. Now we need to address the question: what kinds of similar systems need to be considered?

Two sorts of characteristics of Polish society are especially relevant for exploring social capital. The first is the legacy related to the former communist regime and the subsequent systemic transition. The second is the dominant Catholic tradition. The experiences of the communist regime and the subsequent systemic transitions turn out to be crucial conditions for shaping social capital across Central Eastern European societies (Paldam/Svendsen 2000, 2 ff.; Sztompka 2000, 7 ff.; Salamon et al. 2003, 48-49; Uslaner/Badescu 2003, 226). For this reason, Poland should be compared with a group of post-communist countries. On the other hand, a dominant religious tradition is also an important factor influencing a society's social capital (Putnam 1993, 107; Verba et al. 1995, 282). In the Polish case in particular, religion cannot be neglected as a factor shaping social capital. Catholicism is not only historically anchored in Polish culture and tradition, but also, despite widespread secularisation in Europe, Catholic traditions are widely practiced by a large portion of society today. This is why Poland will also be compared with Catholic societies.

The following sections discuss the potential relevance of these factors (communist legacy, systemic transition and Catholicism) for the development of social capital. Next, the research questions following from these problems are outlined.

1.3.1 Communism

A communist legacy is commonly regarded as hampering the accumulation of social capital (Curtis et al. 2001, 791; Howard 2003, 90; Fioramonti/Heinrich 2007, 38; Valkov 2009, 8). Communism, principally based on the control of the public realm, left citizens little space to associate and create social networks. The few opportunities to get involved in social activities were offered by organisations that were supervised by the authorities, while non-registered groups were controlled or repressed by the authorities. In effect, civil societies based on the voluntary activities of its members were absent in communist societies. Empirical studies confirm there are currently low levels of social participation in post-communist societies (Paldam/Svendsen 2000, 7; Salamon et al. 2003, 48-49). Likewise, communism destroyed social trust by its repressive exercise of power and the widespread surveillance of citizens (Sztompka 1995, 254). Empirical evidence of low levels of social trust in formerly communist societies has also been found in cross-national studies (Kunz 2004, 208; Fidrmuc/Gërxhani 2007). The collapse of communism did not bring about substantial changes in behavioural and attitudinal patterns in Central Eastern Europe (Howard 2003, 105). Apparently, patterns internalised through communist socialisation are difficult to eradicate, and the propensity to associate and trust cannot be evoked simply by introducing basic freedoms.

Although a communist legacy often means current low levels of social capital, it does not explain why social capital in Poland is relatively low compared to other former communist societies in the region. Therefore, when searching for the reasons why Poland is an exception, we need to disentangle the differences in the impact of communism in Polish and other societies. Can we explain the reasons for the present low level of social capital in Poland by the differences in the communist legacies of countries in the region? What dissimilarities can be found in the way people were socialised under the communist regime in Poland when compared to other societies from the region? Why did Polish citizens internalise apparently different attitudinal and behavioural patterns? These questions will be addressed in order to find the reasons – related to the communist legacy – for the low stock of social capital in Poland.

1.3.2 Systemic transition

The systemic transitions following the collapse of communism across Central Eastern Europe were a very dislocating period for post-communist citizens. These transitions resulted in economic hardship and widespread feelings of existential insecurity across these societies. These circumstances did not encourage associational participation, and were not favourable for the building of trust. Scholars analysing societies in transition stress the widespread disillusionment across post-communist citizenries (Howard 2003, 29; Inglehart/Catterberg 2002, 308). And disillusioned citizens prefer to withdraw from the public sphere and are reluctant to take common initiatives or cooperate (Howard 2003, 109).

Since the systemic transitions affected all countries in the region, in order to explain the special situation in Poland we need to search for relevant dissimilarities between Poland and the other post-communist societies in the ways the processes of transition were pursued. The more dislocating the situations and economic troubles that arise from the transition process are, the more disenchantment across society – resulting in reduced citizens' engagement, or in the worst case, in withdrawal and apathy – we can expect (Howard 2003, 109). We should address the question: what was different in Poland during the systemic transition? Were the social costs of systemic transition in Poland higher than in other post-communist societies? Was social disillusionment indeed stronger in Poland than in other societies in the region? Addressing these questions will provide us with the reasons – related to systemic transition – for the lower social capital in Poland.

1.3.3 Catholicism

Poles are exceptionally devoted Catholics, more than people in other post-communist societies. Could strong Catholicism be regarded as an explanation for the low stock of social capital in Poland? Actually the role of Catholicism in the production of social capital is fairly complex, multidimensional and not unequivocally negative. On the one hand, the Roman Catholic tradition is regarded as a negative context for social capital (Putnam 1993, 107; Verba et al. 1995, 245). However on the other hand, churchgoing is principally positively related to social engagement (Putnam 2000, 66; Campbell/Yonish 2003, 94; de Hart/Dekker 2005, 176). Therefore it is important to pinpoint the arguments for the positive and negative influences of Catholicism.

The negative influence of the Catholic tradition on social capital is apparently a consequence of the hierarchical structures of the Roman Catholic Church, which reinforces vertical – instead of horizontal – relations within a Catholic society (Putnam 1993, 175). Horizontal networks are pivotal for social capital, while vertical networks "cannot sustain social trust and cooperation" (Putnam 1993, 174). Furthermore, Catholic tenets do not maintain individualism and do not encourage the faithful to take initiative and responsibility for their own sake, in contrast to other denominations, for instance Protestantism (Jagodzinski/Dobbelaere 1995a, 81). Therefore we need to address the question of whether the hierarchical structures of the Roman Catholic Church and Catholic tenets indeed matter for social capital in Poland. Is this influence similar in other Catholic societies, or is Catholicism more deeply rooted in Polish culture, and therefore has more influence on social capital in that society?

Church attendance has a positive influence on the development of social networks, since people meet in parishes on a regular basis: "churches provide an important incubator for civic skills, civic norms, community interests, and civic recruitment" (Putnam 2000, 66). And religious participation itself is a kind of social participation. So why in Poland, which has one of the highest levels of church attendance in Europe, is religious and secular engagement modest? What is the role of religious observance in Poland for the development of social capital? Can we find similarities when compared to other Catholic societies? Or is the impact of church attendance in Poland different?

Answering these questions concerning the role of Catholicism for social capital in Poland, compared to other Catholic societies, will help elucidate the reasons for the low stock of social capital in Poland.

1.4 Study design

1.4.1 Research strategy

What is the most effective strategy for explaining the low social capital in Poland? The explanations may depend in general on two things: (1) on initial conditions for social capital building, or (2) on mechanisms for the production of social capital. The dissimilarities in conditions and mechanisms may concern all three factors that are relevant for Poland – the communist legacy, the systemic transition and Catholicism. For instance, we would explain the dissimilar mechanisms of social capital building in Poland, when it occurs, by saying that churchgoing has (in general) a positive effect on social capital building, though not in Poland. In such a case we would say that the reasons for the lower stock of social capital building in Poland lay in its dissimilarities concerning the mechanism of social capital production. Another example is that we may deal with dissimilar conditions for social capital building in Poland: the social costs of the systemic transition in this country were more severe (for instance unemployment and inflation were higher for several years during the transition) than in other countries, which resulted in more disappointment in Poland. In this case we could say that the reasons for the low stock of social capital in Poland lay in dissimilar conditions for social capital building in this society.

When we combine both approaches, we get four possibilities, three of which help explore Polish exceptionality (Figure 1.1).

Figure 1.1 How can Polish exceptionality be explained?

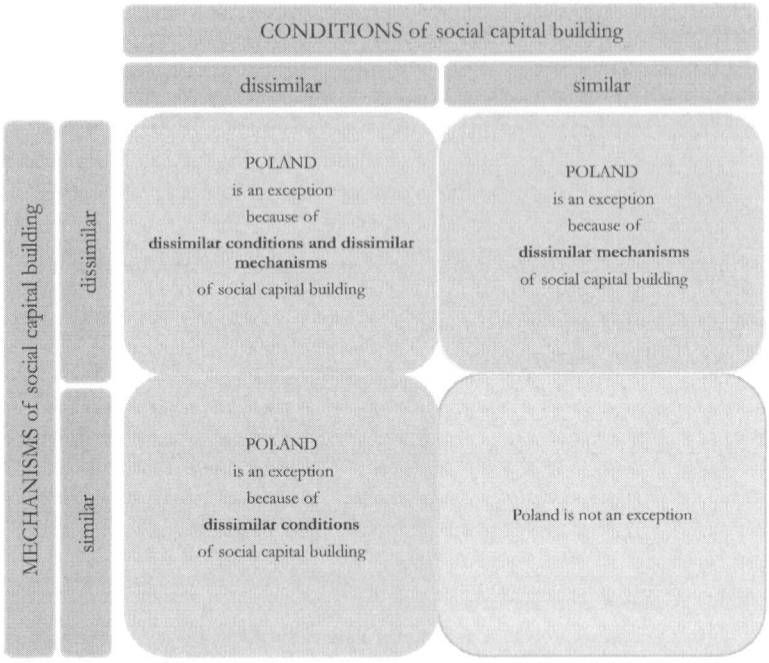

So, we expect to find one of three possible ways to explain Polish exceptionality (the three grey-coloured fields in the Figure 1.1). In the first step – the exploration of conditions – I disentangle similarities and dissimilarities in the conditions for social capital building in Poland and in reference countries. These analyses encompass the three factors discussed above: conditions related to the communist legacy, to the systemic transition and to the Catholic tradition. The reference countries change according to the factors under consideration: when analysing the conditions of the communist legacy and the systemic transition, I compare the situation in Poland with those across post-communist societies. In contrast, when analysing conditions related to Catholicism, the country reference group consists of European

Catholic countries. Societies dominated by other denominations remain excluded from this part of the analysis, since the objective is to assess the influence of Catholicism on social capital. In this part I include an examination of Western Catholic societies, which allows me to analyse the relevance of Catholicism in a non-post-communist context as well. This way of proceeding allows the comparison of Poland with similar societies each time – as the "Most Similar System" design requires – whereby the criterion for this *similarity* in each part of the examination concerns the factor that is relevant for social capital.

In the second step – the exploration of the mechanisms of social capital building – I focus on comparing the determinants of social capital in Polish society and in other societies. In this part the components of social capital are dependent variables, while the factors related to communism, the systemic transition and Catholicism are independent variables. I scrutinise whether the same factors that are relevant for social capital building across reference countries are also relevant for social capital building in Poland. If certain determinants are relevant for Poland, yet are irrelevant for the remaining societies, this will be evidence of dissimilar mechanisms of social capital building in Poland – and will thus help explain Polish exceptionality. In this step of the analyses, the country reference group contains both post-communist and non-post-communist Catholic countries. In this way the assessment of determinants related to Catholicism can be compared in a post-communist and a non-post-communist context.

The results of this study will focus in particular on the exceptional low social capital in Poland *in comparison to other post-communist societies*, while Western Catholic societies will be used for a background analysis of the post-communist context only.

1.4.2   Data sources

The nature of the problem under scrutiny – social capital in the European post-communist context – and the need to consider the wider Catholic context in this study put certain requirements on the dataset that should be used. Commonly used datasets in comparative political science are cross-national surveys. For this study, a suitable dataset should comprise, on the one hand, questions allowing the measurement of the stock of social capital across societies – in principle, questions concerning social networks, trust, norms and values. On the other hand, the data should cover a possibly wide range of post-communist countries, including Catholic societies (such as, for instance, Czech Republic, Hungary, Slovakia and Slovenia) and Western Catholic societies (for instance, Austria, Belgium, France, Ireland, Portugal and Spain). The World Values Survey (WVS) seems to fulfil the requirements, since it contains a substantial amount of questions concerning social capital components, and covers a wide range of countries of Central Eastern and Western

Europe, including societies stamped by a Catholic tradition. The fourth wave, including fieldwork conducted between 1999 and 2001, will be the main source of data for the analysis pursued in this study.

Using the fourth wave of the WVS allows the comparison of Poland with 14 post-communist countries – Belarus, Bosnia and Herzegovina, Bulgaria, Croatia, Czech Republic, Estonia, Hungary, Latvia, Lithuania, Romania, Russia, Slovakia, Slovenia and Ukraine – when the communist context is examined. For the analysis of Polish society in the Catholic context, we will be able to consider 13 Catholic European countries, six of which are from Central Eastern Europe (Croatia, Czech Republic, Hungary, Lithuania, Slovakia and Slovenia) and seven from Western Europe (Austria, Belgium, France, Ireland, Italy, Portugal and Spain).

1.5 Plan of the book

The outline of the book reflects the specific logic of the analyses. Before examining the conditions and mechanisms of social capital building, we first need to know what is understood by the term "social capital." Therefore chapter 2 presents the theory of social capital, its conceptualisation and measurement. The conceptualisation of social capital used throughout this book considers – by including informal networks alongside institutional ones – aspects of social networks that are particularly relevant for Central Eastern Europe. In this way we challenge the reproaches that social capital is a Western-oriented concept. Furthermore, when dealing with the problems of the dimensionality of social capital and the related dilemmas of its measurement, I consider three components of social capital separately. This approach seems to best suit the comparative character of the analyses and allows the assessment of differences across societies. The second part of chapter 2 considers the endowment of social capital in Poland in comparison to other post-communist societies, taking Western societies as a background. In this way we explore to what extent Polish society is exceptionally poorly endowed with social capital, and which components of social capital are especially weak in this country.

Chapter 3 addresses the problem of the conditions of social capital building related to communist legacies and the systemic transitions across post-communist societies. The main question is how the level and nature of social capital in Poland are affected by the communist legacy and the systemic transition when compared to other societies in Central Eastern Europe. This examination reveals a number of dissimilarities and similarities in the conditions of social capital building between Polish and other societies with prior communist experience. Dissimilarities in conditions allow initial conclusions to be drawn concerning the reasons for Poland's exceptionally low endowment with social capital. At the same time, these findings are a baseline for further examining the differences in the mechanisms of social capital building pursued in chapter 6.

Continuing the examination of the conditions of social capital building, the next two chapters deal with the multifaceted relationships between religion and social capital. Chapter 4 disentangles the positive and negative aspects of religious influences on social capital in the literature, to lay the foundation for further empirical comparative analyses. The focus is put, in particular, on understanding the assumed negative impact of Catholicism on social capital. Furthermore, an overview of the arguments concerning the positive role of churches in producing social capital is presented, to assess any potential "counterbalancing" positive effects of widespread church affiliation in Poland. Understanding the link between religion and social capital allows the formulation of specific questions concerning the situation in Poland when compared to other societies shaped by Catholicism.

In chapter 5 the arguments ascertained in the literature review are tested across Catholic societies. An empirical examination of the relations between religion-related factors and social capital across the Catholic countries in the sample is pursued. The purpose is to compare the situation in Poland to that of other Catholic societies, in order to identify which similarities and dissimilarities of Polish conditions of social capital building are related to religion. In addition to conditions, the relationships between religious factors and social capital are also investigated in a preliminary way, because the evidence across studies is often ambiguous. Results of the analyses answer the question: in what respect do dissimilar conditions and mechanisms of social capital building related to Catholicism explain the reasons for the low endowment of social capital in Poland?

Chapter 6 compares the mechanisms of social capital building that are related to all considered factors. The examination is pursued in the form of multivariate regression models encompassing factors that are relevant for social capital building, including conditions – similar and dissimilar – identified in the previous chapters. It turns out that Polish exceptionality can be explained by different mechanisms of social capital building that occur in this society. This method of analysis enables us to understand the nature of Polish exceptionality – whether the reasons for the low stock of social capital lay in different conditions of social capital building, or different mechanisms, or both.

The evidence found for Polish exceptionality and the reasons for this are presented in concluding chapter 7. It seems that certain cultural traits of Polish culture, which is influenced by Catholicism, as well as specific legacies of communism and the recent difficult systemic transition are partly responsible for the low stock of social capital in Poland. On the other hand, Poland today benefits from relative political and economic stability; Polish citizens enjoy more freedom than ever before, and they are more exposed to different worldviews and religious traditions. These new circumstances could be a favourable ground for change, and could also help Poland catch up on the development of social capital. Perhaps this is the last opportunity to capture Polish exceptionality before Poland gets "tediously normal," as Michael Moran believes.

2 Social capital – conceptual framework and empirical findings

2.1 Introduction

The collapse of communism brought new perspectives for people in Central Eastern Europe. However with these changes many new questions arose and new challenges appeared. Why are certain societies better off than others? Why do institutions in certain countries perform better than in other countries? To what extent do these differences have cultural roots? Can these discrepancies be somewhat smoothed by certain policies? Such questions are especially relevant for countries undergoing systemic transitions or facing problems related to the implementation of a new political order. The concept of social capital, introduced to political science by Robert Putnam at the beginning of the 1990s, contributes to our understanding of the relationship between society and institutional performance. The relevance of the "habits of hearts," consisting of the readiness to self-govern and self-organise, is not a new idea – Alexis de Tocqueville emphasised the benefits of associational activity for the cohesion of local communities in 19th century America.

Although intensively examined empirically, the conceptualisation and measurement of social capital varies substantially among studies (Halpern 2005, 2-9; van Deth 2007, 151). Therefore it is advisable to define the concept of social capital and describe how it is measured in this study before starting an empirical investigation of social capital in Poland and other countries in the region (van Deth 2007, 154). The first section of this chapter presents the concept of social capital, while the second section discusses its importance for Eastern Europe. An empirical examination of the endowment of Polish society with social capital compared to other European countries is the main objective of the third section. The concluding part examines to what extent Polish society is exceptional as far as the stock of social capital is concerned.

2.2 Social capital: functions and definition

Social capital is "usually understood as a functional concept" (van Deth 2007, 152). The principal functions of social capital are supporting social cohesion and facilitating cooperation among individuals. The more face-to-face interactions, mutual trust and dense social networks a society has, the higher its contribution to a common well-being: "social capital makes us smarter, healthier, safer, richer, and better able to govern a just and stable democracy" (Putnam 2000, 290).

The interest in social capital and its beneficial impact on a nation's well-being goes beyond narrow clusters of political scientists. Evidence for the benefits of substantial stocks of social capital in a society found its echo in Organisation for Economic Co-operation and Development (OECD) recommendations directed to policy-makers (OECD 2001). Likewise, the International Monetary Fund, which provides financial support for low- and middle-income countries, also places a great emphasis on developing "Civic and Community Relations"[3] across recipient countries, because "the economic function of social capital is to reduce the transaction costs associated with formal coordination mechanisms like contracts, hierarchies, bureaucratic rules, and the like."[4] Social capital, through its contribution to economic development, attracts the attention of national and supra-national institutions, including Poland. In the guidelines for its strategic objectives, increasing social capital over the next 20 years was mentioned as one of the Polish government's ten main challenges (Ministrów 2009).

Before discussing single components of social capital, let us first pinpoint its definition. Putnam's proposed definition is probably the most common: social capital "refers to features of social organisation, such as trust, norms, and networks, that can improve the efficiency of society by facilitating coordinated actions" (Putnam 1993, 167). These three components (norms, networks and trust) are self-reinforcing, cumulative over time and mutually interdependent: "social trust (...) can arise from two related sources – norms of reciprocity and networks of civic engagement" (Putnam 1993, 171). At the same time, "networks of civic engagement foster robust norms of reciprocity" (Putnam 1993, 173). According to Halpern, the components of social capital "have some degree of functional equivalence" (Halpern 2005, 28), meaning that one component could to some extent substitute or compensate for another. This is one of the reasons why it is advisable to investigate the components of social capital separately. Social networks and social trust are the most frequently empirically examined, while far fewer studies pay attention to the norms and values (van Deth 2003, 83). In this study, all three components of social capital are examined separately, whereby norms and trust comprise a cultural basis of social capital, while social networks refer to its structural aspect.

---

[3] See the IMF website: http://www.imf.org/external/np/cpac/index.htm, accessed on 09.05.2011.
[4] Ibid, accessed on 09.05.2011.

2.2.1 Components of social capital

2.2.1.1 Social networks

What functions are social networks said to perform? In a networked community individuals cooperate with each other in order to achieve common goals. Through this cooperation they accomplish common objectives, which would probably be more difficult to achieve individually. For instance when residents of a newly built neighbourhood convince the city council together to build a new road in this neighbourhood, or parents lobby for a new school building for their children, they create and benefit from social capital in this neighbourhood. When a goal is attained, people get a feeling of accomplishment, and indirectly, are more satisfied with political processes in general (Gabriel et al. 2002, 20). Furthermore, through the process of mutual cooperation they learn certain skills – to take responsibility, to keep their own commitments, to convince others of their own proposals or ideas, to rely on others and to be a reliable partner, etc. Only through mutual cooperation can people become effective as a group. This kind of cooperation can be issue oriented and spontaneous.

The more that cooperation among people is regular, the more chances they have to practise their cooperation skills. Other forms of networks are formally established groups such as voluntary organisations or associations. Members of such groups cooperate on a regular basis, so they have more opportunities to learn civic skills such as running meetings, giving speeches or writing a letter or petition (Almond/Verba 1963, 309 ff.). Formal groups – organisations or associations – are "schools of democracy," to use Tocqueville's phrase. Regular contacts and cooperation also create opportunities to develop mutual trust among group members: "those more engaged in community life are both more trusting and more trustworthy" (Putnam 2000, 137); as a consequence they have more opportunities to stockpile their "relation social capital" (discussed in section 2.2.2). The question of what comes first – trust or social engagement – remains open: "the efficacy of voluntary organizations in creating trust and reciprocity has so far only been assumed in the literature and has not been empirically tested or explored" (Stolle 2003, 23).

The type of organisation matters for the quality of the social capital that is produced. Voluntary groups of a heterogeneous nature create "bridges" in a society: "bridging social capital refers to social networks that bring together people who are unlike one another" (Putnam/Goss 2002, 11) and in effect produce positive external effects for society. In contrast, bonding social capital "brings together people who are like one another in important aspects (ethnicity, age, gender, social class)" (Putnam/Goss 2002, 11) and provides social and emotional support for their members rather than social cohesion in general. In extreme cases, in societies with sharp social divisions, an abundance of bonding and a scarcity of crosscutting allegiances could lead to violent conflicts. This problem seems, on one hand, to be rather irrelevant for the ethnically and religiously homogenous Polish society. On the other hand, "we don't need to worry quite so much about always measuring both bonding and bridging social capital – if an individual or community is rich in one, then they will probably be rich in the other too" (Halpern 2005, 21). So, though aware of these differences in bridging and bonding social capital, I do not make an analytical distinction when measuring social capital in Central Eastern Europe.

Most of the empirical studies investigating social capital focus on formalised social networks, which are operationalised as membership in diverse types of organisations or associations (van Deth 2003, 82-83; see for instance Gabriel et al. 2002; Paxton 2002). Some authors consider the density of social networks (Howard 2003, 63 ff.), while others concentrate on the level of associational membership and consider different types of organisations (Gabriel et al. 2002, 44-45; Paxton 2002, 269-270). Membership in organisations might be a somewhat misleading measurement of social networks for two reasons. First, some organisations might be "check-book" organisations that give few opportunities for face-to-face interactions (Stolle 2003, 26; Grant et al. 2007, 88). Second, in post-communist societies, membership rates in certain types of organisations, like trade unions, are relatively high, which is more a legacy of communist times than evidence of an eager readiness to struggle for the rights of working people (Howard 2003, 63-67). This is why, when operationalising social networks, active engagement in an organisation is considered as a secondary indicator, after membership. An exploration of volunteering complements our analysis of social capital, since through volunteering people can benefit from joining social networks and from externalities resulting from interactions within these networks.

When exploring social networks across Central Eastern European societies, we need to bear in mind another specific societal characteristic of this region. Scholars emphasise the strength of informal ties as one of the consequences of the communist legacy (Rose 1998, 9-10; Paldam/Svendsen 2000, 8; Grabowska/Szawiel 2001, 155; Howard 2003, 107-109). Informal bonds were developed in communist regimes for two main reasons. First, networks of acquaintances and friends were needed as a counterbalance for the coerced membership in officially supported organisations. Second, people needed to rely on informal networks to survive in an economy with a permanent shortage of goods and services (discussed in detail in chapter 4). Furthermore, informal networks probably remained after the collapse of the communist system because habits and social patterns do not change overnight: "in post-communist societies (...) many people are still extremely invested in their own private circles and simply feel no need, much less any desire, to join and participate in organizations, when they feel that, socially they already have everything that they could or need want" (Howard 2003, 28). For these reasons, when analysing social networks in post-communist Europe we will consider both kinds of networks – formal (membership and volunteering in organisations) and informal (contacts with acquaintances and friends).

2.2.1.2 Social trust

Social trust is a cultural component of social capital. Trust entails certain assumptions about future behaviour and attitudes concerning other people (Sztompka 1995, 256). Furthermore, those who trust assume that others will behave appropriately and hope for positive results of the intended actions of others (Gabriel et al. 2002, 52); this belief exists under uncertain circumstances that are beyond an individual's control (Sztompka 1995, 256; Sztompka 2007, 62-67). Putnam emphasises that trust is an "essential component of social capital" (1993, 170), which "lubricates cooperation" (1993, 171). In other words, social trust is crucial for social cohesion and the readiness to cooperate. The tangible results of cooperation lubricated by trust are lower transaction costs, which contribute at the macro level to economic development. This is partly why high-trust societies are in general more developed ones (Fukuyama 1995, 29).

Social trust is conceptually close to generalised trust, which refers in general to trust in other people. In contrast, "particularized trust is faith only in people like yourself" (Uslaner 2007, 104). Similarly, "thick trust" is "a belief that rests on intimate familiarity with *this* individual" (Putnam 1993, 171, emphasis in original). When referring to social capital, "a more impersonal or indirect form of trust is required" (Putnam 1993, 171). This is why I focus on generalised trust as a measure of social trust.

Where does trust come from? The debate over the origins of trust is vibrant among scholars. Putnam claims that social trust is a societal resource, the roots of which can be traced back to the historic legacy of a given society. For instance in the regions where the social order was dominated by vertical social links, and the accumulation of wealth was based on the exploitation of one social stratum by another, it is likely that the stock of social trust is now low. On the other hand, in societies with a social order founded on horizontal social links in the past, the stock of social capital could remain high (Putnam 1993, 174 ff.). His claim is mostly based on the comparison between Northern and Southern Italy. Fukuyama's line of argumentation is similar – social trust is a resource with roots in historical legacies, and some societies are low-trust while others become high-trust societies (Fukuyama 1995, 26 ff.). For both scholars, the historical dominance of the Catholic tradition is a prerequisite for rather low social trust, though they describe different mechanisms: while Fukuyama emphasises strong family bonds in Catholic countries (Fukuyama 1995, 55-57), Putnam attributes the low generalised trust to the hierarchical structures (Putnam 1993, 175). Furthermore Fukuyama, along with other scholars, highlights the negative impact of communist experiences on civil society, and in effect on generalised trust (Fukuyama 1995, 54-55; Sztompka 1995; see also Paldam/Svendsen 2000, 7). Another pattern stressed at the macro level is a positive relationship between equality (income equality specifically) and social trust, which explains the high level of social trust among Scandinavian societies (Uslaner 2003b,

180 ff.). Uslaner emphasises that in general, "*collective* experience – including, but not limited to, the distribution of resources in society – plays a critical role in shaping trust" (2007, 113; emphasis in original). Likewise Sztomkpa stresses the relevance of collective experience for the production of a "culture of trust" (Sztompka 2007, 292). Sztompka points to five main macro-level features of a society that enhance social trust: normative cohesion, stability and continuity of social order, transparency of societal organisations, familiarity with the societal environment, and an institutional and individual sense of responsibility (Sztompka 2007, 276-281).

However social trust is not entirely shaped by a society's collective experiences and cultural legacies; there are also individual determinants for trust. On the one hand, trust is a strategic individual decision, which could be based upon previous experiences (Uslaner 2007, 102); on the other hand, "moralistic trust is a moral command to treat people *as if* they were trustworthy" (Uslaner 2007, 102; emphasis in original). Uslaner emphasises two key personal traits – optimism and a sense of control – that shape an individual's propensity to trust. Both traits depend merely on education, group identity, family background and childhood experiences (2007, 108-110). The role of the family in early socialisation is critical for the development of generalised trust in adulthood. In particular, growing up in an open, self-respecting and tolerant environment and experiencing parental tolerance and openness towards strangers results in a trustful attitude towards others (Stolle 2003, 29-30). Furthermore, such a tolerant and open worldview is highly correlated with socio-economic status, and especially with education, which is "a powerful predictor of trust (...), [which] especially through university broadens one's perspective on the world – and brings one into contact with a wider variety of people" (Uslaner 2007, 108). Likewise Sztompka stresses that "more affluent individuals (understood broadly, not explicitly in a material sense) are more prone to trust" (2007, 282).[5] There are two reasons for this. First, with a rise in self-confidence resulting from higher social status, the propensity to take a risk related to trust grows. Second, individuals with a higher status are more trusted by others, and because of the interactive character of the formation of trust, they are also more ready to trust others (Sztompka 2007, 283).

In turn Putnam, when conceptualising social capital, highlighted the role of networks and norms in the formation of social trust: "trust itself is an emergent property of the social system, as much as a personal attribute. Individuals are able to be trusting because of the social norms and networks within which their actions are embedded" (Putnam 1993, 177). Indeed, high-trust societies seem to be characterised by more dense networks (Gabriel et al. 2002, 35); these relationships, however, cannot be found in general at the individual level (Gabriel et al. 2002, 90). The debate focuses on the direction of causality: "membership does indeed influence trust toward the other group members and personal engagement within the group, but with regard to *generalized* trust, the self-selection effects were more pronounced than

---

[5] Translation KL.

the membership effects" (Stolle 2003, 25, emphasis in original). In other words, the assumption that membership in associations engenders generalised trust is not supported by empirical evidence. It seems that self-selection mechanisms are in play here – more trusting individuals are more likely to be members of voluntary associations (Stolle 2003, 25).

There are several approaches to measuring social trust in empirical studies. By far the most popular way is to measure generalised trust with a survey question such as: "Could you say that most people could be trusted, or you can be never be too careful?" While in some survey there are only two possible answers to this question (for instance the WVS), others capture fine-grained differences by using an 11-point scale (for example the European Social Survey). Some scholars measure social trust using an index composed of several questions (Letki/Evans 2005), while some distinguish between "thin" and "thick" trust, which refers to other people in general and to a specific group (e.g., family members, neighbours, or ethnic group), respectively (Badescu 2003, 131). Zmerli and Newton argue that the method used to measure trust affects the results of empirical analyses, and that a multi-point scale measurement is more reliable, than dichotomised measurements (2008, 719-720). Unfortunately the WVS dataset used in this study has considerable constraints, and measures generalised trust using a dichotomised method.

2.2.1.3 Norms and values

Norms and values are the second cultural component of social capital. Putnam refers to norms of reciprocity when describing the different aspects of social capital: "generalized reciprocity refers to a continuing relationship of exchange that is at any time unrequited or imbalanced, but involves mutual expectations that a benefit granted now should be repaid in the future (...); the norm of generalized reciprocity is a highly productive component of social capital" (Putnam 1993, 172). Given the expectations, hope and uncertainty included in his concept of reciprocity, it appears very close to the other cultural component – generalised trust. Norms of reciprocity enhance cooperation and help to overcome the dilemma of collective action. Individuals with faith in the cooperative attitudes of other community members tend to collaborate and initiate actions that contribute to a common benefit. If such norms of reciprocity are commonly shared in a community, mutual cooperation aiming at realising common goals has solid normative foundations (Putnam 1993, 171-173). Several studies on social capital have contributed to distinct concepualisations of norms and values, though a large part of this research limits the concept of the cultural aspect of social capital to merely social trust.

Halpern, emphasising multi-level dimensions of social capital, does not limit the study of norms to individuals and generalised reciprocity, but also stresses the importance of norms such as mutual respect, out-group understanding and community customs at the meso-level – and gives human rights, aid and international treaties as examples of norms and values at the macro level (2005, 27). This framing of norms and values is broader than reciprocity and more abstract. Halpern argues that with modernisation, the norms of cooperation and reciprocity need to be shared by a wider public:

> "as cities and nations have grown, formed on the back of wider and wider circled of shared understandings and perceived group membership, this same growth has both facilitated co-operation with groups and, at the same time, aggravated the scale of conflicts between these groups (...) Conflicts are only reduced when social networks, shared understandings and systems of sanctions (...) expand and converge across groups, to encompass the conflicting parties." (2005, 226)

Gabriel and colleagues highlight the importance of such norms and values, which enhance cooperation and acting *with* others, when referring to the cultural aspects of social capital (2002, 69-71). They conceptualise norms and values as pro-social orientations, the rejection of free-riding behaviour and support for law-abidingness. Pro-social orientations are related to such values as solidarity and social connectedness, and refer in general to attitudes that are other-directed. The higher the appreciation for pro-social orientations, law-abidingness, solidarity, etc. in a society, the more socially cohesive the society should be.

In my study a wider conceptualisation of norms and values is applied as pro-social orientations, and support for norms regulating social coexistence and cooperation in a more general sense than reciprocity is explored. On the one hand I consider social capital at the individual and aggregated levels, so that a wider conceptualisation of norms and values is required. On the other hand, norms of reciprocity are very close to the concept of trust, which is already considered in my analyses of social capital.

2.2.2   Double nature of social capital

The double nature of social capital is often stressed by researchers – social capital is both a societal and an individual resource (Gabriel et al. 2002, 26-30; Esser 2007, 24). As a societal resource it is labelled "system capital" and contributes to the benefits of a community, while the profits of "relation capital" remain mostly personal. So a community or society with a high stock of social capital is characterised by dense social networks, trustful relations among people, and widespread values and norms regarding cooperation. In such a community or society some individuals might have low "relation capital" – i.e. they distrust others and would rather withdraw from social networks – though they benefit from a community's "system capital" for instance by enjoying the trust of others, by using dense networks for gathering information or by enjoying low costs when closing a transaction. In Central Eastern Europe we probably deal with just the opposite: individuals with relatively high "relation capital" need to cope with low "system capital" within their communities. Neither norms of reciprocity nor trust get generalised: "networks in communist societies were generally specific (oriented to bring in a specific range of goods or services not available through normal means) and simultaneous (the favour would be returned in the future); but because they were not highly transitive (..) they were consequently low on generalization" (Kolankiewicz 1996, 438). Authors describing post-communist countries refer to a "privatisation of life," meaning a withdrawal from the public to the private sphere of networks (Bozóki 1994, 123; Grabowska/Szawiel 2001, 155), or "pre-modern" societies (Rose 1998, 1) as typical problems in this region. They refer to narrow informal networks and to the short radius of trust, to use Fukuyama's terminology (Fukuyama 1999, 2). It seems that there are more bonding ties and a few bridging ties among these groups, which restrains the accumulation of "system capital." The reasons for these developments are discussed in more detail in chapter 3.

By examining social capital, especially in post-communist societies, we face the problem of the imperfect measurement of "system capital." Using survey questions we learn merely about the "relation capital" of individual respondents, while we can only use aggregated data to measure "system capital."

2.2.3 Social capital as a single construct?

When examining social capital, we can choose between two measurement strategies. Social capital can be measured with one index as a single construct, or we can measure and analyse single components separately. While the first solution seems to be less complicated and is theoretically acceptable, the second option is a more fine-grained approach, and offers more in-depth comprehension of the problem of social capital building. Moreover, despite convincing theoretical arguments for a substantial relationship among single components of social capital, empirical research demonstrates that, especially at the micro-level, there are hardly systematic patterns of relationships among the components of social capital (Gabriel et al. 2002, 92). In other words, a member or volunteer in an organisation is not necessarily someone who trusts more other people and who strongly supports pro-social norms. Furthermore, especially when analysing the determinants of social capital it is advisable to consider the components separately, since single components can be nurtured by distinct individual and contextual factors (Gabriel et al. 2002, 135). As we will see by the end of this chapter, the outcome of the empirical measurement of social capital shows that this approach is appropriate, since the levels of the single components of social capital differ considerably between societies. While in some societies the cultural dimensions of social capital are well developed, and the structural dimensions are underdeveloped, in other societies the level of endowment in all three dimensions is more consistent. Poland has considerable differences in endowment between structural and cultural social capital. So by considering social capital as a multi-dimensional concept, cross-national diversities can be captured.

2.3 Why is social capital an important resource for Central Eastern Europe?

2.3.1 Social capital and democracy

Social capital provides democracy with a structural and cultural foundation. There are many ways in which social capital contributes to better democracy: vital associational life helps to develop a sense of solidarity and fellowship among citizens; social participation contributes to the development of a "culture of trust" not only among fellow citizens but also between the citizenry and institutions – in effect the distance between the citizenry and institutions shrinks, and active citizens have a greater sense of political efficacy (Gabriel et al. 2002, 20). On the other hand scholars stress that social capital is above all a Western-culture-oriented concept (Howard 2003, 48; Letki/Evans 2005, 525; Roßteutscher 2007, 235) and is therefore not fully applicable outside the realm of established democracies in Northwestern Europe and North America. The question is whether it is applicable to the countries of Central Eastern Europe, or only to those with consolidated democracies? Let us begin with democratisation.

In their study on democratisation, Linz and Stepan emphasise the importance of civil society as a mobilising power for anti-regime opposition, especially in Eastern Europe (Linz/Stepan 1996, 7). It turns out, however, that not all types of organisations have a similar impact on democracy. While organisations with a connected nature influence democratisation positively by building bridges among groups of citizens, those with an isolated nature[6] – which produce mostly bonding social capital – affect democracy in a negative way (Paxton 2002, 271). In other words, bridging social capital, which provides better linkages within a society, fosters democracy, while the same does not apply to bonding social capital.

Another cross-national study shows that social capital actually helps stabilise authoritarian regimes and its role in the democratisation process is not unequivocally positive (Roßteutscher 2007, 235; Roßteutscher 2010, 751-752). In addition to questions about whether the impact of structural components of social capital on democratisation is positive, it is also disputable whether social trust contributes positively to democracy: "the level of social trust was irrelevant for the success of

---

[6] To the category 'isolated associations' Paxton counts sport, religious associations and trade unions, whereas the category 'connected associations' consists of organizations related to social welfare, education or cultural activities, local community actions, professional activities, youth work, peace movements, etc. (Paxton 2002, 270).

democratization" in Central and Eastern Europe (Letki/Evans 2005, 523). Scholars suggest that high levels of social capital in Western societies are rather an effect and not a cause of stable democracies (Letki/Evans 2005, 523), or that there is a mutually reinforcing interaction between democracy and social capital (Paxton 2002, 271). For Central Eastern Europe the results of these studies are particularly relevant, at least for those countries that score the highest in democratic performance, because they imply that in countries where democracy is consolidated, social capital and democracy have good prospects to develop. Freedom House counts eight ex-communist countries as consolidated democracies in 2010: Czech Republic, Hungary, Estonia, Latvia, Lithuania, Poland, Slovakia and Slovenia.[7]

Twenty years after the collapse of communism in those countries that are classified as consolidated democracies in Central Europe, there is little likelihood of severe political instability or the return of non-democratic regimes. Democracy seems to be a well-established and commonly accepted political system in these countries (Klingemann et al. 2006, 5), and Poland is one example of a successfully consolidated democracy. Still, there is room for improvement as far as the quality of governance is concerned. Central Eastern Europe falls significantly behind the average of OECD countries in all four measures of the quality of governance: voice and accountability, rule of law, control of corruption, and the quality of public and civil services (Linde 2009, 5-6). Therefore social capital can play an important role in newly consolidated democracies as a means to improve governance. According to Putnam, the quality of governance depends on societal resources:

> "Civic context matters for the way institutions work. By far the most important factor in explaining good government is the degree to which social and political life in a region approximates the ideal of the civic community." (Putnam 1993, 120)

Therefore, a better understanding of the nature of social capital in Central Europe, and the way it is produced, can contribute to improvements in the functioning of democratic institutions and processes in the region and in Poland in particular.

2.3.2 Social capital destroyed by communism?

Explorations of social capital are particularly interesting in the context of the latest political legacies in Central Eastern Europe. Returning to the idea of whether social capital is a Western oriented concept, we could ask where the border is between West and East? Did the communist legacy bring such a long-lasting effect that the Iron Curtain became an enduring line of demarcation? Are post-communist socie-

---

[7] Freedom House Report "Nations in Transit 2010" http://www.freedomhouse.eu/images/nit2010/NIT-2010-Tables1.pdf, accessed on 01.02.2011.

ties indeed so different due to over 40 years of totalitarian rule? Or maybe the religious division between West and East Christianity is the real difference, since Catholic and Protestant countries are more successful in the consolidation of democracy than Orthodox countries. These questions cannot be answered definitively, however when examining social capital building we can see to what extent the mechanisms differ between Eastern and Western democracies and whether the allegedly Western-oriented concept – social capital – is also applicable to Eastern Central Europe.

What are the reasons for a lower stock of social capital across formerly communist societies? The totalitarian regimes are claimed to have destroyed social and institutional trust through the policy of control and surveillance of citizens and civic organisations (Sztompka 1995, 254; Salamon et al. 2003, 48-49; Paldam/Svendsen 2000, 7). The only realms of citizens' life that were excluded from state control were family life and informal ties with friends and acquaintances (Bozóki 1994, 123; Grabowska/Szawiel 2001, 155), which probably remained in post-communist societies as informal social capital (Howard 2003, 27-28). The economic and political turbulences in the transition period contributed additionally to the great disillusionment across post-communist societies and led to a so-called post-honeymoon effect, meaning a decline in political participation a few years after the systemic transformation (Inglehart/Catterberg 2002, 308). In effect there is widespread social apathy and a lack of interest in social engagement across post-communist citizenries. Persisting legacies of communist regimes continue to influence people's attitudes, in particular about the role of the state: "another characteristic behavioural pattern is a wide reluctance to take decisions which may be accountable (...) and a tendency to delegate responsibility (...), while at the same time demanding care, social security, or other free benefits from the authorities" (Sztompka 1991, 303).

The extent to which Poland differs in its communist legacy from other countries in the region is discussed in chapter 3. First, we should learn whether the distributions of single components of social capital are indeed different in Eastern and Western Europe. Second, we should compare the endowment in social capital of Poland and other societies with a communist legacy.

2.4 Social capital in Central Eastern Europe: operationalisation and distribution

"Weakness of civil society" and "culture of mistrust" seem to characterise the societies of Central Eastern Europe (Sztompka 1995; Howard 2003). Furthermore, Poland has allegedly an exceptionally poorly developed civil society, even when compared to other countries from the region (Barnes 1998, 127; Howard 2003, 58). Similarly, social trust is relatively lower in Poland than in other societies in the region (Kunz 2004, 208; Fidrmuc/Gërxhani 2007). The objective of this section is to provide empirical evidence for the endowment with social capital across Central and

Eastern Europe including Poland, whereby Western European countries are considered as references to post-communist societies. Single components of social capital are examined separately.

As mentioned in the introductory chapter, religious influence – specifically the relevance of the Catholic tradition – is one of the factors that will be examined in the following chapters. This is why in this section, the 29 countries under examination are divided in two geographical groups (Western and Eastern European societies) and are also clustered by dominant religious tradition.[8] Across Central Eastern European countries, seven are Catholic (Croatia, Czech Republic, Hungary, Lithuania, Poland, Slovakia and Slovenia), two are Protestant (Estonia and Latvia), and five are Orthodox (Belarus, Bulgaria, Romania, Russia and Ukraine). In the group of Western countries, seven are predominantly Catholic (Austria, Belgium, France, Ireland, Italy, Portugal and Spain), eight are Protestant (Denmark, Finland, Germany, Iceland, Luxemburg, the Netherlands, Sweden and United Kingdom) and one is Orthodox (Greece).[9] First we will analyse structural aspects (social networks); an examination of the cultural aspects (trust, norms and values) of social capital follows.

2.4.1   Social networks

When exploring social networks in Central and Eastern Europe we need to investigate formal networks (membership and volunteering) as well as informal networks (friendship ties). By including informal networks, which are said to have replaced the role of civil society during communism and to have persisted afterwards, I take into consideration the specific nature of networks in post-communist societies. In general, lower levels of formal networks are expected in formerly communist societies compared to Western societies. The East-West discrepancy might be greater in the case of volunteering than in the case of membership, because membership in certain organisations, especially trade unions, could be relatively high in ex-

---

[8] Classification by historically predominant religion is based on Norris and Inglehart (2005, 46-47). This classification is a simplification, since several countries, such as the Netherlands or Germany are dominated by mixed traditions, while some are actually merely secular nowadays, such as Czech Republic or Estonia (see: Britannica World Data 2009. Encyclopedia Britannica Book of the Year 2009. Chicago [u.a.]). Still, for comparative purposes this simplified classification is satisfactory.

[9] The following country name abbreviations are used in the graphs: AU – Austria, BE – Belgium, BU – Bulgaria, BR –Belarus, CR – Croatia, CZ – Czech Republic, DE – Denmark, ES – Estonia, FI – Finland, FR – France, GE – Germany, IE – Greece, HU – Hungary, IC – Iceland, IR – Ireland, IT – Italy, LV – Latvia, LT – Lithuania, LU – Luxemburg, NL – the Netherlands, PL – Poland, PT – Portugal, RO – Romania, RU – Russian Federation, SK – Slovakia, SL – Slovenia, SP – Spain, SE – Sweden, UK – Ukraine; Bosnia and Herzegovina is excluded from this section of analyses, because it is the only Muslim country in the sample, and there is no Western Muslim country available for comparison.

communist societies (Howard 2003, 65). By contrast, informal networks should be quite widespread across Central Eastern European societies.

Formal engagement can take a passive or an active form – one could be a member in an organisation without taking part in any of its activities. A question in the WVS about belonging to an organisation captures both passive and active forms of engagement. In order to capture various forms of active engagement in social networks, unpaid work for an organisation (volunteering) is also included. Both active and passive participation are indicators for involvement in societal networks, though active engagement is expected to contribute more strongly to social cohesion. The question wording is:

> "Please look carefully at the following list of the voluntary organizations and activities and say which, if any, do you belong to?
> - social welfare services for elderly, handicapped or deprived people,
> - religious or church organizations,
> -education, arts, music or cultural activities,
> - trade unions,
> - political parties or groups,
> - local community action on issues like poverty, employment, housing, racial equality,
> - third world development or human rights,
> - conservation, the environment, ecology, animal rights,
> - professional associations,
> - youth work (e.g. scouts, guides, youth clubs etc.),
> - sports or recreation,
> - women's groups,
> - peace movement,
> - voluntary organization concerned with help,
> - other groups."

The second question in the WVS refers to active forms of social engagement:

> "Please look carefully at the following list of voluntary organizations and activities and say which, if any, are you currently doing unpaid voluntary work for?"

The list of organisations is identical.

At this point in the investigation, we are interested in aggregated levels of engagement. Organisational participation is measured at the aggregate level by the percentage of respondents in each country who reported membership in at least one organisation, regardless of type. Figure 2.1 presents levels of belonging to organisations across European countries. Post-communist countries are presented in the right-hand side of the graph, while the Western societies are depicted on the left. Additionally, countries are clustered by the dominant religious tradition, starting with Catholic, followed by Orthodox and Protestant. Poland is displayed in the cluster of Catholic post-communist countries in the middle part of the graph. In addition, Table 2.1 below demonstrates the weighted average levels of membership by country in geographical-religious clusters, while the last column presents the score for Poland. This allows the assessment of the relative level of participation in Poland compared to other countries with similar communist legacies or dominant religious traditions.

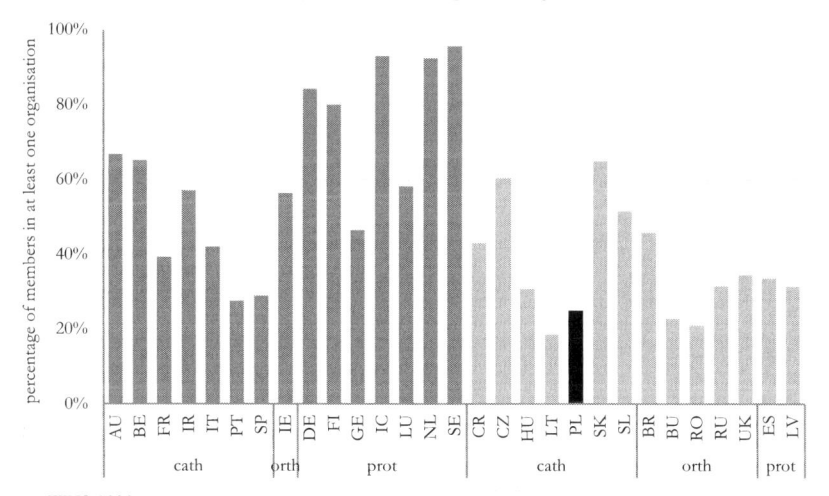

Figure 2.1 Membership in European countries (percentages)

Source: WVS 1999.

Table 2.1 Membership by groups of countries (weighted average percentage by country group)

	Western				Eastern				Po-land
	Catholic	Protestant	Orthodox*	All	Catholic	Protestant	Orthodox	All	
average membership	47%	78%	56%	**62%**	42%	33%	31%	**37%**	*25%*

* only Greece
Source: WVS 1999.

In general, citizens in Western Europe are more engaged in organisations than in Central and Eastern Europe, as expected. In Western Europe the level of membership is highest in Protestant societies (on average 78 percent of respondents participate in at least one organisation). Greece as the only Orthodox Western country takes the second position (56 percent), while participation across countries dominated by Catholicism is the lowest (on average 47 percent). In contrast, in Central

Eastern Europe the highest average participation is reported in the group of Catholic countries (on average 42 percent), Protestant countries are second with one-third of the respondents declaring membership, and Orthodox countries are last (31 percent). In other words, participation patterns related to dominant religions are different between West and East (the impact of religion on participation is addressed in chapters 5 and 6). As far as individual countries are concerned, the highest levels of membership are found in Sweden, the Netherlands and Iceland, followed by Denmark and Finland, which confirms the leading position of Northern European countries in organisational participation (cf. Curtis et al. 2001, 799; Gabriel et al. 2002, 50-52). Across Central Eastern European societies, Slovakia takes the leading position, followed by Czech Republic, Slovenia and Belarus. The aggregated level of participation in Poland, with only one-quarter of respondents declaring membership in at least one organisation, is one of the lowest in Europe. Poland takes the fourth lowest position after Lithuania, Romania and Bulgaria. Interestingly, we can observe similar levels of participation between countries that belonged to one state before the collapse of communism. For instance levels of participation are similar in Slovakia and Czech Republic (around 60 percent), likewise in ex-Soviet countries – Russia, Ukraine, Estonia and Latvia – levels of participation remain at comparable levels (around 30 percent). The outliers in the case of ex-Soviet republics are Belarus, with relatively high participation, and at the other extreme Lithuania, with low participation.

The second measure of social networks is aggregate levels of volunteering. Distribution of volunteering by countries is depicted in Figure 2.2, while average levels of volunteering by country groups is presented Table 2.2, in the same way as membership.

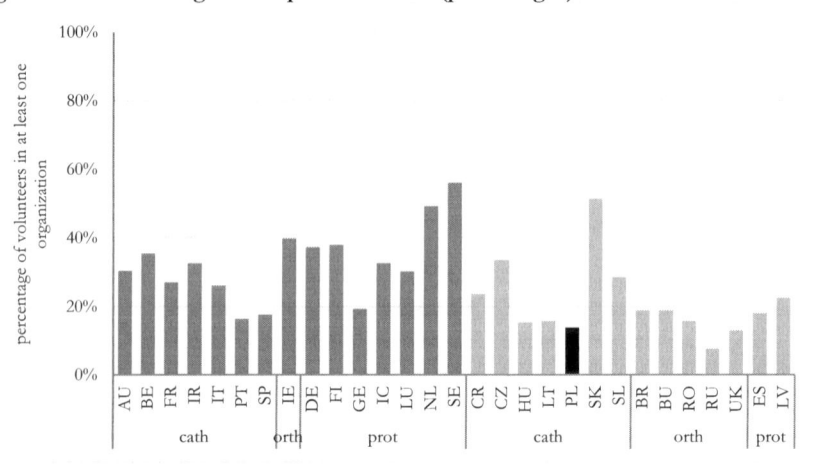

Figure 2.2 Volunteering in European countries (percentages)

Source: WVS 1999.

Table 2.2 Volunteering by groups of countries (weighted average percentage by country group)

	Western				Eastern				Poland
	Catholic	Protestant	Orthodox*	All	Catholic	Protestant	Orthodox	All	
average volunteering	27%	38%	40%	33%	26%	20%	15%	21%	*14%*

* only Greece
Source: WVS 1999.

Similar to membership, the level of volunteering is also generally lower in Eastern Europe than Western Europe, as expected. Across Central Eastern European societies, on average 21 percent of respondents declared doing an unpaid job for at least one organisation, while one-third reported having done so in Western Europe. Furthermore, relationships between dominant religious tradition and volunteering display different patterns in West and East. In Western Europe, respondents in Protestant societies reported higher levels of volunteerism (38 percent) than Catholic societies (27 percent), while the level of engagement in Greece was slightly higher than the average for Protestant publics (40 percent). In Central Eastern Europe patterns were different. While the highest average level of volunteering was reported by respondents in Catholic countries (26 percent), the second position was taken by Protestant Baltic societies with an average of one-fifth of respondents, and Orthodox countries demonstrated lower engagement with only 15 percent of respondents declaring volunteer work. As for individual countries, Sweden and the Netherlands took leading positions, followed, surprisingly, by an Eastern society: Slovakia.[10] Two other Eastern countries with relatively high levels of volunteering are, similar to membership, Slovenia and Czech Republic. On the other extreme, the lowest levels of volunteering are found in Russia and Ukraine, while Poland takes the third lowest position with only 14 percent of people reporting unpaid work for an organisation. In sum, in membership and volunteering Poland takes one of the last positions in Europe.

What about the informal networks? Are they indeed strong in Eastern Europe? How does the situation in Poland look? We again compare Central Eastern European and Western countries. If informal ties were strong in communist countries and the communist legacy is long lasting, we should find stronger informal networks in the East than in the West. Regrettably, the WVS offers limited possibilities to measure informal networks, especially when aiming to compare all 29 countries.

---

[10] This extraordinarily high level of volunteerism in Slovakia is probably overestimated in the WVS. According to Eurobarometer data (No 223) the level of voluntarism is indeed high in Slovakia, though does not reach the level of the leading Western societies. Therefore Slovakia is excluded from the dataset in the following analysis of the mechanisms (chapter 6).

The survey contains questions concerning the frequency of meeting with several types of people such as acquaintances, neighbours or colleagues; unfortunately these items are missing in several countries, including Poland. The only item that captures all 29 countries, including Poland, refers to the frequency of meeting friends. This is an imperfect measure of informal networks, since friends are a specific type of informal network, encompassing well-known persons, so we learn nothing about contacts with broader groups of acquaintances. Furthermore, the question's wording refers to time spent rather than spontaneous cooperation, which would be a more desirable measure of informal social capital. Nevertheless, by measuring the frequency of meeting friends across societies we can get a certain notion of the differences in informal ties across societies, even if it does not include all kinds of networks people are involved in. The question wording in the WVS is:

"I'm going to ask you how often you do certain things. Giving an answer from this card please tell me how often you do each."

One of the four options is:

"Spend time with friends."

The item is scaled from 1 to 4, whereby "1" means "every week," "2" – "once or twice a month", "3" – "a few times a year" and "4" – "not at all." When referring to social capital, the frequency of meeting people is not as essential as the existence of such contacts in general. Therefore the item is dichotomised, so we learn whether respondents report meeting friends or do not meet friends at all. The percentage of people meeting friends at the aggregate level in each country is presented in Figure 2.3, while Table 2.3 outlines the averages across groups of countries.

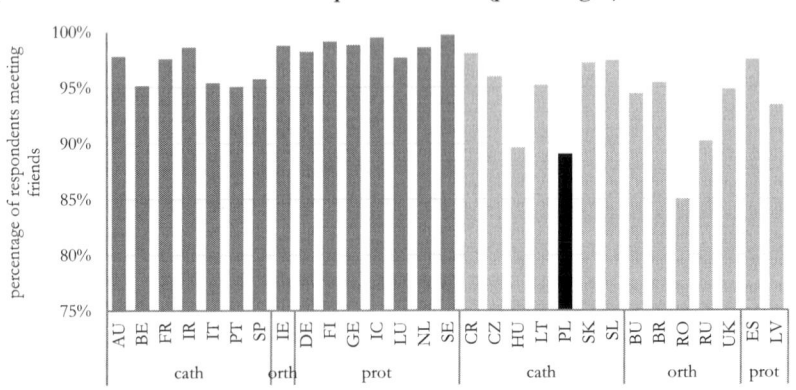

Figure 2.3 Informal networks in European countries (percentages)

Source: WVS 1999.

Table 2.3 Informal networks by groups of countries (weighted average percentage by country group)

	Western				Eastern				Poland
	Catholic	Protestant	Orthodox*	All	Catholic	Protestant	Orthodox	All	
percentage of respondents meeting friends	97%	99%	99%	**98%**	95%	96%	92%	**94%**	*89%*

* only Greece
Source: WVS 1999.

Surprisingly, people from Central Eastern Europe reported fewer informal networks than those in Western Europe. While in the West virtually all respondents reported meeting friends (98 percent), in Central Eastern Europe the score was also very high, though the average was a few percentage points lower (94 percent). In other words, the claim about stronger informal networks in post-communist Europe is not confirmed (Howard 2003, 27-28; Pichler/Wallace 2007, 426). Nevertheless these different findings might result from a different operationalisation of informal networks across studies.[11] Furthermore there are slight differences in informal networks across countries dominated by different religious traditions in Western Europe. It seems that people in Belgium, together with three Southern Catholic countries (Italy, Spain, Portugal), report a slightly lower percentage of respondents meeting friends, around 95 percent, compared to almost 99 percent across Protestant countries and Greece. In Eastern Europe, Orthodox countries have the weakest informal ties on average (92 percent of respondents reported meeting friends), while across Catholic and Protestant countries the average is slightly higher (95 and 96 percent, respectively). In the group of post-communist countries the relative differences among countries seem to be higher than in Western Europe. The highest scores of informal ties are reported by Croatia, Estonia, Slovenia and Slovakia (around 95 percent), on the other hand the least informal networks appear to be located in Romania (85 percent), Poland (89 percent) and Hungary (90 percent). In other words: Poland ranks at the second lowest position in informal ties.

Concluding the analysis of social networks, there are three general findings:
(1) all types of social networks are weaker in Central Eastern Europe when compared to Western Europe, including friendship ties;

---

[11] Howard's operationalisation of friendship networks is broad and encompasses questions concerning relying on friends for fixing one's house or car, or assisting someone in their family, or coping with difficult situations in general; a similar study by Pichler and Wallace is based on Eurobarometer data, and the operationalisation of informal networks in this study is much broader than mine and considers the frequency of contacts with neighbours, colleagues, and ways of giving help.

(2) formal networks are stronger in Protestant societies, though not in Central Eastern Europe (I return to the relevance of religion for social capital in chapters 5 and 6);
(3) Slovakia and Slovenia have the strongest social networks across Central Eastern Europe; and
(4) Poland has exceptionally weak social networks, as expected. For all three types of networks Poland takes one of the last positions across 29 European countries: rates of membership in Poland rank at the fourth lowest level, rates of volunteering are at the third lowest place, and the level of informal networks takes the second lowest position. These findings confirm that Poland is indeed an exception in Europe, even among countries from the region characterised by similar a communist experience, with an exceptionally weak structural dimension of social capital.

What about the cultural components of social capital? Is Poland an exception on the cultural dimension of social capital, too?

2.4.2 Social trust

Is a "culture of mistrust" indeed a widespread phenomenon in post-communist societies? Is Poland also an exception in the region in the case of trust? Using the WVS I analyse the aggregate levels of social trust across Central Eastern Europe. Western European countries are taken into consideration as a reference and, as with social networks, the analysis is conducted in groups of countries clustered according to their dominant religious tradition. As described in the previous section, the roots of social trust are found at the macro and micro levels. At the macro level, the collective experiences of a society are strong determinants for social trust. Therefore both communism and subsequent political and economic turmoil are circumstances that probably negatively influenced trust by evoking fear, uncertainty about the future, lack of reliability in the social and political systems, etc., which characterised the collective experience of Central Eastern societies (Sztompka 1995, 268). At the micro level, post-communist societies seem to display patterns of determinants of social trust that are very similar to those of Western societies: "there are differences between Western states and those in transition to democracy, but overall, the similarities are greater. The variables that are significant for the West are also significant for the formerly communist states" (Uslaner 2003a, 89). Therefore when comparing aggregate levels of trust across societies we should find especially large differences between Western and Eastern societies, which might be the consequence of a negative collective experience related to years under communism and the troubles resulting from the transition period.

Social trust is measured using the standard question for generalised trust:

Social capital in Central Eastern Europe: operationalisation and distribution 53

"Generally speaking, would you say that most people can be trusted or that you can't be too careful in dealing with people?"

The answers are coded as follows: "1" for "most people can be trusted" "2" for "can't be too careful." We are interested in the levels of trust across societies, so the percentage of people selecting the first option ("most people can be trusted") is compared. Figure 2.4 presents the percentage of respondents reporting generalised trust by country, while Table 2.4 demonstrates the average results by country groups.

Figure 2.4 Generalised trust across European countries (percentages)

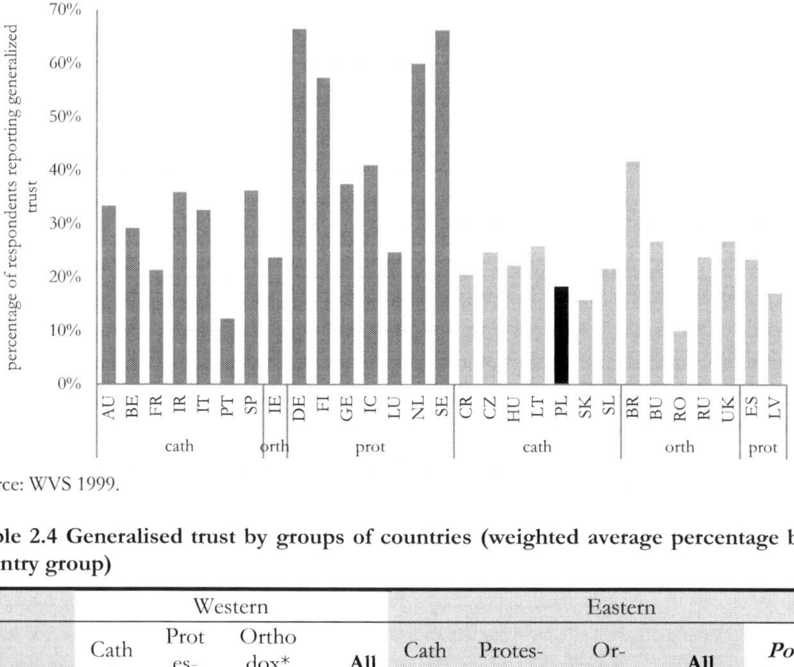

Source: WVS 1999.

Table 2.4 Generalised trust by groups of countries (weighted average percentage by country group)

	Western				Eastern				
	Catholic	Protestant	Orthodox*	**All**	Catholic	Protestant	Orthodox	**All**	*Poland*
weighted average percentage of trusters	29%	51%	24%	**39%**	21%	20%	26%	**23%**	*18%*

* only Greece
Source: WVS 1999.

Levels of social trust differ considerably across countries (Figure 2.4). In general, as expected, citizens in Western Europe are more likely to trust (around 40 percent on average, Table 2.4), than publics from the Eastern part of the continent (around one-quarter on average). The group of Protestant Western societies takes the leading position, with half of the respondents reporting trust on average, while the group of Catholic Western countries, with almost one-third declaring trust, ranks second. In contrast, post-communist European societies with a dominant Orthodox tradition are the most trusting, while Catholic and Protestant publics have similar levels of social trust, around one-fifth of the population. Here, again, patterns related to the dominant religious tradition are different in the West and East. The four most trusting individual countries are Protestant: Denmark, Sweden, the Netherlands and Finland (around 60 percent), while the least trusting are mostly formerly communist societies: Romania, Portugal, Slovakia, Latvia and Poland. Poland is ranked the fifth lowest, with 18 percent of respondents reporting trust. This finding also confirms the weakness of Polish society in regards to cultural social capital. The level of trust in Poland lies below the average of post-communist Europe as a whole, as well as Catholic post-communist countries. This indicates an exceptionally low endowment of cultural social capital in Poland, at least as far as social trust is concerned. What about the second cultural component of social capital – norms and values?

2.4.3 Norms and values

Norms and values are the second cultural component of social capital, the distributions of which will be examined at last. As described in the previous section, when approaching norms and values I refer especially to pro-social orientations: support for norms regulating social coexistence and cooperation. It is difficult to measure the extent to which people support norms of social coexistence and cooperation using the WVS, since such questions were not directly addressed in the questionnaire. We can, however, approximately assess people's value orientations and support for cooperation norms by analysing the answers concerning their evaluation of actions that could be directly harmful to others, such as cheating on taxes. Justification or rejection of such actions is based on an individual normative framework. Furthermore, these norms are directly related to the values of an individual (van Deth 1995, 6).

There is a battery of questions in the WVS that reports evaluations of certain actions such as the fulfilment of citizens' duties or behaviour that could disturb other people. In general the WVS allows the analysis of value orientations in two realms of life. The first realm is related to state-citizen relations or the "civil" sphere of life. Halpern confirms that there is "ample evidence that high social capital is associated with more 'virtuous citizenry'" (Halpern 2005, 185). The second realm refers to social coexistence, or the "public" sphere. Both *civil* and *public* spheres are complementing realms of social life: "individual taxpayers who believe that others are dishonest or are distrustful of government are more likely to cheat. My willingness to pay my share depends crucially on my perception that others are doing the same" (Putnam 2000, 347). Therefore, exploring the norms concerning civil and public spheres will give us a comprehensive picture of the widespread norms and values in a given society that should sustain social cohesion.

In general I expect a high acceptance of the norms related to social coexistence in both parts of Europe. We might find slightly lower levels of acceptance of the norms of social behaviour in post-communist societies, since there is evidence of lower solidarity across societies from this region, whereby in Poland solidarity seems to be at a relatively high level (Roßteutscher 2004, 186). The same study demonstrates higher levels of law-abidingness across formerly communist countries compared to Western Europe (Roßteutscher 2004, 185). On the other hand, Gabriel and colleagues report inconsistent patterns of acceptance of social norms and communitarian values in Central European societies. While Poland and Eastern Germany rank relatively high in approval of social norms and communitarian values, Hungary takes the lowest position among 13 European countries and the USA (Gabriel et al. 2002, 81-83). The results of both studies can only be used as a guideline for the purposes of this study, since the conceptualisation of norms and values differs among them and the number of countries is larger in my study (which also includes the ex-Soviet countries).

First, the acceptance of norms concerning the civil sphere is examined. The WVS contains a number of items concerning the justification of cheating actions – claiming state benefits without entitlement, avoiding paying taxes and corruption. These items are considered as an operationalisation of the acceptance of *norms of civil behaviour*. The question wording is as follows:

> "Please tell me for each of the following statements, whether you think it can always be justified, never be justified, or something in between"

Following four items are considered:

- "Claiming state benefits which you are not entitled to,"
- "Cheating on tax if you have a chance,"
- "Someone accepting a bribe in the course of their duties,"
- "Paying cash for services to avoid taxes."

Respondents assess their level of acceptance of these actions on a scale from 1 (never) to 10 (always).

Using Principal Component Analysis, evidence was found of one-dimensional latent construct behind these four items, with 53 percent of the variance explained. The results of the extraction of the latent factor, shown in Table 2.5, are satisfactory, since all coefficients reach the level above 0.6. Cronbach's alpha is at a satisfactory level of 0.7.

Table 2.5 Extraction of a one-dimensional indicator for "norms of civil behaviour" (factor loadings)

Items	One component extracted (norms of civil behaviour)
Not justifiable: claiming government benefits	0.673
Not justifiable: cheating on taxes	0.809
Not justifiable: someone accepting a bribe	0.680
Not justifiable: paying cash	0.735
R^2	**0.527**
Cronbach's alpha	**0.698**
N	**34,812**

Notes: extraction method: Principal Component Analysis, items coding: 10-1, "never justifiable" - "always justifiable."
Source: WVS 1999.

In the course of further analyses, the acceptance of norms of civil behaviour is measured with the index of norms of civil behaviour (NCBI), which values equal factor scores, rescaled from 0 to 1. Low values of NCBI mean low acceptance of norms of civil behaviour in a society. Figure 2.5 presents mean values of NCBI in each of the examined countries, while Table 2.6 summarises the results by groups of countries according to region and dominant religious tradition.

Figure 2.5 Norms of civil behaviour in European countries (mean index scores)

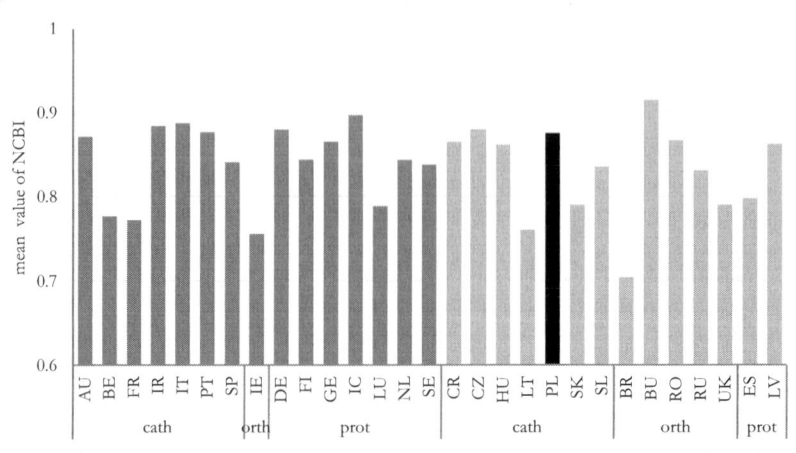

Source: WVS 1999.

Table 2.6 Norms of civil behaviour by groups of countries (weighted average value of NCBI by country group)

	Western				Eastern				Poland
	Catholic	Protestant	Orthodox*	All	Catholic	Protestant	Orthodox	All	
weighted average mean value of NCBI	0.844	0.851	0.756	**0.842**	0.839	0.831	0.822	**0.831**	*0.876*

* only Greece
Source: WVS 1999.

As expected, acceptance of norms of civil behaviour is in general widespread across most of the countries: the mean value of the index reaches a high level of 0.8 in most cases. The strongest outlier is Belarus with the lowest acceptance of norms, which is not surprising regarding the oppressive form of regime in this country. Otherwise, publics report relatively low approval for civil norms in Belgium, France, Greece and Lithuania. In contrast, Poland takes one of the leading positions in approval of civil norms, after Bulgaria and Czech Republic, in the group of post-communist societies. The highest levels of acceptance are demonstrated by Iceland, Italy, Ireland and Denmark, so that Poland ranks seventh among all countries studied. Furthermore, the differences between Eastern and Western Europe are rather modest – the average value of the NCBI is only 0.01 lower in the group of formerly communist countries when compared to the Western countries.[12] The East-West differences according to the dominant religious tradition are similar in Protestant and Catholic countries. On the other hand, average acceptance of norms is higher in Eastern Orthodox societies compared to Western Greece. In Poland, approval of civil norms is higher than the averages in every group of countries. Is the level of acceptance of social norms so high in Poland, too?

Acceptance of norms related to social behaviour is operationalised with other items contained in the same battery of questions. The items concern justification of such deviant behaviours as drunk driving, taking somebody's car for a joyride or littering. The item concerning corruption is also taken into consideration. The introductory statement and the scale used for the justification are identical to the civil norms item. The wording of the relevant answers is as follows:

-"Someone accepting a bribe in the course of their duties,"
-"Taking and driving away a car belonging to someone else (joyriding),"
-"Throwing away litter in a public place,"

---

[12] The T-test provides evidence of significant (p<0.05) differences between mean values of NCB Index in the groups of Eastern and Western countries.

-"Driving under the influence of alcohol."

As in the case of civil norms, a Principal Component Analysis is used to find evidence of a latent structure that might be hidden behind these items. The findings are encouraging, since all four items concerning the justification of deviant social behaviours seem to have one latent construct behind them, which explains 52 percent of the variance of input items (Table 2.7). All factor loading coefficients reach an acceptable level above 0.6, while Cronbach's alpha is the acceptable value of 0.7. In further analyses, a single index of the norms of social behaviour is used (NSBI), rather than four individual items.

Table 2.7 Extraction of a one-dimensional indicator for "norms of social behaviour" (factor loadings)

Items	One component extracted (norms of social behaviour)
Not justifiable: someone accepting a bribe	0.695
Not justifiable: joyriding	0.699
Not justifiable: throwing away litter	0.728
Not justifiable: driving under influence of alcohol	0.751
R^2	**0.517**
Cronbach's alpha	**0.679**
N	36,816

Notes: extraction method: Principal Component Analysis, item coding: 10-1, "never justifiable" - "always justifiable."
Source: WVS 1999.

The NSBI resulting from factor scores, and subsequently rescaled from 0 to 1, is used to analyse the acceptance of norms across the countries examined. The levels of NSBI across the Eastern and Western countries are displayed in Figure 2.6, and the average acceptance of norms by country groups is presented in Table 2.8.

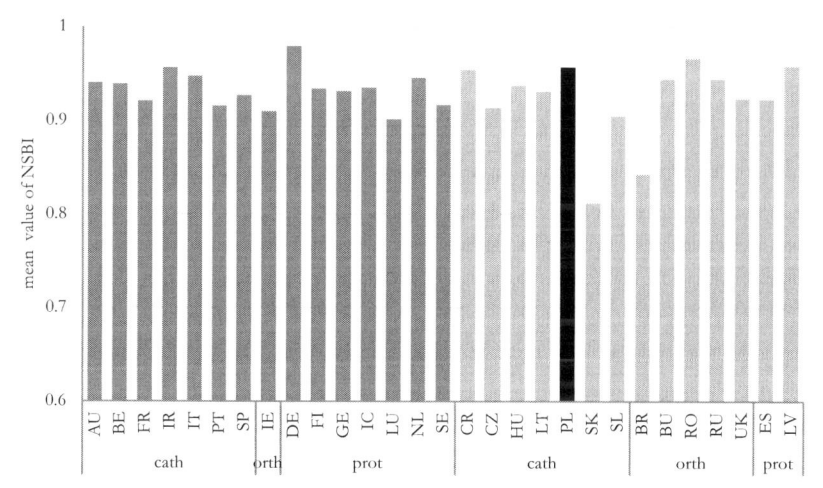

Figure 2.6 Norms of social behaviour in European countries (mean index scores)

Source: WVS 1999.

Table 2.8 Norms of social behaviour by groups of countries (weighted average value of NSBI by country group)

	Western				Eastern				
	Catholic	Protestant	Orthodox*	**All**	Catholic	Protestant	Orthodox	**All**	*Poland*
weighted average mean value of NSBI	0.935	0.935	0.910	**0.934**	0.916	0.941	0.924	**0.922**	*0.957*

* only Greece
Source: WVS 1999.

The average level of acceptance of norms of social behaviour is even higher when compared to norms in the civil sphere: the average for all countries is close to the maximum value of 1 (Table 2.8). Across all but two countries, the mean level of NSBI is higher than 0.9. Two countries, Slovakia and Belarus, are outliers with the lowest levels of approval for social norms (Figure 2.6). On the other end of the spectrum, Poland ranks fourth after Denmark, Romania and Latvia. The comparison between the average NSBI in Western and Eastern Europe shows a lower average acceptance of social norms in the group of post-communist countries, which contradicts expectations.[13] Otherwise, there is no difference in acceptance of norms between Catholic and Protestant countries in the West, while in the East the highest acceptance seems to be widespread in Protestant countries, followed by Orthodox ones, and at last Catholic countries. The level of norms acceptance in Poland is higher than the averages of all groups of countries.

In sum, Poland seems to be a society that displays exceptionally high levels of acceptance of norms in both the social and civil spheres. In both cases, Poland's score is higher than the averages in the East and West. This finding points to an exceptionally high endowment in cultural social capital in Poland (norms and values).

2.5 Conclusions: is Polish society exceptionally weak endowed with social capital?

Having analysed the aggregated levels of all three components of social capital in Europe, we can compare the situation in Poland to other societies. Table 2.9 summarises the scores of calculated indicators for social capital across European countries and presents the weighted averages of the aggregated data of the countries grouped by region and dominant religious tradition. The most striking finding is that lower endowment with social capital in the group of post-communist societies is systematically found across all components – structural and cultural, whereby the relative difference is the lowest in cultural social capital (norms and values). The evidence for Poland is a bit more positive. On the one hand, structural components of social capital and social trust are indeed exceptionally low in Poland, not only when compared to Western societies, but also compared to formerly communist countries. Engagement in social networks is systematically the lowest across Orthodox Eastern countries, including informal networks, and in Poland the percentage of networking respondents is even lower. The situation looks a bit different in the case of trust. The least trusting are Protestant societies, but the level of trust in Poland is lower than the average levels of trust in Protestant countries. On the other hand, norms and values in Poland are at an exceptionally high level in both social and civil spheres. It seem that Halpern's claim about "functional equivalence" is confirmed in the case of Polish society (Halpern 2005, 19). We can say that low structural social capital and social trust are counterbalanced in Poland by a high cultural dimension of social capital (norms and values).

---

[13] The T-test provides evidence of significant (p<0.05) differences between mean values of NSB Index in the groups of Eastern and Western countries.

Table 2.9 Indicators for social capital, weighted averages across groups of European countries

Components of social capital	Social capital indicators	Western countries	Eastern countries	Poland	Rank of Poland in Europe (out of 29 countries)
Social networks	Membership	62%	37%	25%	4. lowest score
	Volunteering	33%	21%	14%	3. lowest score
	Informal networks	98%	94%	89%	2. lowest score
Trust	Trust	39%	23%	18%	5. lowest score
Norms and values	Civil norms	0.84	0.83	0.88	7. highest score
	Social norms	0.93	0.92	0.96	4. highest score

Source: WVS 1999.

We learned from this chapter that Poland is indeed an exception across post-communist Europe as far as endowment with social capital is concerned. However, the good news is that this exceptionality is not purely negative. Polish society seems to be less networked in the form of associations and friendship ties. Poles are one of the least trusting peoples, too. Nevertheless this deficit seems to be somewhat compensated by a relatively high acceptance of norms that support social coexistence.

The aim of the next chapters is to investigate the reasons for Polish exceptionality. In general, three main influences will be taken into consideration – communist legacy, systemic transition and Catholicism as the dominant religion. As the above findings show, the communist past seems to be a negative context for social capital, since low endowment with social capital has been systematically found though all its components in Central Eastern Europe. Therefore chapter 3 presents a review of the literature on diverse aspects of the communist legacy and ensuing systemic transitions, which might have affected social networks, social trust, and norms and values. In this analysis a special emphasis will be placed on any dissimilarities between Poland and other post-communist countries, as potential reasons for the exceptional situation in Poland. Furthermore, chapters 4 and 5 discuss the influence of religion on social capital, with a special emphasis on Catholicism, which is the dominant religious tradition in Poland. As displayed in Table 2.9, social networks and social trust are weaker in Catholic countries, though this applies only to Western societies. In contrast, in Eastern Europe Catholicism appears to be a favourable context for building networks, while it seems hardly to affect informal networks, social trust and norms and values. The way in which Catholicism, the communist legacy and systemic transition affect social capital in Poland remains the problem to be explored.

3 Communist legacy and systemic transition

3.1 Time perspective

Living under a communist regime is an experience shared by people across Central Eastern Europe. Yet, are the consequences of the communist past for social capital the same in all countries in the region? In general, scholars unanimously point to a low endowment of social capital across post-communist societies, which involves a low level of social trust and low levels of associational and volunteering activities (Curtis et al. 2001, 791; Howard 2003, 90; Salamon et al. 2003, 48-49; Fioramonti/Heinrich 2007, 38; Valkov 2009, 8). Authors stress a number of societal similarities between countries in this region. Howard, in his study on civil society in post-communist countries, found common adaptive behaviour mechanisms across the region:

> „the variation among post-communist countries appears to be differences 'in degree,' and not 'in kind' (…) a country's prior communist experience has a very strong negative impact on the organizational membership of its citizens today." (2003, 90)

He assumes that behavioural and attitudinal patterns that were developed under communist regimes persist after the collapse of the communist systems. When analysing social trust in this region, scholars find unique patterns across societies (Mishler/Rose 1997, 437; Uslaner 2002, 244). Inglehart and Welzel observe "a massive period effect" across post-communist societies in value changing processes (2005, 133). Similarities across ex-communist countries become evident when they are compared with a group of established democracies, or a group of other ex-authoritarian regimes (Howard 2003, 90; Salamon et al. 2003, 48-49). What are the reasons for such striking similarities across post-communist societies? How do scholars explain the impact of the communist past on social capital?

The term "communist past" encompasses a wide spectrum of societal, political and economic phenomena. In order to structure my descriptive analysis, I discuss the communist past with reference to two aspects: (1) societal developments crucial for social capital during the communist regime (communist legacy); and (2) societal changes during the systemic transformation after the collapse of the communist regime (consequences of systemic transition). Systemic transition brings new and different experiences, profound changes in citizens' everyday lives, and often a deterioration in living standards – especially at the beginning of transition. When analysing social capital building shortly after the collapse of a political system, the impact of both the prior system and the consequences of transformation should be taken into account. Therefore it is reasonable to distinguish between conditions prevailing in Central Eastern Europe under the communist regime and those that dominated in the aftermath.

3.2 Before the collapse of communism – similarities across countries

My analysis begins with a description of conditions that are crucial for social capital that dominated across communist societies before the collapse of the communist regimes. Phenomena and patterns discussed in this section were similar across communist societies, including Poland. I discuss single components of social capital – social networks, social trust, norms and values – according to the theoretical approach presented in chapter 2.

3.2.1 Social networks

People living in communist countries needed to develop certain strategies in order to survive under a hostile system. Far-reaching caution in relationships between people was one widespread survival strategy. Compulsory or coerced associational activities – such as trade unions or memberships in professional associations – failed to generate trust or help develop civil skills, while informal networks became a substitute for the inadequate formal networks.

3.2.1.1 Involuntary communist organisations

Formal organisations enjoyed a low degree of trust across communist societies: "the communist practice of compulsory membership and the misrepresentation of members' views has left a legacy of distrust" (Rose 2009, 62; see also Fioramonti/Heinrich 2007, 38). Membership in state controlled organisations, for instance youth groups, trade unions, peasant or worker groups, was often mandatory or coerced by circumstances: "people joined organizations because they had to, or because they were threatened with negative consequences if they did not join, or because they improved their career chances by joining" (Howard 2003, 27). Widespread membership in intermediate "politically correct" organisations was an instrument of control and indoctrination used by regimes and served as a source of legitimacy.

Membership rates in these "official" organisations were quite high, so theoretically such broad networks could create (bridging) social capital. Principally, membership in some types of organisations provided an opportunity to build horizontal networks among members, or among members of different groups. Moreover, activity in these organisations could provide an opportunity to learn civic skills, since members had a common goal to achieve together. However, the difference between *voluntary* social activity and *enforced* social activity is *the motivation and the level of engagement*:

> "if we consider the motivation, the circumstances of becoming a member on the one hand, and the predominantly façade range of activity and bureaucracy on the other hand, all this can be hardly conducive to authentic and engaged membership."[14]
>
> (Grabowska/Szawiel 2001, 148)

Members of such involuntary networks lacked trust as well as sincere motivation. In other words, such "official" organisations failed to produce the horizontal networks characterised by civil society. Scholars describe characteristically weak relations among citizens in communist societies as "atomization" (Paldam/Svendsen 2000, 5; Grabowska/Szawiel 2001, 149). Furthermore, spontaneous and voluntary foundations of civil or cultural organisations, or loose citizens' initiatives, were always treated with suspicion and were restricted, if not directly prohibited. Thus membership for communist citizens had nothing to do with a voluntary action and creation of horizontal networks. Poland was in this regard an exception. Polish citizens managed to create organisations, which to some extent enjoyed autonomy – the very first horizontal networks appeared primarily in the 1970s among the activists of underground opposition (Grabowska/Szawiel 2001, 148-149; Wnuk-Lipiński 2007, 35). Civil society under communism in Poland is discussed in section 3.3.

In general, in a context of coerced membership and intimidation, communist citizens were obliged to create substitutes for civil society that was lacking, such as creating informal networks.

3.2.1.2 Informal networks – an alternative for inadequate associational networks?

Two kinds of informal networks dominated across communist societies. One type of informal network resulted from the "privatisation of life," which means a withdrawal from the public sphere and a focus on private networks of family and close friends. These behavioural patterns were the consequence of oppressive policies

---

[14] Translation KL.

enforced by communist regimes. A second type of informal network, "provisional" or "instrumental" ties, appeared as a consequence of shortages of basic goods and services.

3.2.1.2.1 The privatisation of life

The "privatisation of life" was a common survival strategy in communist societies (Bozóki 1994, 123; Grabowska/Szawiel 2001, 155; Howard 2003, 28; Wnuk-Lipiński 2007, 35; Rose 2009, 25). This term refers to the withdrawal of ordinary people from the public sphere and a focus on the private sphere, including family and close friends. It was an inevitable adaptive behaviour for people living under such systems, in which one could not rely on any public forms of networking, and distrusted any official organisations. This phenomenon was described in the 1970s by Polish sociologist Nowak, who labelled it the "social vacuum" (Nowak 1979). Rose attributes the term "the hour-glass society" to this phenomenon (Rose 2009, 25), pointing to two barely overlapping worlds in which the elites and ordinary citizens were living. This situation ultimately led to a strong emphasis on the private sphere and strengthened family ties (Wallace 1995, 104). Young generations failed to learn to be independent and autonomous; contrarily, they relied on the "instrumental" ties and social capital accumulated by parents. In addition, housing shortages resulted in the preservation of multigenerational families and reinforced the dependencies of children on their parents (Schöpflin 1994, 198; Wallace 1995, 98; Rose 2009, 33).

What impact do strong family ties have on social capital? Banfield, who analysed the impoverished village of Montegrano in Southern Italy, argues that family-based isolation leads to a lack of cooperation among community members and, in effect, backwardness and impoverishment become stronger. He terms this pattern of behaviour and attitudes "amoral familism" (1958, 85). Putnam argues that people who live under an authoritarian government and are trapped in "amoral familism" tend to lack civic-mindedness as a consequence: "Force and family provide a primitive substitute for the civic community" (1993, 178). Without widespread social capital, a community can hardly function in a civic way.

In countries where the collapse of communism was followed by economic development, housing shortages should weaken gradually. And if housing shortages contributed in part to strong family dependencies, this should change after the rise in housing availability. Furthermore, the "privatization of life" is no longer needed in a free society. People can express their opinions and join the public sphere without being intimidated. It remains an open question to what extent these behavioural patterns can promptly adjust after a change in political system. Many authors subscribe to the thesis that behavioural patterns remain after institutional changes and need much more time to evolve (Howard 2003, 105; Uslaner/Badescu 2003, 224-225, see also next section). We probably need to wait for a generational change to observe the evolution in behavioural patterns in post-communist societies.

3.2.1.2.2 "Provisional" or "instrumental" ties

"Provisional" networks were the second common type of informal networks in communist societies. Establishing networks of informal connections was indispensable to coping with the shortages of goods and services in official, dysfunctional markets (Wallace 1995, 98; Paldam/Svendsen 2000, 8; Howard 2003, 25 ff.; Uslaner/Badescu 2003, 222). Since centrally planned economies were ineffective, people needed to find alternative ways of acquiring desired goods or services. Howard calls these networks "instrumental" because they existed to satisfy people's basic needs (Howard 2003, 28). Considering the size and importance of informal "provisional" ties in communist societies, we should address the questions (1) whether these ties persisted in post-communist societies after the dismantling of the planned economy, and (2) whether the ties can be considered an alternative source of social capital.

If goods and services are widely accessible in the developing market economy, the "instrumental" ties are not needed any more. Howard proves empirically that in Eastern Germany, compared to Russia, these informal ties lost much of their relevance (2003, 113). He explains:

> "This is not surprising given that, although most goods and services can now be purchased in Russia, prices are prohibitive for most people, who still have to rely on friends for assistance. In Eastern Germany, however, the advantage of living in a stable market economy and a more free and safe society is that most people now have enough income and peace of mind to get things done through official channels, rather than having to rely on friends as much as they used to." (2003, 109)

Likewise, Rose observes that the transformation phase is related to economic hardship, therefore: "ordinary people continued to rely on informal networks to cope with the stress of transformation" (Rose 2009, 26). So it seems that the "instrumental" ties do not disappear until the market economy functions properly and goods and services are commonly available and affordable. This is probably still not the case in certain Central Eastern European countries, as Rose explains. The empirical study conducted by Pichler and Wallace on informal ties across Europe reports a higher propensity to build informal ties in post-communist societies than in Western ones, even 14 years after transformation (2007, 431). In other words, the reminders of "provisional" networks are still to be found in the former communist societies.

To answer the second question, whether "provisional" networks can be an alternative source of social capital, we need to return to the function of social capital stressed by its conceptualisation (section 2.2). The main difference between social capital as conceptualised by Putnam and the "provisional" networks under communism is the strictly individualistic character of the "provisional" networks. Social capital in Putnam's sense is both an individual and a collective resource (Putnam 1993, 170; see also Esser 2007, 24). However, trust and open "credit slips" (to use the terminology of Coleman 1988) is particularised in the case of "provisional" networks:

> "networks in communist societies were generally specific (oriented to bring in a specific range of goods or services not available through normal means) and simultaneous (the favour would be returned in the future); but because they were not highly transitive (…) they were consequently low on generalization."   (Kolankiewicz 1996, 438)

"Provisional" networks were created to meet a specific need, and the kind of trust or "credit slips" related to these type of networks were not transferable (Wallace 1995, 98). The core idea of social capital lies in the contribution to the common good, by contrast "provisional" networks remain an individual resource: a form of "personal social capital." The aim of "provisional" ties is rather to maximise a short-term profit for an individual or close family member. Similarly, Uslaner and Badescu argue that trust developed in provisional networks has no moral basis, and therefore cannot be understood as generalised trust (Uslaner/Badescu 2003, 222; see also section 3.2.2.1. on 'distrust syndrome').

In disputes over social capital, scholars do not agree whether the informal networks constitute an alternative to social capital or a part of it. On the one hand, numerous empirical studies on social capital limit its measurement to the vitality of associational activity. On the other hand, researchers of social capital in post-communist societies emphasise that informal networks can overstrain the function of inadequate formal ties: "those East Germans whose friendship networks have persisted or even intensified are less likely to join voluntary organisations, whereas those who have experienced more disruption in their own networks are more likely to participate" (Howard 2003, 113). Pichler and Wallace emphasise it more strongly: "substitution takes place in Eastern Europe: low levels of formal social capital are replaced by rather high levels of informal social capital" (Pichler/Wallace 2007, 431).

Despite the doubts about whether the functions of informal networks are similar to those of formal ones, I include informal ties, as another form of social networks, in order to more fully examine the allegedly unique character of networks in post-communist societies.

3.2.2 Social trust

3.2.2.1 "Distrust syndrome"

Widespread low social trust is a common characteristic in Central Eastern European societies. Sztompka (1995) describes this phenomenon as a distrust syndrome that affects virtually all spheres of life, including society and political and economic institutions such as local and national authorities, private enterprises, state health systems, etc. He directly attributes this distrust to the experiences of communism (1995, 268). Communist systems were totalitarian, and aspired "to the total domination of each single individual in each and every sphere of life" (Paldam/Svendsen 2000, 5). Totalitarian regimes use an ideology that is "elaborate, guiding [and] articulates a reachable utopia" (Linz/Stepan 1996, 44) to help maintain power. A core difference between totalitarian regimes and other non-democratic systems, such as dictatorships, is the range of control a system exerts. While a non-democratic system endeavours "only" to exercise power in the broad political sphere, a totalitarian system strives to control even the thoughts of its subjects: "the communist party-state claimed total ownership of all resources of society, including the lives and minds of its subjects" (Rose 2009, 20). Repression and intimidation were common instruments of control: "creation of fear and distrust is an important element in totalitarian control" (Paldam/Svendsen 2000, 7). Citizens under communist regimes "learned to trust nobody, to obey authority, and take no initiative of their own" (Paldam/Svendsen 2000, 7). They were forced to develop survival strategies, for instance by creating informal networks.

However, another group of scholars maintain that state-citizen relations are distinct from those among citizens:

> "distrust of state structures should not be mistaken for distrust of fellow citizens. Co-operation, reciprocity and trust in others were resources necessary for survival in situations of economic scarcity and political arbitrariness," (Letki/Evans 2005, 524)

But if this were true, we would not see such striking differences in the level of social trust between Western and Central Eastern European countries. In short, social trust was a scarce resource among communist citizens.

3.2.2.2 Short-radius trust

During communism, the family remained the only sphere of life beyond state control: "the family was also a refuge from a public world in which people were distrusted" (Wallace 1995, 99). Therefore "the radius of trust," using Fukuyama's terminology (Fukuyama 1999), was very short in communist societies and was mainly narrowed to family members and contingently to a circle of close friends. Due to its short radius, this kind of trust failed to become generalised trust. In fact, just the opposite occurred – trust was a personal resource, hardly transferable, and was attributed to specific individuals. "Provisional" networks were another type of social tie outside state control (see section 3.2.1.2. about informal ties). Uslaner and Badescu argue that the kind of trust that appeared in communist societies was "experienced-based trust" (2003, 222) and failed to have a moral basis, which is crucial for the development of generalised trust. Therefore trust among individuals connected within "provisional" networks could not be a source of generalised trust:

> "The fundamental bases of generalized trust are optimism and control, the beliefs that the world is a good place, that it is going to get better, and you can make it better. In a world of shortages and rationing, it would be foolhardy to be too optimistic (…) It is hardly surprising that neither close friends nor the provision networks are related to generalized trust (…) Crucially, trust in one's close friends and family does *not translate into a more generalized sense of trust in strangers.*"
> (Uslaner/Badescu 2003, 223 emphasis in original)

3.2.3 Norms and values

Certain norms and values were common among people living under communist regimes. Specific patterns of attitudes and values, for instance passive and disinterested *"homo sovieticus"*[15] was an unavoidable reaction of citizens living in a state that rejected plurality and abused its power. In anti-modern societies, citizens were deprived of the opportunity to gain civic skills, therefore they were socialised as "incompetent citizens."

---

[15] This term was used for the first time in a book of Aleksandr Zinovyev *"Homo sovieticus."* (Grove: Atlantic. 1986); and it was subsequently popularised by J.Tischner, P. Sztompka and other sociologists and scientists describing social characteristics under communist regimes.

3.2.3.1 "Homo sovieticus"

People living in communist regimes, which acted paternalistic and repressive at the same time, developed certain strategies and attitudes sarcastically called "*homo sovieticus*." This term refers in general to an opportunistic survival strategy, and highlights certain attitudes: "collectivism, emphasis on security, acceptance of status stability and conformity, seeking state protection, blaming the system for personal failures, privatization of life, demand for egalitarian distribution, dogmatism and intolerance" (Sztompka 2004, 14). Marody ascribes similar attitudes and values to "*homo sovieticus*": "passivity, avoidance of responsibility, learnt helplessness, disinterested envy, and primitive egalitarism" (Marody 1987; after Koralewicz/Ziółkowski 2006, 187). One of the reasons for these developments lays in state policies that compensated low wages and low living standards by a certain existential security. Communist citizens did not experience unemployment, and their wages were hardly related to the professional performance delivered. In this way "a modest but stable life did not require much individual initiative" (Berend 2007, 275). In a nutshell, communist citizens accommodated to their communist reality through passivity and conformist norms and values, and in exchange they got a certain level of economic security.

3.2.3.2 "Anti-modern" societies

Rose applied another term to communist societies: "anti-modern" (2009, 17 ff.). This term stresses deep differences between communist (anti-modern) and Western (modern) societies. In anti-modern societies, the process of modernisation was not the product of economic and societal development. Modernisation was forced by communist rulers onto an unprepared foundation: "whereas pre-industrial institutions of West European societies had provided a solid foundation for political and economic modernization, the legacy of Communism did not" (Rose 2009, 17). Therefore economic modernisation was not followed by societal changes:

> "urban enclaves exhibited Western characteristics, but social modernization trailed economic development (…) occupational structure radically changed and the rural-peasant society disintegrated; while urbanization and industrial occupation became dominant; several pre-modern elements of the society survived and were strengthened."
> (Berend 2007, 277)

Modernisation in communist style meant industrialisation at any cost, even at the expense of society.[16] Economic progress and performance were indispensable means for the legitimacy of the system. In case of economic failure or crisis, "appropriate" positive statistical data were produced. However, "the communist system did not fail because it was ineffective, but because of how it achieved its effects" (Rose 2009, 21), namely it produced an anti-modern society. These societies were characterised by arbitrary and political rule of law, a lack of transparency, false accounts (statistics), bribes and informal contacts, where causes and effects were uncertain and the output inefficient (Rose 2009, 21 ff.). In other words, modernisation referred mainly to the economic realm, and hardly reached the societal one.

The rise of anti-modern societies would not have been possible without a certain historical background in this region. As Berend observes, Central Eastern European societies had a rural character even at the beginning of 20th century, in contrast to the Western societies, which had established a bourgeoisie by this time. In Central Eastern Europe nobility-peasant vertical relations were deeply rooted across societies: "Central European gentry's culture penetrated the peasantry, the entire society and became Polish and Hungarian culture in general" (2007, 276). The rural character of societies strengthened the prevalence of hierarchical structures. These horizontal bonds were eagerly supported by communist regimes, so that "communist societies become neo-feudal structures" (Zarycki 2007, 492). Vertical ties were reinforced by the paternalistic character of state-citizen relations in communist countries: "the traditional paternalistic community and the people's dependence on it became 'institutionalised' as state patronage in state socialist society" (Berend 2007, 277). Vertical bonds appear not only in traditionalist family models, but also at the workplace and in political and social organisations. Following Putnam's logic (1993, 174-175), hierarchical bonds hamper the generation of social capital, which is nurtured by vertical, fellowship ties.

In short, forced modernisation carried out in hierarchic structured societies resulted in anti-modern societies in communist countries.

3.2.3.3 Incompetent communist citizens?

Sztompka postulates that communist citizens lacked "civilisational competence," since they were subjects of communist regimes: "political autocracy alienated the masses and blocked the emergence of citizenship" (2000, 7). Rose observes similarly: "Communist ideology did not allow for the expression of diverse opinions" (2009, 24). Sztompka stresses that post-communist citizens need to develop certain

---

[16] The existing communist regimes still execute such policies, for instance today in China, intensive industrialisation leads to environmental catastrophes; the regime in North Korea develops expensive nuclear programs while allowing the starvation of the population.

civilisational competencies, in a Toquevillean sense, in order to become citizens of democratic Europe in the full sense. They need to become responsible for their own sake and become ready to cooperate for the common good. Similarly, Lipset claims:

> "Totalitarian systems, however, do not have effective civil societies. Instead, they either seek to eliminate groups mediating between the individual and the state or to control these groups so there is no competition. And while by so doing they may undermine the possibility for *organized* opposition, they also reduce group effectiveness, reduce the education of individuals for innovative activities." (1994, 13, emphasis in original)

Under such circumstances citizens could hardly gain civic skills and become competent citizens. Staniszkis points to the historical background when explaining the differences in the development of civil societies and nation-state formation between Western and Eastern Europe. Across Western societies, "the formation of the nation-state and of civil society generated the consciousness and institutional foundations for *contractual civilization*" (Staniszkis 1995, 43, emphasis in original). In contrast, processes of state formation across Central and Eastern Europe have been disrupted by "foreign annexation, occupation, or the lack of statehood" (Staniszkis 1995, 43), and many of these states have been for long years part of the Russian, German, Habsburg or Ottoman empires. Their citizenship developed under circumstances of opposition to state structures. Moreover, for centuries Central Eastern European states constituted peripheral parts of the empires, which was an additional impediment their societal development: (Staniszkis 1995, 43). Later communist regimes were also perceived as imposed from the outside, and "as such did not generate feelings of shared civic pride and responsibility for the common good" (Tworzecki 2008, 50).

The conditions presented above related to social networks, social trust, norms and values have been dominant across communist societies, including Poland – i.e., they are similar conditions of social capital building between Poland and other post-communist societies. The following section discusses the *discrepancies* in conditions between Poland and other countries in the region.

3.3 Before the collapse of communism – dissimilarities

Despite the similarities resulting from communist rule, each individual society differs to some extent from other ones. In Poland we can find a number of differences in its communist experiences. First, probably partly due to their country's poor economic performance, Poles were more likely to manifest discontent through relatively frequent protest actions. Second, the steady challenge of Soviet hegemony resulted in relative pluralism and autonomy, reflected for instance in a relatively independent position in the Catholic Church and the appearance of the proto-civil society and *"Solidarność"* movement in the 1980s.

3.3.1 Frequent protest action in Poland

The emergence and achievements of the Polish social movement *"Solidarność"* are an exception among communist societies. However, the appearance of *"Solidarność"* would not have been possible without previous developments in citizen-state relations. Poland experienced five major political crises (in 1956, 1968, 1970, 1976 and 1980-81) which included the wide involvement of various social and professional groups (Ekiert/Kubik 1999, 21 ff.). Protest actions were not as frequent in other communist countries as in Poland (1953 in East Germany, 1956 in Hungary and 1968 in Czechoslovakia). A rebellious nature characterised the Polish working class in particular (Pomian 1985, 10), and was also reinforced in other groups of society by a long history of strong anti-Russian sentiments and over 100 years of uprisings against foreign domination[17] (Ekiert/Kubik 1999, 24). The Polish communist regime needed to deal from the very beginning with challenging social pressures and was more vulnerable than other regimes in communist Europe to protest activities from below. Scholars especially stress the relevance of the first protest action in 1956 and see these events as a milestone for subsequent political developments in Poland:

> "communist Poland was an extreme example of both institutional weakness of the party-state and strength of various groups within society who were able to openly challenge state policies (…). After 1956, the Polish communist regime became institutionally more diverse, culturally more tolerant, and economically more constrained than most of its East European neighbours (…) the specific resolution of the de-Stalinization crisis in 1956 created institutional and cultural foundations for Poland's subsequent turbulent political history."
>
> (Ekiert/Kubik 1999, 24; see also Grabowska/Szawiel 2001, 147)

The outcomes of this event were a first contribution to the long history of the underground struggle against Soviet domination: "the 1956 revolt in Poznań had a crucial significance for Poland's internal autonomy" (Djilas 1983, 145).

Why are Poles more rebellious than people in other communist societies? Ekiert and Kubik stress the cultural-political dimension of collective action in Poland during the communist era (1999, 4). However, when analysing the origins of Polish

---

[17] During Poland's partition between 1795 and 1918, numerous uprisings took place: in 1794, 1806, 1830, 1846, 1863 and 1905.

protest actions during the communist period, scholars point to the economic situation as a trigger for these events: "demands for immediate economic betterment underlay most of Poland's upheavals" (Curry 1996, 10; see also Ekiert/Kubik 1999, 27 ff.). So, in addition to the political-cultural dimension, economic hardship has played an important role in mobilising collective protests. In order to explore whether the economic situation constituted a strong stimulus for protests in Poland, I analyse the economic conditions in other countries in the region. It is hard to compare the past economic situations across these societies, due to the fact that statistical data, especially those concerning economic performance, was considered a political instrument. Thus official national statistics should be analysed with suspicion.

Nonetheless, there are a number of demographic statistics provided by international organisations that allow comparisons of the general living conditions across countries. Infant mortality, for instance, is an indicator of a country's economic conditions, as well as its living and healthcare situation, since the probability that a baby survives its first year depends not only on hygiene and medical care, but also on the health and living conditions of the mother. Lower infant mortality in a country, therefore, reflects the better economic and social conditions of its population. Thus I compare infant mortality rates across Central and Eastern European countries from 1955 to 2005 provided by the United Nations demographic statistics. Infant mortality successfully declined in communist countries after 1955, and these developments had similar rates of progress across countries in the region (Figure 3.1). Infant mortality rates were higher in Central Eastern Europe than in Western Europe, and the relative difference between West and East diminished during the 20th century. Poland's infant mortality rate was the highest in Central Eastern Europe, and this discrepancy shrank in the 1950s and 1960s. In the 1990s Poland's infant mortality rate was slightly higher than the average in Central Eastern Europe and in 2000s it equalised to the average in other countries. In light of this fact, relatively poor living conditions could be a plausible cause of the high frustration of Poles during the communist era, which could partly account for the numerous protest actions.

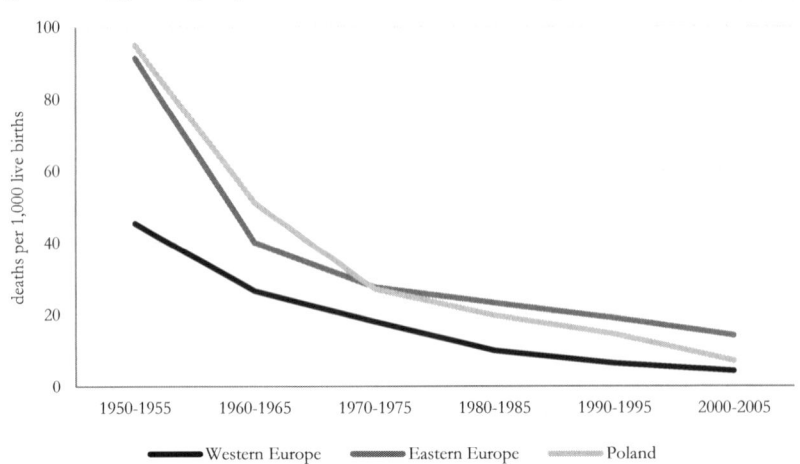

Figure 3.1 Infant mortality rates in Europe 1955-1990 (deaths per 1,000 live births; weighted averages for groups of Eastern and Western European countries)

Notes: Central Eastern Europe: Czech Republic, Hungary, Slovakia, Slovenia; Western Europe: Austria, Belgium, France, Germany, Liechtenstein, Luxembourg, Monaco, Netherlands, Switzerland
Source: United Nations, Department of Economic and Social Affairs, World Population Prospects; http://data.un.org/Data.aspx?d=PopDiv&f=variableID%3A77, visited on 28.07.2011.

Similarly, we can find evidence of an economic background to protest activities in the 1980s in Poland. The economic crisis in Poland became dramatic in the 1980s. After reaching its lowest level during the Martial Law period (1981-1983), an economic disequilibrium became chronic despite economic reforms (Castle 1996, 213 ff.; Eysymontt 1989, 40 ff.; Myant 1989, 13 ff.). Living conditions worsened dramatically, real wages dropped sharply and inflation rose to double digits (Socha 1989, 50). In no other communist country were living conditions in the 1980s as difficult as in Poland. In macroeconomic terms, Poland was trapped in a severe external debt crisis, which was not solved until the liberalisation in 1990, when Poland started negotiations for external debt abolition with the International Monetary Fund and the World Bank. The chronic economic crisis in the 1980s led to massive protests in 1989 and in effect to the Round Table elite negotiations and the collapse of communism in Poland. The relationship between economic hardship and protest activity in the 1980s in Poland is clear (Castle 1996, 221-222).

In sum, the high frequency of protest actions in Poland during the communist period can be partly explained by the relatively harder economic conditions compared to other communist countries. However, economic hardship alone seems insufficient to explain frequent protest activity under a repressive regime. The following section compares the degrees of autonomy and pluralism allowed by communist regimes across Central Eastern European countries, especially in Poland.

3.3.2 Relative pluralism and autonomy in Poland

Communist systems are usually labelled as totalitarian regimes. However the classification of individual communist regimes remains a subject of debate among scholars. Some authors claim that not all communist systems in Central Eastern Europe fit the label "totalitarian," and that particularly in the Polish case, totalitarianism was never fully established:

> "Polish society resists classification as having ever been a fully installed totalitarian regime. We certainly do not deny that there were some efforts to install a totalitarian regime in Poland and that much of the totalitarian state apparatus and official party ideology found elsewhere in Eastern Europe was found in Poland. However some fundamental elements of Polish politics do not really fit the totalitarian regime type."
> (Linz/Stepan 1996, 255)

The regime in Poland seems to have been authoritarian rather than totalitarian (Djilas 1983, 137; Sanford 1994, 191; Linz/Stepan 1996, 255-256; Parrott 1997, 13; Wnuk-Lipiński/Fuchs 2005, 43-44). The debate about the definition of totalitarianism has an overwhelmingly theoretical character and is, therefore, beyond the scope of my descriptive analyses. However, some arguments in this debate are important for my analyses of the conditions for developing social capital during communism.

In general we can distinguish three main conditions that differentiate the Polish one-party system from others in the region: (1) a relatively independent Roman Catholic Church, (2) a failed peasant collectivisation, and (3) a military and party leadership that was relatively autonomous of Soviet hegemony. For Linz and Stepan the independent Catholic Church and non-collectivised peasants are both indicators of limited pluralism,[18] "a mark of incomplete state penetration and a sign of social power and autonomy outside the grip of the totalitarian state" (Linz/Stepan 1996, 258; see also Parrott 1997, 13; Michta 1997, 73-74). Moreover, military and party leaders in Poland needed to cope, on the one hand, with Polish anti-Soviet sentiments and strong nationalism, which was "one of the most emotionally and historically intense in Europe" (Linz/Stepan 1996, 258). Polish stateness, in trouble for over 200 years, was a particularly highly appreciated value, and thus from the very beginning "provided a deep reservoir of sources of resistance" (Linz/Stepan 1996,

---

[18] According to Linz and Stepan pluralism is one of key dimensions, in which non-democratic and totalitarian systems differ. In their analysis of political systems they refer to pluralism in different spheres: social, political and economic (Linz/Stepan 1996, 38-45).

258; see also Sanford 1994, 190-191). On the other hand, Polish party leaders, in order to remain in power, needed to implement the compulsory policies and ideology forced on them by Soviet hegemony. These difficult circumstances resulted in ambiguous stances of military and communist party leaders in several crisis situations[19] and underline that "Poland was the weakest link in the Soviet bloc in Eastern Europe" (Sanford 1994, 190). The Polish regime was unusually autonomous of Soviet domination in comparison to other Eastern-bloc regimes. In Hungary and Czechoslovakia, for instance, both the Kádár and Husák regimes originated in the Soviet military intervention, and by consequence enjoyed a low degree of autonomy (Batt 1994, 168). Comparable degrees of internal autonomy in domestic affairs were only found in Yugoslavia (Linz/Stepan 1996, 261).

Pluralism, at the beginning encompassing only independent Church and non-collectivised peasants, stepwise spread out across the political sphere in Poland (Ekiert/Kubik 1999, 29; see also Wnuk-Lipiński/Fuchs 2005, 43-44). By the 1960s, the first "independent intellectual activities [emerged] outside the party's control" (Michta 1997, 74). The 1970s brought an alliance between two major resistance groups – intellectual elites and the industrial working class (Michta 1997, 74). After 1976, the opposition could act to a limited extent in an open (not only underground) and institutional way (for instance in the form of the Workers' Defence Committee, *Komitet Obrony Robotników*), which was an exception across communist Europe (Grabowska/Szawiel 2001, 146 ff.). Between 1976 and 1980 more oppositional institutions became active in the public sphere, for instance the educational institution "Flying University," free trade unions, political parties, etc. (Grabowska/Szawiel 2001, 146; Michta 1997, 74; Linz/Stepan 1996, 261). Oppositional groups were controlled by the state and could only act in a limited way, however their degree of internal autonomy was still higher than before 1955 (before the beginning of the de-Stalinisation process). This limited degree of freedom and autonomy turned out to be crucial for later political developments in Poland. It laid a baseline for the emergence and eventual success of the "*Solidarność*" movement many years later.

---

[19] Few examples: party leader Gomułka rejected coercive collectivisation in the 1950s, acting against Soviet policies (Linz/Stepan 1996, 257; Sanford 1994, 190), another party leader Gierek allowed in 1970s limited opening to the world in economic, cultural and travel terms (Sanford 1994, 191); Polish army conducted civil war against Soviet forces in 1945-47 (Linz/Stepan 1996, 259), Polish army did not fire upon the Poznań strikers in 1956 (Linz/Stepan 1996, 260); Polish General Jaruzelski remained autonomous against Kreml in 1981 when introducing the Martial Law (Sanford 1994, 190).

3.3.3 Why was "Solidarność" ephemeral?

When explaining the phenomenon of the "*Solidarność*" movement we need to address several questions: Why did this massive social movement turn out to be so ephemeral and fail to build the basis for a vibrant civil society in the aftermath of communism? Was "*Solidarność*" a civil society organisation, or was it rather a short-term and massive social mobilisation? On the one hand, some scholars stress the need to distinguish between social mobilisation and civil society (Bozóki 1994, 134). On the other hand, Wnuk-Lipiński develops a concept of "ethical civil society" (see also Linz/Stepan 1996, 271) and explains the volatile nature of civil society in Poland by the extraordinary context of its emergence:

> "ethical civil society emerges usually on a very limited scale, predominantly in a non-democratic context, and particularly within a monocentric system which derives its legitimacy from the predominant ideology of public discourse (…) Under such circumstances, civic initiatives that are alternative to the omnipotent state seek for the legitimacy in the axiological sphere (moral norms) rather than in the area of group interests."
> (Wnuk-Lipiński 2007, 31-32)

In other words, involvement in "ethical civil society" is morally driven and its activists remain in opposition to the non-pluralistic system. However, once these initial conditions disappear, ethical civil society dissolves as well:

> "when a non-democratic system collapses and general moral values (that were main driving force of opposition to a monocentric system) are preserved and even protected in public life, they become taken for granted (…) This is what leads to erosion of ethical civil society. In short, being a powerful tool for challenging an oppressive social system, ethical civil society can hardly survive its collapse as the struggle for values is extensively replaced by the struggle for group interests."
> (Wnuk-Lipiński 2007, 32)

Ethical civil society is volatile by definition, since its goal is to establish a certain ethical standard in political and social realms. "*Solidarność*" is an example of an ethical civil society organisation (Wasilewski 1995, 118-119; Linz/Stepan 1996, 271 ff.; Wnuk-Lipiński 2007, 31 ff.). Therefore, from the moment when its main ethical goal – the introduction of pluralism into the political sphere – was achieved, it dissolved and split into a few political currents: social democrats and socialists, Christian democrats, Catholic-nationalists, populists and radical rightists (Wasilewski 1995, 119; see also Grabowska/Szawiel 2001, 150). Open pluralism became possible with the system change. In effect, groups of interests that were suppressed and marginalised until that moment emerged slowly in a long consolidation process of the post-communist political elites. Post-*Solidarność* movements were part of these emerging groups and political parties (Wasilewski 1995, 119).

3.3.4 The Catholic Church's support of the opposition

To claim that the appearance of an opposition movement was a uniquely Polish achievement among communist regimes would be an exaggeration. In Hungary and Czechoslovakia dissident movements were also established, for instance Charter 77, the Civic Forum and the Hungarian Democratic Forum (Luers 1990, 86 ff.; Bernhard 1993, 319). The main difference is that they were unable to gather broader social support (Bernhard 1993, 323). Only in Poland did elites succeed in evoking a massive response to their oppositional activity (Wnuk-Lipiński 2007, 34, 37). In turn, the key differentiating factor was the existence of an institutionally strong and politically independent Roman Catholic Church, which contributed considerably to the development of the massive opposition movement (Lipset 1994, 13; Grabowska/Szawiel 2001, 149; Kurczewska 2005, 331; Wnuk-Lipiński/Fuchs 2005, 44). No other communist country took advantage of the supranational institutional strength of the Catholic Church to such an extent (see: Luers 1990, 89). Besides, the "Pope factor" played a crucial role in strengthening the position of the Church. The first visit of Polish Pope John Paul II in 1979 in Poland was a trigger for the first mobilisation of civil society. Connections built at that time constituted a basis for networks of the "*Solidarność*" opposition movement afterwards (Grabowska/Szawiel 2001, 149-150). Wnuk-Lipiński describes:

> "the Papal visit was a huge organizational undertaking which succeeded largely due to the effort of eager volunteers. This army of volunteers was a resource which less than a year later was utilized by elites and by the masses to create Solidarity."
> (Wnuk-Lipiński 2007, 36)

In addition, this organisational effort and engagement of numerous volunteers created an opportunity for them to learn civic skills:

> "this visit became the key experience in grass-root social self-organisation shared by several thousand people (...) it evolved into a massive educational institution 'teaching' democracy and citizenship. Horizontal relationships prevailed."
> (Wnuk-Lipiński 2007, 35-36)

Scholars stress that in that moment, a proto-civil society emerged under communism for the first time (Grabowska/Szawiel 2001, 148-149; Wnuk-Lipiński 2007, 35-36). Until the Papal visit human relationships in Poland were atomised and dominated by distrust, as in other communist societies. The events in 1979 changed this perception, and even the subsequent repressions during the period of Martial Law could not really dismantle the already awakened civil society and the feeling of solidarity.

Besides creating horizontal networks and providing opportunities for civic skills training, the Pope's visit brought also moral support, encouragement for resistance and created a new sphere of social communication, which was up to that point impossible in an atomised society:

> "It turned out that the space not controlled by the Communist state suddenly enlarged and comprised vast masses. Those 'thinking alike' who met during Papal religious events and meetings took a quick head count and, to their amazement, discovered an army of people (…) Furthermore, the fresh and consoling message of the Pope that would not have been tolerated earlier in the public sphere became the ready-made model of social communication for the initial phase of democratization."
>
> (Wnuk-Lipiński 2007, 35-36)

In addition to the Pope, the institutionalised Roman Catholic Church in Poland also played a crucial role, especially in building civil society networks after his visit. As mentioned above, after 1956 the Church in Poland acquired limited autonomy and was to a certain extent independent from the state. In this regard, it was an "external" institution, and therefore trustworthy for the citizens. Church and Church-related structures provided support for the organisation of "*Solidarność*" networks in the 1980s (Grabowska/Szawiel 2001, 149; Kurczewska 2005, 331).

The institutional strength of the Catholic Church throughout Polish history is also reflected in the broad acceptance of Catholic moral teachings, which are crucial elements of the Polish traditionalist value system. The strength of family ties in Poland is the subject of the following section.

3.3.5 Strong family ties and traditional values

Polish society is characterised by strong traditional values[20] whereby family takes a prominent place in the value system. It results in very strong family bonds in Polish society. Wallace, for instance, observes in her empirical study particularly strong tendencies of inter-generational dependencies in Poland, though compared only with German and British societies (Wallace 1995, 99). Results of another comparative study show a higher importance of the family in Poland in comparison to other societies from the region, since in this regard Poles are "closer to West European

---

[20] Polish traditionalist value orientations and commitment to family values are discussed in chapter 5.

Catholic countries than to other post-communist countries" (Giza-Poleszczuk/Poleszczuk 2004, 207). The same authors stress that in addition to the importance of family, the bonds between parents and adult children are also stronger in Poland when compared to other post-communist societies. In Polish society the percentage of multi-generation households is quite high: "particularly worthy of attention in Poland is the high percentage of adults who live with their parents" (Giza-Poleszczuk/Poleszczuk 2004, 222); only Estonia ranks higher (out of 26 Western and Eastern European countries). These particularly strong family bonds are on the one hand a consequence of the historically long-term dominance of the Catholic tradition and traditionalist value orientations. On the other hand, strong family relations were reinforced during communism through the privatisation of life, housing shortages and vertical social relations (Schöpflin 1994, 198; Wallace 1995, 102; Ziółkowski 1998, 29; Grabowska/Szawiel 2001, 151; Berend 2007, 277; Rose 2009, 33). This reinforcement of family bonds occurred in other communist societies, too (see section 3.2.2.1). So we need to address the question: were family bonds indeed stronger in Poland than in other communist societies?

Besides the above-mentioned study by Giza-Poleszczuk and Poleszczuk, other empirical cross-national studies do not actually confirm stronger family relations in Poland when compared to other European countries. The frequency of meetings with family members (nuclear and extended) in Poland remains at a similar level to other Catholic countries,[21] but Poland ranks almost at the lowest position (after Latvia) among post-communist countries (van der Meer 2009, 59; Murphy 2008, 31). Similar findings concern the frequency of contacting family members: Poland ranks second to last among post-communist countries (Murphy 2008, 31). In an earlier analysis I also did not find more frequent contacts between family members in Poland than in other societies (Lasinska 2009). This evidence shows that family ties in Poland are strong, but are not remarkably stronger when compared to other post-communist countries.

Moreover, another Polish study shows that the new generation, entering their adulthood after the collapse of communism, chooses different, "modern" strategies of family building. Young people in Poland marry and have their first child later than generations who were socialised under communism (Giza-Poleszczuk 2007, 310-314). This evidence suggests that the generational interdependence among family members that was observed in Poland was probably more a consequence of the situation under communism than a normative imperative. In terms of the strength of family ties, Poland does not seem to be an exception among countries with a communist legacy.

---

[21] In general, family ties seem to be stronger in Catholic than in Protestant countries. The nuclear family bonds are actually the strongest in the Southern Catholic countries of Italy and Spain (van der Meer 2009, 59).

3.4 Conclusions – conditions before the collapse of communism

When considering the dissimilarities in conditions of social capital building during communism between Poland and other post-communist societies, we surprisingly found that conditions distinguishing Poland from other countries in the region were mostly favourable for social capital. Disentangled factors that influence social capital in a positive way are interrelated and mutually reinforcing: numerous protest actions contributed to pluralism and internal autonomy, which allowed the Catholic Church to strengthen its independence and subsequently to mobilise the mass movement "*Solidarność.*" Another claimed difference – stronger family ties – failed to find broader empirical evidence.

How can the lower social capital in Poland be explained if the conditions there were positive? It is important to stress that during the communist regime, the main effort of social mobilisation focused **on opposing the current system**. After the collapse of this system, however, the situation changed completely, and the efforts focused **on acting within the political system**. As a consequence, the favourable conditions required for the generation of social capital in a democratic system probably differ from those indispensable in a non-democratic one – "ethical civil society" has different goals and motivations than a "regular" civil society. An empirical study conducted in Poland provides evidence that those who opposed the system during communism display different political preferences than prior communist-party members (Grabowska 2001, 215). These findings suggest that socialisation as an opposition member may influence an individual's later political orientation. Whether this type of socialisation also matters for the propensity to generate social capital should be tested empirically. Furthermore, in this new society, frequent protests and the strong position of the independent Catholic Church could potentially hamper the development of social capital. In the next section I address the question of whether the conditions in democratic Poland remain favourable for social capital building, while the role of the Catholic Church in generating social capital is addressed in chapter 5.

3.5 After the collapse of communism – similarities and dissimilarities

The collapse of communism was a first important milestone for Central Eastern Europe in a long process of development into modern and democratic societies. As discussed earlier, communist societies were characterised by low social trust ("distrust syndrome"); weak civil societies resulting from compulsory membership in organisations, combined with relatively high levels of informal networks such as "provision networks;" and the privatisation of life. Value orientations internalised during the years of communism were far from supportive of societal cooperation, or community oriented. In a nutshell, one can hardly speak about widespread social capital under communism.

What changed after the collapse of the communist regimes? Why do citizens not make use of the newly gained freedom of speech and freedom to gather and associate? Why is social capital not generated in the post-communist era? In the following sections I discuss several explanations proposed in the literature for the low social capital endowment across post-communist societies. Scholars exploring this problem focus on the one hand on the persistence of patterns of participation and distrust, and on the other hand on the negative effects of the systemic transition. In those respects conditions in Poland do not differ much from those in other societies – in Poland we find the persistence of patterns of low participation and distrust, and the negative effects of transformation occur there as well. In the aftermath of communism, the Polish situation seems to differ "in degree" rather than "in kind," when compared to the other countries in the region. The unique difference seems to be related to Catholicism and to the strong role of the Catholic Church, which will be discussed separately in chapter 4 and chapter 5.

3.5.1   Persistence of behavioural and attitudinal patterns

The first explanation for low social capital across post-communist societies is the persistence of behavioural and attitudinal patterns: "the collapse of communism did not create a tabula rasa by erasing people's prior experiences; rather, those very experiences influence people's current behaviour" (Howard 2003, 105). These patterns do not change as quickly as the economic and political systems. The latter can be introduced by law and regulations, in contrast to the former. Societal changes need time; people socialised in an atmosphere of intimidation are not likely to change their habits overnight (Rose 2009, 5). It is a long way from *"homo sovieticus"* living in communism to *"homo economicus"* living in capitalism.

After the collapse of the communist regimes, citizens' negative perception of social organisations and resulting reluctance to join social groups did not really change. Citizens socialised under communism also perceived new organisations, founded under the democratic system, with distrust and disinterest. As Uslaner and Badescu argue: "changing one set of institutions for another is not sufficient to reshape a country's political culture (…) Democracy raises expectations, but is insufficient to reshape society, at least in the short term" (2003, 224-225). Some empirical studies show analogies between attitudes during communism and afterwards. Howard demonstrates a direct correlation between mistrust in organisations under communism and the reluctance to volunteer in organisations in the aftermath (2003, 107). He describes this pattern in the following way:

"the more people mistrusted communist organizations, and the more they avoided them during the communist period, the less likely they will be to participate in voluntary organizations today." (Howard 2003, 105)

In other words, Howard discovers a certain continuity in the reluctance to volunteer nowadays that results from communist experiences. His findings based on survey analyses confirm the results of his in-depth interviews in Russia and East Germany. Likewise, patterns of political behaviour seem to be preserved from the communist era, since membership in the communist party appears to be one of the most powerful predictors of political participation after the collapse of communism: "membership in a Communist party before 1989 is a very good predictor of conventional political participation in the new ECE [Eastern Central European] democracies, and its influence on participation in politics after 1989 is positive" (Letki 2003, 22; see also Grabowska/Szawiel 2001, 179). Thus a readiness for both social and political participation remains relatively stable after the systemic change. Additionally, informal ties, which played a crucial role in communist societies due to the "privatisation of life" still remain strong: "At the bottom of the hour-glass, ordinary people continued to rely on informal networks" (Rose 2009, 26). While friendship ties remained, "provisional" networks seem to be partially unnecessary (Howard 2003, 113).

From a pessimistic perspective, changes in participation, trust and values will not occur until a new generation, socialised under the democratic system, comes of age. Analyses of social capital endowment between "communist" and "postcommunist" generations could provide evidence for the persistence of behavioural and attitudinal patterns. If those born after 1990 (when major changes happened in most of the countries in the region) indeed demonstrate higher participation, trust and norms of cooperation than citizens born earlier, it would provide evidence for the explanation based on the persistence of patterns.

3.5.2 Negative effects of transition

The second explanation for the poor endowment with social capital in Central Eastern Europe may be the negative impact of transition processes and the ensuing disillusionments. Transformation took place in all political, economic and social systems almost simultaneously. The procedures and outputs of this experiment, unique in history, were not clear for anybody – policy-makers, economists or ordinary people (Rose 2009, 1). For Central Eastern European citizens, transformation meant tremendous turmoil in their lives, related to high levels of insecurity and economic hardship. These conditions were far from favourable for social capital development in post-communist societies.

3.5.2.1 Transition processes

In order to understand the negative effects of transformation at the societal level, we first need to know how systemic transition proceeds. In general, researchers exploring transformation processes distinguish four phases: (1) initial phase: "honeymoon" – common euphoria about newly acquired freedoms; (2) mid-systemic phase: "hour of lawyer" (Koralewicz/Ziółkowski 2007, 215) – introduction of new political institutions, by the end of this phase a restoration of the old political regime is unlikely; (3) advanced phase – equality becomes the more powerful mobilising power, and materialist values become dominant; (4) consolidation phase – solid and stable social legitimisation of democracy, and a slow shift toward postmaterialist values (Koralewicz/Ziółkowski 2007, 214-223; Wnuk-Lipiński/Fuchs 2005, 54-60). Most of the countries of Central Eastern Europe went through the first three phases, yet the last one – consolidation – was not achieved by all of them.[22] While during the first two phases feelings of hope and uncertainty prevail, the third phase brings the risk of disappointment. At that point, when there is no return to the old regime and democratic institutions are established (beginning of the advanced phase), people start to evaluate the performance of the new system. In the process of transformation two values (liberty and equality) constitute the main mobilising power across different stages:

> "In the initial and mid-systemic phases of transition, *liberty* remains a major value mobilising people from various social strata to collective actions in public life. Subsequently the state, along with various agencies, goes through a process of liberalisation of the rules of the game and the value of *equality* defined in terms of social justice begins to emerge." (Wnuk-Lipiński/Fuchs 2005, 55 emphasis in original)

In other words, at the beginning of the advanced phase, citizens take freedom for granted, and they expect the new system to meet their expectations and needs. Economic performance and elimination of social inequality are, among other things, salient requirements for a positive evaluation of the system's performance.

---

[22] Freedom House, which classifies regimes according to political rights and civil liberties, classifies some ex-Yugoslav and most ex-Soviet republics, including Russia, as non-democratic. Among the ex-communist states Czech Republic, Hungary, Poland, Slovakia, Slovenia, Estonia, Latvia, Lithuania, Bulgaria, Croatia and Romania fulfil the criteria of "liberal democracies" (Diamond 2008, 276). In other words, democracy is now consolidated only in these countries, according to the Freedom House evaluation.

3.5.2.2 Economic performance

Did the new political systems in post-communist Europe meet the expectations of their citizens? How did new democracies perform, and what were the main problems they needed to cope with? What are the differences between the economic performance of Poland and that of other countries? The macroeconomic performance of the new market economies between 1990 and 2007 seems promising – after years of deep crisis (which began even before the collapse of communism), the economies experienced recovery after 1994. Since 2000, annual GDP growth in this region even exceeds dynamic growth in Western European countries (Figure 3.2). In Poland, the first signs of recovery appeared as early as 1991. Annual growth rates in Poland since 1991 were above the post-communist average until 2000.[23]

Figure 3.2 GDP growth per capita in Europe 1990-2007, PPP[24] (annual growth rates in percentages; weighted averages for groups of Eastern and Western European countries)

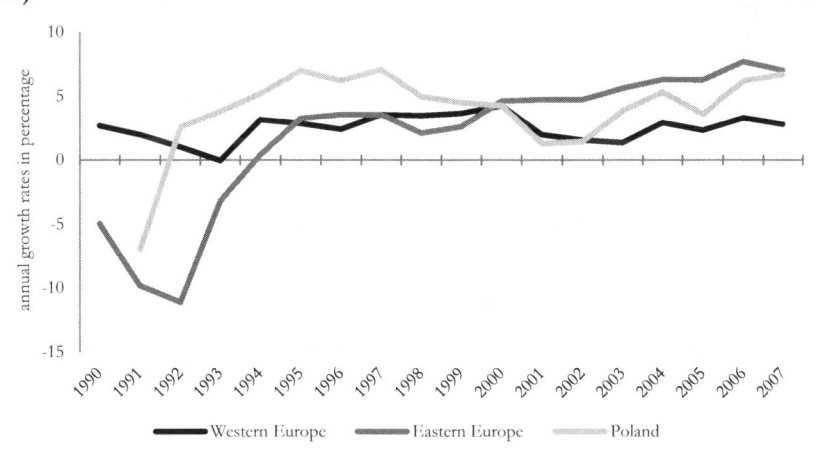

Notes: *Eastern Europe*: Czech Republic, Estonia, Hungary, Latvia, Lithuania, Poland, Romania, Russian Federation, Slovakia and Slovenia (1990 only for: Estonia, Hungary, Latvia, Hungary, Romania, Russian Federation and Slovakia);
Western Europe: Austria, Belgium, Denmark, Finland, France, Germany, Greece, Italy, Luxembourg, Netherlands, Norway, Portugal, Spain, Sweden and United Kingdom.
Source: World Bank (http://ddp-ext.worldbank.org/ext/DDPQQ; visited on 20.10.2009).

---

[23] Growth of GDP is only one measure of recovery, and does not take income distribution into account. A fast path of GDP growth in Poland was a direct result of drastic liberalisation and deregulation packages in 1990 (the so-called Balcerowicz plan). Yet the Polish economy, after chronic crisis in the 1980s, was weak and GDP was at a relatively low level – therefore relative growth rates were high in numerical terms.
[24] PPP: Purchasing Power Parity

However, rapid economic growth brings new risks. According to Kuznet's hypothesis (1955), income inequality rises over time with economic development and then, at a certain critical point, it starts to decrease. In other words, Kuznet's curve showing the relationship between economic development and income inequality has an inverted "U" shape.

To what extent does Kuznet's hypothesis apply to the situation of Central Eastern Europe? Did income inequality rise with economic development? Changes in GINI coefficients for income inequalities[25] seem to corroborate these expectations (Figure 3.3[26]). On the one hand, the transition to a market economy, liberalisation of currency exchange course and prices, privatisation of state-owned enterprises etc., brought the expected effect of economic growth. On the other hand, not all groups within transforming societies profited to the same extent from these developments. During rapid macroeconomic growth, discrepancies between poor and rich increased. As we can see in Figure 3.3, these discrepancies were higher between Eastern European countries (GINI coefficient between 30 and 50), when compared to the average in Western countries (around 30), with the exception of Bulgaria, Czech Republic, Hungary and Slovakia. The situation in Poland seems to be more difficult compared to other countries in Central Europe. In Poland the GINI coefficient is higher than in Bulgaria, Czech Republic, Hungary, Slovenia and Slovakia. Higher income discrepancies are found only in ex-Soviet countries: Latvia, Lithuania and Russia.

---

[25] A higher value of GINI coefficient means higher income inequalities. The GINI coefficient may take values from 0 (perfectly equal distribution) to 100 (perfectly unequal distribution).
[26] Values of GINI coefficient for income inequalities are not available for all examined countries in the same periods of time. Therefore in Figure 3.3 presents the values of GINI coefficient for all available periods and can serve as a proximal assessment of the situation across individual societies.

Figure 3.3 Income inequalities in Europe 1988-2005 (GINI coefficient for income in Eastern European countries; weighted average for groups of Western European countries)

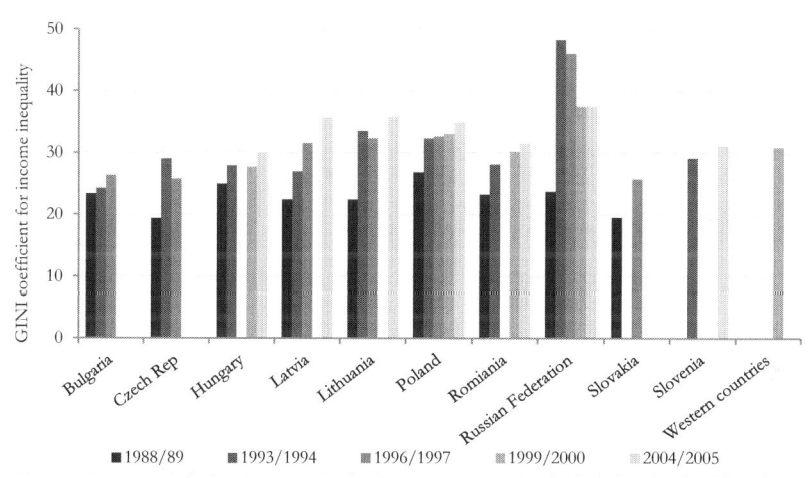

Notes: Western countries: Austria, Belgium, Finland, France, Germany, Greece, Italy, Netherlands, Norway, Spain, Sweden and United Kingdom.
Source: World Bank (http://ddp-ext.worldbank.org/ext/DDPQQ; visited on 20.10.2009).

Another study of income inequalities across European Union (EU) countries confirms that Poland has one of the highest discrepancies in material status between rich and poor, which ranks second among EU member states; a worse situation is found only in Romania (Alber et al. 2010, 10). I return to this problem in section 3.5.2.4.

Besides income inequalities, unemployment and inflation rates were also at high levels – much higher than in Western Europe – during the transformation in Central Eastern Europe (Figure 3.4 and Table 3.1). Average unemployment rates in post-communist countries exceeded 10 percent for more than ten years until 2005. In Poland unemployment rates exceeded the average in the group of post-communist societies. Especially after 2000, unemployment rates exploded and reached 20 percent in 2002. In general, average unemployment in Central Eastern Europe is systematically higher than in Western Europe, though since 2001 there has been a downward trend. The average unemployment rate in 2007 in Central Eastern Europe was close to the average in Western Europe.

Figure 3.4 Unemployment in Europe 1992-2007 (annual unemployment rates in percentage of total labour force; weighted averages for groups of Eastern and Western European countries)

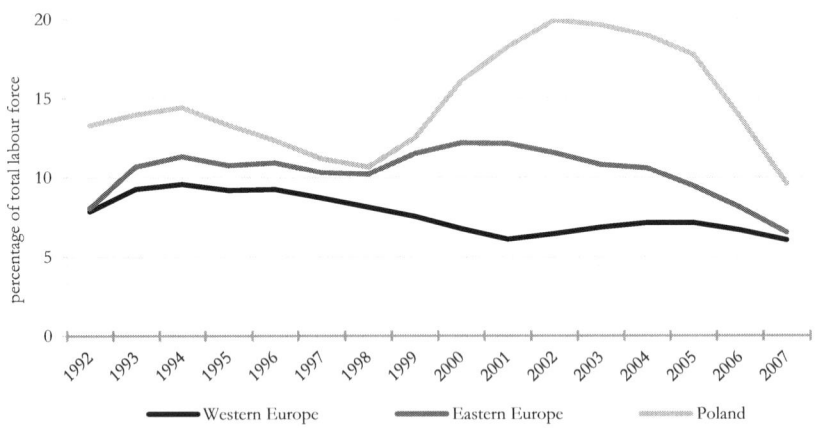

Notes: Eastern Europe: Czech Republic, Estonia, Hungary, Latvia, Lithuania, Poland, Romania, Russian Federation, Slovakia and Slovenia (1992 only for: Estonia, Hungary, Poland and Russian Federation; 1993 without Lithuania, Romania and Latvia; data for Latvia missing for 1994 and 1995, data for Bulgaria missing for 2007);
Western Europe: Austria, Belgium, Denmark, Finland, France, Germany, Greece, Italy, Luxembourg, Netherlands, Norway, Portugal, Spain, Sweden and United Kingdom.
Source: World Bank (http://ddp-ext.worldbank.org/ext/DDPQQ; visited on 20.10.2009).

Inflation rates (Table 3.1[27]) in Central Eastern Europe were extremely high at the beginning of the transformation (above 1,000 percent in Russia and around 900 percent in the Baltic countries in 1992), and remained at more than five percent annually until 2005. Inflation was systematically higher for the whole period than the average in Western Europe. Poland seemed to deal with the problem of inflation worse than other Central European countries, such as Czech Republic, Hungary and Slovakia.

---

[27] Inflation rates cannot be presented in a graph due to large relative differences in inflation rates across countries and years – annual inflation rates take value from 1,000 to -0.29 percent.

Table 3.1 Annual inflation rates in 1992-2008 in Bulgaria, Czech Republic, Hungary, Latvia, Lithuania, Poland, Romania, Slovakia and Slovenia; and weighted averages of annual inflation rates for group of Western European countries

	1992	1995	2000	2005	2008
Bulgaria	59.58	62.85	6.69	3.76	11.36
Czech Republic	12.92	17.03	1.51	-0.29	1.70
Estonia	873.64	n.a.	n.a.	5.27	7.78
Hungary	21.51	26.73	12.91	2.28	3.86
Latvia	932.52	27.53	4.19	10.17	15.18
Lithuania	942.31	48.66	0.79	6.61	10.29
Poland	**38.51**	**40.76**	**7.19**	**2.64**	**3.07**
Romania	200.10	35.24	44.25	12.29	14.00
Russian Federation	1490.42	144.00	37.70	19.22	15.00
Slovakia	11.43	9.13	9.41	2.38	2.89
Slovenia	208.18	28.45	5.34	1.60	4.02
Western Europe (weighted average)	4.31	3.33	3.21	2.75	3.19

Notes: n.a. – not available; Western Europe: Austria, Belgium, Denmark, Finland, France, Germany, Greece, Italy, Luxembourg, Netherlands, Norway, Portugal, Spain, Sweden and United Kingdom.
Source: World Bank (http://ddp-ext.worldbank.org/ext/DDPQQ; visited on 20.10.2009).

In sum, the systemic changes brought a rise in income inequality, unemployment and price levels across Eastern Europe, which means that post-communist societies paid for the economic and political transformation with high social costs. The situation in Poland seems to have been more difficult than in other Central Eastern European countries, above all with regard to relatively high levels of unemployment and income inequalities.

3.5.2.3 Societal consequences of the transition

What do we know about the consequences of transformation turmoil at the societal level? What are the conditions for social capital development? Numerous authors exploring the situation in post-communist societies report widespread disillusionment, pessimism and withdrawal from the public sphere as consequences of difficult economic conditions and political instability during the transformations. These are direct causes of reasons for low social trust and low social engagement.

Disillusionment about the new situation prevailed as early as the 1990s. For instance in Poland in 1994, only 15 percent of people declared that the systemic change brought them more gains than losses; and 42 percent declared the opposite opinion (Kozarzewski 2007, 28). In a report concerning the situation in Poland in 1999 we find the remark: "the public is simply tired with the reforms under way and the public mood is deteriorating" (Lubiński 2000, 18). This disenchantment found its expression in the political sphere as well. In many countries at the beginning of the 1990s, ex-communist policy-makers returned to power in democratic elections. Publics, electing "old" communist leaders, expressed their disappointment with the government of the new parties that emerged after liberalisation, which have been in power since that time. Lipset emphasises the burden of deregulations as one of the key factors for these widespread reversals in political preferences: "these situations are (…) exacerbated by the fact that replacing command economies by market processes is difficult, and frequently conditions worsen before they begin to improve" (1994, 13).

In the civic sphere, disillusionment resulted in withdrawal from social and political activity: "many east Europeans had engaged in unconventional politics during the democratic transitions of the late 1980s and early 1990s, but these forms of action diminished after the transition in a kind of 'post-honeymoon' effect" (Dalton/Klingemann 2007, 16). Howard points to disappointment as the reason for withdrawal from engagement, too:

> "the political and economic systems that have taken root seem to have disappointed most people who had believed and hoped that a new political and economic system would live up to their ideals. This disappointment has only increased people's demobilization and withdrawal from public activities since the collapse of communism."
>
> (2003, 29)

Besides social engagement, social trust also had poor conditions for development during the systemic transition, since: "people in transitional societies are both pessimistic about the future and feeling helpless" (Uslaner 2003a, 83). While optimism is one of the key determinants of trust (Uslaner 2003a, 95), widespread pessimism contributed to the rise of distrust during the transitional phase. Sztompka (1995) refers to the difficult economic situation (unemployment, inflation, instability of the financial system, etc.), as well as aggressive and uninhibited business behaviour in the very first phase of the capital accumulation in the new capitalist systems (forcing up of prices, low quality of goods and services, fraud, corruption) as crucial factors that hampered the development of trust among people after the systems collapsed (1995, 269).

Income inequality was also detrimental for social trust. And as we have seen in Figure 3.3, income inequality was relatively high during the transformation across post-communist countries. Uslaner and Badescu see low trust as direct consequences of inequality:

> "inequality leads to less generalized trust. A growing income gap leads to greater pessimism for the future, especially among those who have become worse off under democratic capitalism (…) The democratic transition seemed doomed to subvert a rise in social capital." (2003, 225)

In sum, neither social trust nor social engagement had favourable conditions to develop in post-communist societies during the transformation.

3.5.2.4 Social costs of transition and disappointment in Poland

The situation in Poland compared to other countries in the region seems to differ "in degree" rather than "in kind." Poles have reasons to be more disappointed than other post-communist citizens – the social costs of transformation were higher in Poland, especially as far as unemployment and income inequality are concerned (see Figures 3.3 and 3.4). The trajectories of economic transformations across Central Eastern European countries are different, and in Poland, the economic adjustment reforms were probably the most radical. There are at least two reasons for this: the long-lasting economic crisis, which began in the 1980s, and exceptionally high social support for economic reforms:

> "shock therapy strategy was necessary and possible due to a specific combination of factors. The inherited economic crisis was much worse than in other countries, the new government was highly autonomous and insulated from entrenched interests, and it enjoyed a high level of public trust and confidence." (Ekiert/Kubik 1999, 63)

Exceptionally broad social support for reforms in Poland is also emphasised by other authors: "Only Polish reformers could rely, at least in the first critical phase of economic stabilization, on the organized support of the society" (Bruszt 1994, 111; see also Mohr 2005, 188).

On the other hand, the income discrepancies in Poland seem be to have grown larger than in other countries across the region:

> "In the short run, however, the political and economic price for the success of the stabilization program was high. Unemployment grew rapidly, industrial output and real wages declined dramatically, and the poverty rate increased. (…) Another set of measures used to assess the economic situation of the people deals with the gap between the rich and poor. By all accounts, during the early postcommunist years in Poland, this gap opened much wider than before 1989 (…) in Poland the ratio of incomes of people belonging to the top percentile of the population to the incomes of the people belonging

to the bottom percentile was 3.31 in 1989. In 1994, it rose to 6.57 and was then much higher than in any other Central European country." (Ekiert/Kubik 1999, 64-67)

In short, the radical adjustment reforms, which were introduced with a high level of social support, brought probably the highest economic costs: a rise in poverty and income inequality. The higher levels of GINI coefficients (Figure 3.3) confirm that the discrepancy between rich and poor, as well as unemployment, was highest in Poland (Figure 3.4).

Poles are probably more disappointed than other post-communist citizens. If we use the level of satisfaction with one's life as a proxy for disappointment, an empirical study provides evidence of higher dissatisfaction among Poles when compared to other European – Western and Eastern – citizens (Neller 2004, 34 ff.). The level of disappointment is the subject of further empirical analysis presented in chapter 6.

Besides withdrawing from social engagement and maintaining a low level of social trust, how else did citizens express their disappointment? Some sources report high protest activity, especially among Poles. Disappointment and protest actions have a mutually reinforcing effect: "protest actions have a strong impact on popular perception of the political and economic situation" (Ekiert/Kubik 1999, 20). And this negative perception of economic and political developments led to further protest action. The next question is: to what extent did citizens express social dissatisfaction in the form of protest actions? Was the situation in Poland similar to other post-communist countries? What consequences did protest actions have for social capital?

3.5.2.5 High level of protest actions in Poland

Polish citizens under communism showed a higher propensity for collective protest actions than other societies across Central Eastern Europe (see section 3.3.1). Ekiert and Kubik provide evidence in their thorough study for the relatively high frequency of protest events in Poland after the collapse of communism: "our research indicates that during the first five years of democratic consolidation, Poland had a higher number of protest events than the other East Central European countries we studied" (Ekiert/Kubik 1999, 112).[28] Another cross-national study of unconventional political participation by the end of 1990s, however, shows that Polish levels of protest were similar to levels in Czech Republic, Slovakia, Hungary and Bulgaria – and were even lower than in Romania (Siemienska 2006, 227). Unfortunately, the

---

[28] Some critics of this study point to its limitations, for instance the number of protest actions in East Germany is relatively high for its population size, and the intensity of protests in the Czech Republic and Slovakia were not considered (Kramer 2002, 218-221).

results of both studies are not comparable, since they refer to different forms of protests. Nevertheless, it seems plausible that in Poland the level of protests was higher than in other countries as a result of the relatively high social costs of reforms. Since economic conditions were a trigger for protest actions during the communist period, it is plausible that the economic situation prompted protests in the aftermath of communism, too. The level of protest actions in Poland is discussed and examined in more detail in chapter 6.

What is the relationship between protest activity and social capital? Dekker and colleagues (1997) show inconsistent patterns at the micro and macro levels when analysing relations between protest and social activities. Initially their protest indicator did not include strikes, therefore the level of protest activities across southern Europe is underestimated (Dekker et al. 1997, 232). After including strikes, they were able to observe a pattern across Southern European societies, mainly Spain and France:

> "the second pattern, exemplified by Spain, combines low organizational participation with high protest levels, radical protest forms and a predominance of mobilization around traditional cleavages." (Dekker et al. 1997, 229)

And they propose an institutional explanation for this relationship:

> "The negative correlation between organizational and protest participation can be explained by seeing them as strategic alternatives within the action repertoire of social movements. In open, inclusive political systems, where success can be achieved by less demanding conventional strategies, social movement activists find less need to resort to unconventional protest. If they do, they rely primarily on accepted forms of protest. In closed, exclusive systems, conversely, conventional strategies are not likely to induce authorities to give in to movement demands. Hence, challengers are forced to use radical, unconventional strategies in order to make themselves heard."
> (Dekker et al. 1997, 229)

The patterns found across the countries of Southern Europe – high protest activity combined with low organisational engagement – could have appeared in Central Eastern Europe after the collapse of communism as well. One reason could be the weakness of new democratic institutions, which need time to fully consolidate. A second reason could lay in the lack of "civilisational competence" among citizens in this region (Sztompka 2000), they may see protest as the only effective way to achieve their goals. Thus the institutional weakness of new democracies, combined with a lack of civic competence, could result in high protest activity instead of positive social engagement. Ekiert and Kubik suggest a direct causal link between a weak civil society and the intensity of protest actions in Poland: "the poor institutionalisation of the relationship between the state and its citizens seems to be a reason for the high intensity of collective protest" (Ekiert/Kubik 1999, 7). In further analyses (chapter 6) I examine the relationship between the intensity of protest actions and social capital.

3.6 Conclusions – is the communist legacy and systemic transition different in Poland?

The conditions for social capital building differ between post-communist societies, and the goal of this chapter was to disentangle the conditions that were specific for Poland – during communism and during the transition. The communist legacy in Poland was actually *less detrimental* for the development of civil society compared to other societies in the region. In contrast the conditions for social capital building in Poland related to the systemic transition were definitely *more detrimental* in Poland compared to other post-communist societies.

During the communist era, social engagement was mostly motivated by ideology – acquiring basic freedoms, in addition to economic improvements – and was directed against the regime. In a non-democratic system, these activities had a positive effect on social capital and political developments and eventually resulted in liberalisation. However after the collapse of communism, the high propensity to protest against policies made in a democratic decision-making process had a negative effect on political stability: "the mass character of the movement – would have a strong, *adverse* impact on the consolidation phase, since they delayed the development of pragmatic, issue-oriented politics" (Ekiert/Kubik 1999, 6; emphasis in original). Furthermore, other factors – such as the high social costs of reforms and disappointment – appear to have had an additional negative impact on social capital in the transition phase.

Table 3.2 summarises the results of the analysis of conditions related to communism and to systemic transition presented in this chapter. This overview also shows the relations between analysed conditions and single components of social capital.

Table 3.2 Similarities and dissimilarities in conditions for social capital building between Poland and other post-communist countries

COMPONENTS OF SOCIAL CAPITAL	PERIOD	CONDITIONS	SIMILAR to other post-communist countries	DISSIMILAR to other post-communist countries in degree	DISSIMILAR to other post-communist countries in kind
Social networks	during communism	coerced membership	+		
		"provisional" networks	+		
		privatisation of life	+		
		protest actions			+
		pluralism and autonomy			+
		strong and supportive position of the Catholic Church			+
		strong family ties	+		
	after the collapse of communism	"provisional" networks	+		
		social costs of transition (disappointment)		+	
		protest actions			+
Social trust	during communism	distrust syndrome	+		
		short-radius trust	+		
	after the collapse of communism	social costs of transition (income inequalities)		+	
		dissatisfaction and pessimism			+
Norms and values	during communism	"homo sovieticus"	+		
		incompetent citizens	+		
	after the collapse of communism	"homo sovieticus"	+		
		incompetent citizens	+		

One important conclusion can be drawn from the overview of the results outlined in Table 3.2: dissimilarities in conditions for social capital building in Poland affect mostly two components of social capital – **social networks** and **social trust**. As far as conditions for norms and values are concerned, no dissimilarities related to the communist legacy and to the systemic transition were found in Poland. In the course of further analyses, we need to address the question of whether there is empirical evidence for the relevance of dissimilar conditions in Poland for social networks and social trust. Positive evidence of the importance of dissimilar condition would contribute to the explanation of Polish exceptionality.

Before searching for this evidence, I continue to examine dissimilarities in conditions for social capital building between Poland and other countries. Specifically the focus in the following two chapters is on exploring the conditions related to religion. Does it matter for social capital in Poland that Catholicism is the dominant religious tradition? Does it matter that Poles are an especially religiously devout society? These questions are addressed in chapter 4 and chapter 5, while the analyses of the impact of the dissimilar conditions in Poland on social capital will be pursued in chapter 6.

4 Catholicism and social capital

4.1 Introduction

The legacies of communism and the consequences of the systemic transitions are not the only factors that affected social capital building across post-communist Europe. The long-term influence of religious traditions also plays a crucial role in the development of social capital. Central Eastern Europe is diversified with regard to dominant religions: among post-communist countries there are Catholic, Orthodox and two Protestant countries (three when including East Germany, see section 2.4). However, what distinguishes Poland from all other countries, including Catholic ones, is an exceptionally high level of religiosity. Catholicism is more strongly embedded in tradition and culture in Poland than in any other post-communist country. Poland is also, along with Ireland and Italy, one of the most devout countries in Europe. Since many authors emphasise the relevance of the religious impact on social capital (Putnam 1993, 107; Wuthnow 1996, 17; Putnam 2000, 69; Smidt 2003, 216-218; Welch et al. 2004, 319; de Hart/Dekker 2005, 176; Roßteutscher 2009, 37), religion could be a crucial explanatory factor when exploring Poland's exceptionally low endowment with social capital.

The main objective of this chapter is dealing with the question: to what extent does strong Catholicism influence social capital building in Poland? To address this question we need to overview relevant arguments in the literature concerning relations between religion and social capital, with a specific focus on the impact of Catholicism. Religious influence is discussed on the one hand as a cultural factor (for instance as a moral imperative for social engagement), and on the other hand as a structural condition (affiliation in church-related networks) that is crucial for social capital building. Both types of religious influences are discussed in the two following sections.

4.2 Why does religion matter for social capital endowment?

The impact of religion and churches on the creation of social capital is emphasised by several authors, and a number of studies provide empirical evidence for it. Yet the relationship between religious traditions and social capital is complex, and findings are contradictory. For one thing, it seems that different denominations have distinct effects on the propensity to build networks and on social trust. Catholicism is apparently a hampering factor for generating social capital (Putnam 1993, 107, 173), while other denominations, especially Protestantism, seem to create favourable conditions for social engagement (Verba et al. 1995, 245). In section 4.2.1 I use the term "denomination effects" when referring to the allegedly negative impact of Catholicism on social capital. For another thing, many authors demonstrate positive relationships between churchgoing and the individual stock of social capital. When referring to this relationship in section 4.2.2 I use the term "affiliation effects" meaning the relatively high propensity of churchgoers to get connected in social networks (Wuthnow 1991, 125; Greeley 1997, 590; Putnam 2000, 66; Campbell/Yonish 2003, 94). "Affiliation effects" are empirically confirmed by several cross-national studies, and these findings concern also Catholics[29] (Norris/Inglehart 2005, 188; de Hart/Dekker 2005, 176). This is why in Poland, which has a history and culture strongly influenced by Catholicism and where churchgoing is one of the most frequent in Europe, the "resulting" direction of religious impacts seems to be difficult to assess. We can formulate the question in another way: why in Poland, despite the high level of church attendance, do social networks remain weak? I address this question by analysing arguments concerning the negative impacts of Catholicism (denomination effects) and the positive influences of church affiliation (affiliation effects) on social capital.

4.2.1   Exploring "denomination effects"

4.2.1.1   Evidence of "denomination effects"

Before we discuss theoretical arguments concerning the negative impact of Catholicism on social capital, let us overview the empirical evidence in the literature. This approach allows us to explore precisely which components of social capital are influenced by the allegedly negative "denomination effects" of Catholicism.

The negative relationship between Catholicism and social capital can be seen primarily at the macro level, while evidence concerning the micro level is not consistent. Several empirical cross-national studies show that predominantly Catholic countries rank low in social involvement (Curtis et al. 2001, 791; Gabriel et al. 2002, 52; van Deth 2004, 306). Similarly, social trust at the macro level seems to be lower in Catholic countries compared to countries with other religious traditions (La Porta et al. 1997, 336; Inglehart 1999, 92; Gabriel et al. 2002, 59; Kunz 2004, 209). For the third component of social capital – norms and values – there is little evidence of the

---

[29] This effect seems to be weaker for Catholics than for Protestants (Norris/Inglehart 2005, 188).

differences between Catholicism and other traditions. Two cross-national European studies based on different datasets analyse patterns of support for such values and norms as law-abidingness, solidarity, socially oriented child-raising values, and acceptance of community oriented norms (Gabriel et al. 2002, 69-78; Roßteutscher 2004, 183-187). Both studies demonstrate the absence of a direct relationship between a country's dominant religious tradition and support for norms and values related to social capital. In turn a considerable difference across European societies seems to lay in the value orientations situated along an axis: traditional and rational-secular value orientations. A study by Inglehart and Baker demonstrates that traditional value orientations dominate across Catholic societies, in contrast to Protestant ones (2000, 29). The question remains unanswered whether traditional value orientations are relevant for the values and norms related to social capital. I return to this question when discussing the "dogmatic explanation" of the impact of Catholicism on social capital.

At the micro level, denominations are relevant in explaining differences in social participation between Catholics and Protestants in US society (Verba et al. 1995, 245; Lam 2002, 414). Similar results concerning the relevance of denomination were found in a cross-national study explaining the propensity to volunteer (Ruiter/De Graaf 2006, 200). Nonetheless, examinations of European societies demonstrate much weaker differences between Catholics and Protestants in participation rates (van Deth 2004, 308-309). Furthermore, the evidence on the relationship between generalised trust and Catholicism at the micro level is not consistent. Analyses encompassing European populations show that Catholics are more likely to trust than non-religious individuals; furthermore, the effects for the adherents of other denominations (for instance Protestants) are stronger (Guiso et al. 2003, 256, 263). Another study of social trust among the members of different churches in American society (Catholic and a variety of Protestant denominations) does not find differences in trust between Catholics and Protestants:[30] "individuals from a variety of denominational backgrounds do not differ appreciably from their mainline Protestant counterparts in the levels of trust they display. Catholics do not differ from the mainliners" (Welch et al. 2004, 325). The only significant difference concerns members of a conservative Protestant denomination (Pentecostals), who show a low level of generalised trust.[31] Otherwise there is no empirical study on the relationship between values widespread among Catholics and the third component of social capital — norms and values. Table 4.1 summarises the empirical findings concerning Catholic influence on social capital.

---

[30] The patterns among American Catholics may not always be applicable to European Catholics. I return to this aspect later.
[31] Scholars explain it as a high in-group collective identity of Pentecostals (Welch et al. 2004, 325).

Table 4.1 Summary of empirical evidence of "denomination effects" at macro and micro levels by components of social capital

	Macro level	Micro level
Networks	-	-
Trust	-	-/+
Norms and values	0	0

Notes: "-" refers to empirical evidence on the negative relationship between Catholicism and a component of social capital;
"+" refers to empirical evidence on the positive relationship between Catholicism and a component of social capital;
"0" refers to the absence of empirical evidence on the relationship between Catholicism and a component of social capital.

In summary, the evidence on the relationship between Catholicism and social capital concerns mostly social networks at both the macro and micro levels. Furthermore, Catholic societies (macro level) demonstrate less social trust, though this does not apply to the micro level – individual Catholics are not less trusting (Table 4.1). How do scholars explain the negative impact of Catholicism on social networks and trust?

4.2.1.2 Explaining "denomination effects"

The explanations concerning the impact of Catholicism on trust and networks in the literature can be divided into two streams of argument. First, scholars refer to the hierarchical structure of the Catholic Church, which is supposed to have a negative impact on horizontal networks and generalised trust. Second, some authors argue that the dogmatic characteristics of the Catholic tradition that have shaped the normative framework of the Catholic worldview discourage Catholics from getting involved.

4.2.1.2.1 The hierarchical structure of the Catholic Church

Putnam is the first scholar who pointed to the hierarchical structure of the Catholic Church as a crucial explanatory factor for the low stock of social capital in the Southern part of Italy. Social networks, which are crucial components of social capital, should be characterised by their horizontal nature (Putnam 1993, 173-175). In contrast, vertical bonds, such as patron-client relations, create encouraging conditions for the exploitation of those trapped in a "client" position and are detrimental to social cohesion. Only horizontal networks are conducive to the development of generalised reciprocity and trust among their members. In every society both types of networks exist; the important question is which type prevails. In Southern

Italy, for instance, vertical networks dominate horizontal ones, and Putnam sees the strong influence of the Catholic Church as a reason for these patterns (1993, 173, 175). The Catholic Church in this region of Italy "retains much of the heritage of the Counter-Reformation, including emphasis on the ecclesiastical hierarchy (...); vertical bonds of authority are more characteristic of the Italian Church than horizontal bonds of fellowship" (Putnam 1993, 107). These characteristics of the Catholic Church seem to be reflected in the nature of the prevailing bonds among community members. Citizens in this region are relatively uninterested in community activities and are reluctant to cooperate with each other.

Not only social networks appear to be negatively correlated with Catholicism; there is a similar correlation with social trust at the macro level. Scholars draw their argumentation on Putnam's emphasis on the role of the hierarchical structure of the Catholic Church, which "by imposing a hierarchical structure on the society (...) has discouraged the formation of trust" (La Porta et al. 1997, 336). An empirical study by La Porta and colleagues shows that the general predominance of a religious tradition that is characterised by a hierarchical structure – not only Catholic, but also Eastern Orthodox and Muslim – could be an explanatory factor for low social trust at the macro level (La Porta et al. 1997, 336-337). When explaining the mechanisms of this relationship Inglehart stresses the importance of a hierarchical organisation (such as Roman Catholic Church), which dominates and controls local communities:

> "it seems to reflect the principle that horizontal, locally-controlled organizations are conducive to interpersonal trust, while remote hierarchical organizations tend to undermine it. The Roman Catholic Church is the very prototype of a hierarchical, centrally-controlled institution; Protestant churches were smaller, relatively decentralized and more open to local control. Though these factors may not count for much today, historically the respective churches played immensely influential roles in shaping their societies. The contrast between local control and domination by a remote hierarchy seems to have important long-term consequences for interpersonal trust."
>
> (1999, 92-93)

Inglehart's explanation does not specify in what way churches' "remote hierarchy" could shape interpersonal trust across societies. Furthermore, the Lutheran Church in Scandinavian countries is also characterised by a hierarchical structure (Roßteutscher 2009, 89); yet despite this, Scandinavian countries have the most trusting societies in Europe (Gabriel et al. 2002, 58-59). In this respect the argument that the hierarchical structure of the Catholic Church diminishes social trust is not convincing. There must be something more than the Church's structure that hampers social trust in Catholic societies.

A study by Verba and colleagues confirms at the micro level Putnam's claims about the relevance of Catholicism[32] for lower participation in voluntary networks (1995, 245-247). The reason seems to lie in the organisational features of Catholic parishes, which are large and hierarchical:

> "Protestant congregations tend, on average, to be smaller than Catholic parishes; compared to the Catholic Church (...) and most of the Protestant denominations are organized on a congregational basis with authority vested in the congregation itself rather than a church hierarchy." (Verba et al. 1995, 245)

The argument of Verba and colleagues, which refers to the differences in the structural features of the churches is, to a certain extent, inconsistent with the claims of other American scholars, who stress that the American Catholic Church changed dramatically after Vatican II adopted a congregational structure similar to that of the American Protestant churches[33] (Coleman 2003, 36-37; Welch et al. 2004, 319). Besides these objections, one main problem appears when applying the findings of Verba and colleagues to my study: it concerns the situation in the USA. In Europe, relationships between social networks and religion are more complex, and the patterns of church structures differ considerably between Europe and the USA (Roßteutscher 2009, 88). Not all Protestant churches in Europe are egalitarian and characterised by small congregations. As mentioned earlier, the Lutheran churches in Scandinavian countries are characterised by hierarchical structures, similar to the Catholic Church (Roßteutscher 2009, 89). So, following the argumentation of Verba and colleagues, we would expect that members of Scandinavian Lutherans' large and hierarchical churches would be reluctant to participate in voluntary organisations. But the opposite is true – participation rates among Scandinavians are the highest in Europe.[34] On the other hand, Roßteutscher finds that large, hierarchical organisations are actually more prone to the generation of social capital among their members because they are more professionalised and institutionalised (Roßteutscher 2009, 417). According to this argument, Catholics – embedded in the large hierarchy of the Catholic Church – can take advantage of connections to a wide web of Catholic parishes (Roßteutscher 2009, 399).

---

[32] Verba and colleagues compare the rates of participation between Catholics and Protestants in the USA (1995, 245).
[33] Verba and colleagues suggest that the differences in the structures of Catholic parishes and Protestant congregations, though smaller, still remained after Vatican II but will disappear in the future (1995, 245-246).
[34] Roßteutscher claims that the differences between churches' capacity for social capital building can be explained in Europe by the **size** of church-related organizations, and not by the hierarchical or egalitarian structures of a church (2009, 404-409).

What is meant by "hierarchical structures"?

The principal problem about the "structural approach" is the inconsistent use of the term "hierarchical structure" in reference to the Catholic Church. Some scholars, when using the term "hierarchical," refer to relations between the faithful and the church authorities or priests (Putnam 1993, 175; Verba et al. 1995, 245). In contrast Inglehart and La Porta refer to the structure of the Roman Catholic Church as such (La Porta et al. 1997, 336; Inglehart 1999, 92). Other authors argue that the structure of the church as such does not affect social capital, but that the *structure of church-related organisations* is particularly relevant, since this is where the participation actually takes place (Wuthnow 1996, 35; Wuthnow 2002, 678). And specifically, as Roßteutscher emphasises, it is important whether the relation between church authorities (or clergy) and parishioners has a hierarchical nature or is based on egalitarian principles. She shows that within big hierarchical churches (e.g., Catholic and Lutheran), religion-based groups are small and have an egalitarian nature (2009, 338). Furthermore, social capital is generated most efficiently by big hierarchical organisations within small churches (Roßteutscher 2009, 437, 441). This is why structural approaches seem to be convincing when focusing on the nature of cooperation between the clergy and the congregation, for example regarding church-related activism.

Religious participation matters

Empirical studies confirm that church-based groups are the key source of social capital (Wuthnow 1996, 36; Roßteutscher 2009, 417). Among parishioners, social capital can be built through social interactions that happen through activities in religious groups or church-based organisations, otherwise attending the religious services alone creates only favourable conditions for social interactions among parish members. I return to this aspect when discussing the positive impact of religiosity on social capital building. What is important at this point is how many congregation members participate in church-related activities across different denominations. Catholics, when compared to Protestants, are less involved in church-based organisations, due to a lack of encouragement from the Church itself: "compared to the Catholic Church, most of the Protestant denominations allow for greater participation in the liturgy" (Verba et al. 1995, 245).

This characteristic of the Roman Catholic Church has changed to some extent after the Vatican II Council (1962-1965), which introduced tremendous changes in such issues as lay participation, liturgy and attitudes towards ecumenism. The Roman Catholic Church became a more open and modern institution, encouraging more lay involvement in church-related activities (Adloff 2010, 195). However, despite the fact that the Catholic Church is one institution, the "spirit of Vatican" did not reach Catholics to the same degree in different societies. Apparently national context mattered considerably for the introduction of the changes across societies. For instance, while in the USA parish structures changed considerably after Vatican II (Warren 2003, 56) and church activity is a widespread form of social participation, in Western Europe the Church's position was in general weakening and a secularisation across many Catholic societies took place (meaning for the Catholic Church a considerable decline in social church activities and in churchgoing rates Jagodzinski/Dobbelaere 1995a, 82). In general, despite efforts to enhance and modernise the clergymen-laymen relationship, church-related participation in Europe is still lower in Catholic societies than in Protestant ones (Figure 4.1).

Figure 4.1 Membership in religious organisations in European countries (percentages)

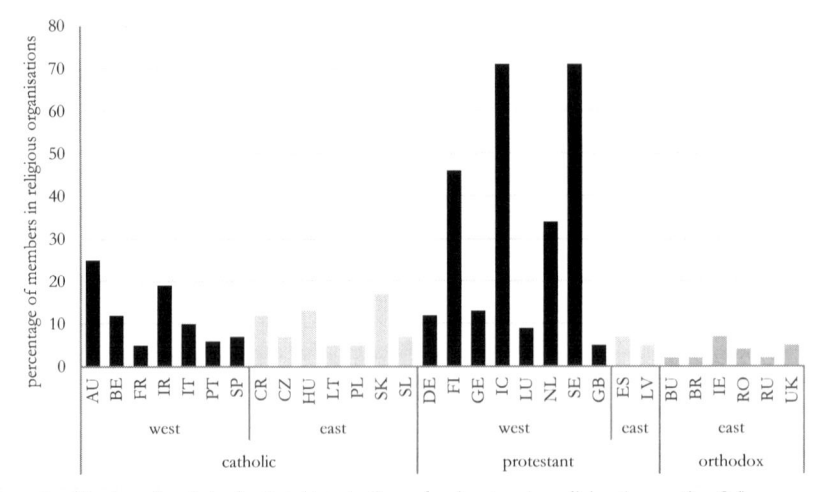

Note: classification of societies by their historically predominant major religion (see section 2.4)
Source: WVS 1999.

Table 4.2 Average membership in religious organisations in European countries (weighted averages)

	Western			Eastern				Poland
	Catholic	Protestant	**All**	Catholic	Protestant	Orthodox	**All**	
average membership in religious organisations	12%	33%	**23%**	9%	6%	4%	**7%**	*5%*

Source: WVS 1999.

Figure 4.1 depicts the levels of religious participation across European societies. Countries are grouped according to their dominant religious traditions.[35] Within the category "religious tradition," I also categorised societies according to the East-West axis. We can see that while religious participation is highest in Western Protestant societies (see Table 4.2. – on average, 33 percent of respondents declare membership in church-related organisations), Catholic societies display lower religious involvement, irrespective of geographical location (on average, 12 percent in Western countries and 9 percent in Eastern ones). This is evidence of only modest success of the Vatican II in promoting lay participation, since these reforms failed to prompt lay involvement in church-related groups to the level observed, for instance, in Protestant societies. In Poland the level of participation in church-related groups is low, which points to the limited success of Vatican II in Poland, too. Let us look closer at the effect of Vatican II in Central Eastern Europe.

Religiously based participation in Central Eastern Europe

Since the goal of this chapter is to assess the impact of Catholicism on social capital in Poland, it is important to understand what Vatican II has meant for religious participation in Poland and other countries across Central Eastern Europe. The outcome of Vatican II for lay participation in this region is difficult to compare with the changes in Western European countries, particularly during the communist era. Therefore we should consider the consequences of Vatican II in two periods: before and after the collapse of communism. Under communist regimes the Catholic Church was banned from the public sphere and its institutional survival was a big issue:

---

[35] For details on the classification of societies according to their historically predominant religion, see section 2.4.1.

"Communist states excluded religion from public life. They nationalized or closed denominational institutions and urged people to abandon or to hide religious convictions. Persecution of religion created a gap between individual faith, which was denied space to express itself in social terms, and collective religious practice."

(Tomka 2002, 485)

Therefore support for the lay participation in church-related groups was especially difficult under the official ban of the Church from the public sphere. On the other hand, after Vatican II the Catholic Church supported societal efforts for democratisation across Central Eastern Europe, and Catholicism helped facilitate the development of social, and particularly political, participation under communism (Huntington 1991, 78-80). The character of political activities organised through the Catholic Church was obviously anti-systemic. When compared to other religious traditions, through its supranational character the Catholic Church had in general more potential to resist against communist authorities and contributed to the overthrow of communist regimes across Central Eastern Europe (and other countries worldwide, see Huntington 1991, 77 ff. and section 3.3.4). This is an apparent advantage over Protestant and Orthodox churches, which have institutional structures that limit their influence on the national level. The Catholic Church has resources that could be allocated among different countries and regions. Its clergy is, to a higher extent, independent from the secular authorities in a country, in contrast to Protestant pastors[36] or to Orthodox clergy, who are often subordinate to the secular authorities (Borowik 2000, 26). This embedding of the Catholic national churches in international structures creates advantageous circumstances for political anti-regime engagement in a crisis situation: "Protestantism in regular times, Catholicism in a crisis![37]" (Roßteutscher 2009, 83). In this sense the Catholic Church stimulated the development of social capital across communist Catholic countries to a greater extent than other churches.

However "in regular times," after the collapse of the communism, lay participation in church-related groups in Catholic countries in Central Europe remains low, and only exceeds 10 percent in Croatia, Hungary and Slovakia (Figure 4.1). Church-related involvement changed its focus after the collapse of communism – from politically oriented to a more religious or social orientation (Kamiński 2008, 17; Žaloudková 2003, 273-280; Krizek 2003, 191-197). Additionally, some scholars report that lay participation across post-communist countries meets several constraints, such as a low level of professionalisation, a lack of experience in the enforcement of democratic structures and the rejection of the principle of a pluralistic society (Krizek 2003, 187-189; Žaloudková 2003, 280; Lenschen 2003, 434). Generally, empirical data show (Table 4.2) that church-related activities are not considera-

---

[36] Protestant pastors are financially dependent on the congregations (Roßteutscher 2009, 78-79).
[37] Translation from German KŁ.

bly lower across Central Eastern Catholic societies (9 percent) when compared to Western Catholic ones (12 percent).

In summary, the structural approach applied to the explanation of the negative "denomination effects" of the Catholic Church on social participation needs to be refined. For the production of social capital, clergy-lay people relations are more important than the structure of the church. The social capital generated by the churches concerns church-related organisations. It seems that the Catholic Church promotes lay people to be involved in various church-related groups to a lesser extent (compared to Protestant churches), however this line of argumentation fails to explain why **secular participation** is lower in Catholic societies, too. Why should Catholics be less engaged in secular social activity if the problem consists of low encouragement to participate in church-related activities? In a later section I analyse the influence of Catholic tenets, which could explain the reluctance of Catholics to be involved in social activity – religious **and** secular. However, we cannot elucidate the impact of the structure (of the Catholic Church) on social capital while neglecting the normative frame of the Catholic dogma. This is why we need to turn to the "dogmatic approach" to explain Catholics' low endowment with social capital in a general context.

4.2.1.2.2   Catholic tenets and social capital

An important line of argumentation in the literature points to certain values embedded in the Catholic dogma, which in a way curb the propensity to build social networks and are prone to trust. The values one sees as salient and the norms one follows constitute a moral and normative foundation for motivations and behaviours. Van Deth proposes the concept of "value orientations," which is crucial to understanding the relationship between values and behaviour patterns (van Deth/Scarbrough 1995, 529). Each religion imposes a set of norms that concerns, among other things, relations among the faithful (or other people) and promotes certain values based on religious dogma. These sets of norms and values differ between religions, even between denominations that have the same roots, such as Catholicism and Protestantism. Several authors point to a specific set of norms and value orientations that are widespread among Catholics that distinguish them from adherents of other religious traditions; these scholars see a direct link between these value orientations and Catholics' reluctance to build social capital.

The collective character of the church is strongly emphasised in Catholicism. Catholics are embedded in a collective identity through belonging to a large community, their church: "The Catholic Church, with its extensive, dogmatic, collective creed imposes a (...) collective identity upon the faithful" (Jagodzinski/Dobbelaere 1995a, 81). In the Catholic dogma a believer, through the sacrament of baptism, becomes a part of the Church, and is at the same time a part of "a mystical body of Jesus Christ." As the faithful learn from the letter of St. Paul: "now all of you together are Christ's body, and each one of you is a separate and necessary part of it" (1 Cor 12, 27). This dogma strongly emphasises the unification of a Catholic believer with his Christian community (and with God). In addition, the administration of other sacraments and participation in religious rites require church attendance on a regular basis and the intermediation of a Catholic priest. So, a Catholic is not only a part of his church, he also needs intensive bonds with the institutional church to be a good Catholic. This leads to a strong dependency between Catholics and the church.[38] And strong bonds to the church make Catholics apparently less engaged in worldly issues: "they seem more concerned about the city of God than the city of man" (Putnam 1993, 107).

A consequence of this strong dependency on the Catholic community is a weak emphasis on individual achievement: "the seeds of individualism were manifest much earlier in Protestantism. In contrast to Catholics, Protestants are personally responsible before God in religious matters" (Jagodzinski/Dobbelaere 1995a, 81). The emphasis on individualism makes a Protestant more responsible for himself and makes him more motivated to take the initiative to move things forward. In contrast, a Catholic is expected to take his destiny as a will of God and to follow it. Weber pointed to a "protestant ethic" as a driving force for material welfare among Protestants (specifically among Calvinists), while for Catholics, striving for material goods evokes rather pejorative connotations (Weber 2009 [1904], 30). In general a Protestant actively takes individual responsibility for his life and sees God's blessing in his success, whereas a Catholic is supposed to be passive and patient.

Besides individualism, egalitarian values seem to be another "scarce good" across Catholic societies. Moving along the hierarchical-egalitarian axis does not only concern structures of churches, but also values transmitted by a denomination. Uslaner claims that egalitarian values dominate among Protestants "because the Protestant Church has historically been more egalitarian than the Catholic Church" (Uslaner 2003b, 180). His line of argument is based on the assertion that the structural features of a church are reflected in the value systems of the faithful. Egalitarian values are relevant for social capital, since: "more egalitarian societies are more likely to be trusting" (Uslaner 2003b, 180). He gives the example of Scandinavian societies: "Scandinavian societies are so trusting because they are more equal and more Protestant" (Uslaner 2003b, 181 ff.). In his empirical examination he operationalises egalitarian values as economic equality (Uslaner 2003b, 181 ff.). Uslaner's claim that there is a positive relationship between egalitarian values and Protestantism is based on the structural characteristics of the Church, in this case the Protes-

---

[38] A good Protestant is to a lesser degree obliged to keep frequent contacts with his church as a good Catholic is (Roßteuscher 2009, 85)

tant Church. This argument, however, needs to be clarified. As shown in section 4.2.1.2.2, the Lutheran churches in Scandinavian countries are actually hierarchically organised (Roßteutscher 2009, 89). However, the relations between parishioners and pastors are more egalitarian than relations between the Catholic faithful and priests. Therefore Uslaner's argument seems to be plausible if we consider only the relations between the faithful and clergy, not the structure of the Church as an institution. On the other hand, not all Protestant denominations, despite displaying egalitarian relations between the clergy and the faithful, contribute to the development of trust. Adherence to some specific denominations (like Pentecostals in the USA) seems to diminish the likelihood of trusting people in general. On the one hand, the reason for this can be explained by the specific worldview embedded in this religious tradition: "this worldview, which tends to characterize good and evil in personal terms (...) creates a powerful dynamic that seems likely to inhibit the growth of social trust" (Welch et al. 2004, 337). On the other hand, Uslaner argues that value orientations embedded in a denomination play a crucial role in the development of generalised trust:

> "Religious values may lead people to insulate themselves from strangers – and disbelievers (...) People may identify so strongly with their faith that they become suspicious of others." (Uslaner 2002, 87)

In Europe, similar in-group identity building has appeared among Catholics in the past: "in the nineteenth century, the Catholic Church reacted to the anti-Catholicism of the Protestant majority society by withdrawing inwards and building social milieu which kept their distance from that majority society" (Adloff 2010, 198). This appeared, for instance, in Germany as a reaction to the *Kulturkampf* and resulted in bonding social capital and in-group trust among Catholics (Adloff 2010, 196; see also Roßteutscher 2009, 75-77).

A contradictory line of argument holds that the Catholic emphasis on collective identity is a favourable condition for strengthening the feeling of solidarity among Catholics (Offe/Fuchs 2002, 208; see also Inglehart 1997, 71). The virtues of mercy and compassion promoted by Catholic teachings make a Catholic ready to take responsibility for others and for the collective (Offe/Fuchs 2002, 208). This could be a significant motivation for engagement with others, especially for those in need. However, in this regard Catholicism is not really much different from Protestantism. This is why altruistic motivation for social engagement should be seen as an effect of religious commitment that is independent from denomination (Wuthnow 1991, 51; Wilson/Janoski 1995, 138, 143). I return discuss religious motivation for volunteering in section 4.2.2.

The Catholic Church on the one hand emphasises its collective character, and on the other hand praises the family as one of the most salient institutions. A number of scholars argue that strong family ties (especially across Southern European societies) are explanatory factors for the low stock of social capital across these societies (especially as far as social trust is concerned Fukuyama 1995, 55-56; Kunz 2004, 209; see also section 2.2.1.2). Putnam argues that kinship bonds fail to "nourish wider cooperation" among community members (Putnam 1993, 175) because of their inclusive character and limitation to a small group within a society (bonding social capital). Banfield describes an extreme case of an Italian village in the 1950s in which priority was given to the short-term interests of the nuclear family and cooperation with community members was rejected – which brought social atomization, backwardness and impoverishment for the whole community (1958). This phenomenon – "amoral familism" – is an example of the possible negative consequences of strong family bonds for social cohesion (Putnam 1993, 177; Fukuyama 1995, 56). Nevertheless for Halpern (2005) strong kinship bonds (bonding social capital) are not an alternative for widespread bridging bonds, such as associational networks, they are simply another dimension of networks in society, and both are independent from each other (see also section 2.2.1.1). In Halpern's typology of societies, which is constructed using a combination of network patterns (bridging and bonding), "amoral familism" constitutes one of four possibilities and refers to a combination of strong bonding and weak bridging ties (Halpern 2005, 21). Furthermore, a mixture of strong family (bonding) ties and strong associational (bridging) ties is another possible type of societal network pattern, as the examples of Sweden and USA show demonstrate (Halpern 2005, 21). In other words, the salience of family values does not mean implicitly weak associational ties, and the Catholic emphasis on family values can lead to lower social capital, but this is not necessarily a general principle.

By summarising the explanations of the negative effect of Catholicism on social capital, we can draw two main conclusions:
(1) "Structural approaches," which refer to the hierarchical nature of the clergy-faithful relationship, explain a part of the reality, namely Catholics' low engagement in religious-based groups, but fail to explain their reluctance to build social networks in the secular realm. The argument concentrating on the hierarchical structure of the Catholic Church as the reason for the low stock of social trust also captures only a part of the situation, since this argument cannot be generalised to include all churches with a hierarchical structure (such as the Lutheran Church).
(2) "Dogmatic approaches" point to the Catholic tenets that promote certain normative frameworks encompassing, among other things, collectivism, disinterest in worldly affairs, lack of individualism and egalitarianism, and an emphasis on family. This could hinder the propensity to build social networks. Low levels of social trust among Catholic societies are explained by particularly strong family bonds, which discourage social network building outside the family. However, this point of view is not shared universally.

4.2.2 Exploring "affiliation effects"

Some scholars emphasise that the effect of church affiliation is stronger than denominational effects: "how often you go to the church is far more important in predicting whether you volunteer than which church you attend" (Campbell/Yonish 2003, 98; see also de Hart/Dekker 2005, 184). A positive role of churches in the generation of social capital has been stressed by many authors (Wuthnow 1996, 17; Smidt 2003, 216-217; de Hart/Dekker 2005, 184-185). Churchgoing is an important indicator of social integration (Gabriel et al. 2002, 99); furthermore, regular contact with religious teachings provides a moral basis for social engagement (Wuthnow 1991, 51; Harris 2003, 134). The first part of the following section presents an overview of the empirical evidence for the relationships between church affiliation and all three components of social capital. The second part focuses on the explanations for these relationships and discusses the constraints that are especially important in the case of Poland.

4.2.2.1 Evidence of an "affiliation effect"

Networks are fostered by churches. As various empirical studies demonstrate, regular churchgoers, irrespective of their denomination, are more likely to be socially engaged and to volunteer than non-religious individuals: "religious involvement is an especially strong predictor of volunteering and philanthropy; (...) religious adherents are also more likely to contribute time and money to activities beyond their own congregations" (Putnam 2000, 67). Putnam's analyses concern the situation in the USA. Empirical studies of European countries demonstrate similar patterns, though mostly across Western European societies (van Deth 2004, 307-308; Gabriel et al. 2002, 115; de Hart/Dekker 2005, 176, 184). Empirical findings concerning positive relationships between churchgoing and participation can be found mainly at the micro level. Macro-level results are different, since levels of church attendance are lowest in countries with Protestant and mixed traditions, for instance in Denmark, the Netherlands and Sweden (de Hart/Dekker 2005, 173-174; Norris/Inglehart 2005, 72-73), which are characterised by high rates of social participation (Gabriel et al. 2002, 47; van Deth 2004, 305).

The evidence concerning the second component of social capital – social trust – appears blurry. At the macro level, relationships between social trust and religiosity appear to be negative (Berggren/Bjørnskov 2009). Religiosity is operationalised in a study by Berggren and Bjørnskov as the salience of religion in one's life (2009, 13), whereas a low salience of religion is highly correlated with low rates of church attendance in Europe (see de Hart/Dekker 2005, 173; compared with Berggren/Bjørnskov 2009, 37). The evidence at the micro level is contradictory.

While some cross-national studies provide evidence that churchgoers are more likely to trust others in general (Gabriel et al. 2002, 122; Guiso et al. 2003, 249), others prove just the opposite (Norris/Inglehart 2005, 192).

Cross-national studies about the third component of social capital – norms and values – do not demonstrate any relationship with the level of church integration at the macro level[39] (Gabriel et al. 2002, 84; compared with de Hart/Dekker 2005, 172-174). Furthermore, at the micro level a mixed pattern appears: while churchgoing is negatively correlated with socially oriented child-rearing objectives, the relationship with the acceptance of the norms of social behaviour is positive (Gabriel et al. 2002, 126, 130).

Table 4.3 presents an overview of the empirical results of relationships between churchgoing and single components of social capital at the macro and micro levels.

Table 4.3 Summary of empirical evidence of "affiliation effects" at macro and micro levels by components of social capital

	Macro level	Micro level
Networks	0	+
Trust	-	- / +
Norms and values	0	- / +

Notes: "-" refers to empirical evidence on the negative relationship between churchgoing and a component of social capital
"0" refers to the absence of empirical evidence on the relationship between churchgoing and a component of social capital
"+" refers to empirical evidence on the positive relationship between churchgoing and a component of social capital

To generalise the findings (Table 4.3), people integrated in a church are also likely to be integrated socially and are prone to accept norms of social behaviour. However, churchgoers are likely to reject pro-social child-rearing objectives, while there are no general patterns concerning relationships between churchgoing and trust. From a macro perspective, the positive effect of church integration on networks and acceptance of norms seems to fade away. Furthermore, trust is low across more devout societies. How do scholars interpret the positive effect of church integration on networks and partly on the acceptance of norms, and why is this picture different at the aggregated level?

---

[39] For operationalisation of norms and values in these studies, see section 2.4.3.

4.2.2.2 Explaining "affiliation effects"

4.2.2.2.1 Recruitment, rise in civic competence and trust generated through churches

One of the most common explanations of why religion fosters social capital concerns the role of churches as incubators of social networks. Churches are not only places to worship and practice religious rites; they also facilitate the establishment of networks among the parish's or congregation's members. Churches are locations where members of local communities meet on a regular basis, and in this way they support the connections between community members. Such church-related links ease the recruitment for social engagement. As Verba and his colleagues claim, people are reluctant to participate: "because they can't; because they don't want to; or because nobody asked" (1995, 269). Thus recruitment, or just "being asked," is one of three main explanatory factors for participation, as Verba and colleagues propose in the Civic Voluntarism Model (ibid 269). Churches seem to be favourable places to "be asked" to volunteer. Further empirical studies in the USA confirm claims that church-related networks are important sources of recruitment: "churches are the common pathway into the voluntary sector" (Campbell/Yonish 2003, 95). Recruitment happens through congregations or parishes, social capital then rises through direct social interactions, which take place in church-related groups: "if social capital requires firsthand interaction, then small groups are clearly an important source of social capital" (Wuthnow 1996, 36). In these groups people learn to trust each other, become connected and learn civic skills. Religiously engaged citizens gain civic skills though practice: "religiously active men and women learn to give speeches, run meetings, manage disagreements, and bear administrative responsibility" (Putnam 2000, 66). In other words, churchgoing is important for getting an opportunity to be integrated into social networks, but this opportunity is not used until one gets involved in church-related activities.

The fact that churchgoers are involved in church-related groups is not surprising, but whether they are also more likely to be engaged outside the church is less self-evident. Some scholars suggest that a spillover effect takes place, meaning that church-related social activity stimulates secular engagement: "people who are involved in religious volunteering are almost 3.6 times more likely to do non-religious volunteer work as well" (Ruiter/De Graaf 2006, 204; see also de Hart/Dekker 2005, 184-186). A possible explanation is the rise in civic skills and motivation: "the spillover may occur through the civic education function of church participation, and also because additional (competing or complementary) bases for association joining are likely to arise in a climate of vigorous church activity and involvement" (Curtis et al. 2001, 800; see also: Greeley 1997, 591). A cross-national empirical study confirms that church-related activity, not only churchgoing, is positively correlated with civic skills: "membership in religious organizations was significantly associated with various indicators of civic engagement, including social attitudes and political behavior" (Norris/Inglehart 2005, 194).

On the other hand, a few scholars present empirical evidence for just the opposite – involvement in religious organisations creates competition for participation in secular ones: "religious organizations to some degree, compete with secular organizations for the time and energy of their members" (Lam 2002, 415; see also Becker/Dhingra 2001, 328). Similar findings are presented by Campbell and Yonish: "Among people who volunteer, increased church attendance leads to less general-purpose volunteering, instead directing their energies to religious volunteering" (Campbell/Yonish 2003, 101). However, both studies examine the patterns across American society, where religious engagement constitutes the main pillar of social activity: "Congregations are a major source of human and social capital in the American society" (Cnaan et al. 2003, 21; see also Greeley 1997, 591). Moreover, the USA has one of the least developed public social service systems among industrialised nations, thus "religious congregations serve a broader function than in many other countries" (Cnaan et al. 2003, 21). The situation in Europe is different; civil societies across European nations are instead secular (Roßteutscher 2009, 412-413). Thus we can only speculate about whether we would observe competition or spillover effects in Europe. Most probably we would detect a spillover effect, for the reason that secular associations are more widespread in Europe than the USA. I analyse this problem empirically in chapter 5.

Turning to trust, churchgoing is, in principle, positively related to the likelihood to trust (Gabriel et al. 2002, 122; Guiso et al. 2003, 249). However, these effects are weak and not confirmed by all empirical studies (Norris/Inglehart 2005, 192). Scholars found that the differences in contribution to trust between churchgoers are actually related to their adherence to different denominations, which was discussed in section 4.2.1.2.2. Hence, for my further research the impact of churchgoing on social trust in Poland compared to other societies remains an empirical question.

4.2.2.2.2 Does churchgoing reinforce religiously driven motivation to volunteer?

Until now we have focused on the Church as a structural factor that supports social capital building – basically churchgoers have more chances to be recruited to volunteer, and those involved in church-based social networks probably have more civic skills. Besides being connected to the religious community, churchgoers are also more exposed to religious teachings. Therefore religion, especially for those attending religious services on a regular basis, can also be a source of motivation to volunteer, especially when related to activities for others in need. Using Verba and colleagues' Civic Voluntarism Model (1995, 269) we can say that devoted people could be more likely to volunteer "because they want to." Why? The message of Christian religions promotes norms of mutual cooperation and values such as honesty, truthfulness, compassion, mercy and "love of the neighbour." Norms of altruism and compassion are attained through the process of religious socialisation: "religious worldviews and practices – depending on their orientations – have the capacity to diminish the need for material incentives when group cooperation is anchored in religious beliefs" (Harris 2003, 122). Religious people, usually raised by religious parents, are exposed to religious teachings from their childhood on. So, the contribution of religion to social capital building could be considerable and long lasting: "if we assume that religion has a powerful and lasting effect on people's attitudes and behaviours, then religious teachings may contribute to a more civil and caring society" (Cnaan et al. 2003, 29). Empirical evidence shows that churchgoers are more likely to accept the norms of social behaviour. An American study on religious activism brings convincing results: "religious explanations were the strongest justifications for participation in church work (...) church activists were also highly motivated to participate by altruism and desire for social intimacy" (Harris 2003, 134). Other research, however, based on in-depth interviews with volunteers engaged in church-related activities finds that: "social networks, rather than beliefs, dominate as the mechanism leading to volunteering, and it is the social networks formed within congregations that make congregation members more likely to volunteer" (Becker/Dhingra 2001, 329). Intrinsic normative motivations and the need to socialise are probably both primary sources of impulses to volunteer and differ from person to person (see also Harris 2003, 135).

Normative imperatives can be on the one hand sources of motivation for social engagement, on the other hand activists internalise certain values related to religious beliefs through social engagement in religious groups. Wuthow reports that involvement in small-group church-related activities influences the spirituality of the respondents: "the spiritual development emanating from these groups is often significant" (1996, 36). Membership in religious small groups affects an individual's attitudes and values in various spheres of life:

> "members report that they have become more interested in peace or justice as a result of their participation ( ) they have become more interested in social or political issues (...) a fellowship group had a significant impact on a wide range of attitudes and values, including attitudes toward money, the value of material possession, and the meaning of the work." (Wuthnow 1996, 37-38)

Hence, there is a mutual relationship between values and engagement – values can be a source of moral motivation to volunteer, and engagement can nourish the development of altruism, sensibility and spirituality.

4.2.2.2.3   The relevance of the national context

If churchgoing is such a favourable structural and cultural context to encourage volunteering, why in a few of the most devout countries in Europe, for instance in Poland and Italy, are there relatively low proportions of churchgoers ready to participate compared to more secular Sweden or the Netherlands (Figure 4.1)? Are there, besides the denominational explanations discussed above, any other contextual constraints that hamper the participation of churchgoers, particularly across devout countries?

Ruiter and de Graaf (2006) argue that the positive effect of churchgoing on volunteering is much weaker in countries where substantial proportions of the populace attend religious services:

> "the differences between secular and devout people are substantially smaller in religious countries than in secular countries. Our findings imply that individual religiosity is hardly relevant for volunteering in devout nations."   (Ruiter/De Graaf 2006, 206)

They explain these relations by "saturation" of the recruitment effects of churchgoing. While in secular societies frequent churchgoing raises the chances of being recruited, in devout countries the likelihood of being recruited is "saturated," therefore the added value of frequent church attendance is low (Ruiter/De Graaf 2006, 195). This finding is important for explaining the patterns of social engagement in a devout country such as Poland, where the rates of frequent church attendance are high. If saturation effects appear in Poland, it would mean that potential volunteers are already recruited.

Important for my further research on social capital in Poland is that "affiliation effects" (1) were observed mostly at the micro level, and (2) were weaker in devout countries. So I expect that in Poland, attending religious services on a regular basis increases an individual's chance to be a member of a (religious or secular) organisation, though in Poland these effects could be weaker compared to churchgoers from less devout countries. Furthermore, being a churchgoer in Poland could have a positive effect on acceptance of the norms of social behaviour, while the direction of influence of church attendance on social trust is difficult to predict.

4.3   Conclusions

The overview presented in this chapter results in some conclusions, which are crucial for further analyses of the impact of religion on social capital in Poland. Let us summarise the complicated puzzle of relationships between religion and social capital:

1) Studies concerning social capital reveal a webbed pattern of relationships. I distinguished two types of religious influences (Tables 4.1 and 4.2). First, I analysed the cultural aspects of religious influence (specifically Catholicism, which is crucial for Poland). Second, structural aspects of religious influence – embedding in church communities – were scrutinised. Empirical evidence of religious influence on single components of social capital is as follows:
    a. It seems that the impact of religion on social capital is consistent at the micro and macro levels only in reference to structural aspects, and only to one component of social capital – social networks. Specifically, Catholicism is negatively related to social networks at both levels. Relationships between social networks and church attendance are in contrast positive, though evidence was found only at the individual level.
    b. As far as trust is concerned, the negative effects of religion appear principally at the macro level, and here both structural and cultural effects are negatively related to trust (evidence at the micro level is inconsistent).
    c. In turn, norms and values correlate positively only with church affiliation at the micro level, whereby these relationships concern merely the acceptance of social norms. In contrast, church attendance is negatively correlated with support for socially oriented child-rearing objectives. Catholicism remains unrelated to norms and values. Moreover, both religious aspects – cultural and structural – turn out to be irrelevant for norms and values at the macro level.
2) The negative impact of Catholicism on the propensity to build social networks is partly explained by structural features of the Catholic Church, such as (1) the hierarchical nature of relations between the clergy and the faithful, and (2) lower encouragement to get involved in religious groups. The structural approaches, however, refer mostly to religious engagement. Reluctance to build social capital by Catholics in the secular realm could be better explained by (3) specific value orientations influenced by Catholic dogma, such as collectivism, disinterest in worldly affairs, lack of individualism and lack of egalitarianism. Moreover, emphasis on the family as a crucial value in the Catholic tradition could hinder the propensity to generate trust, though not all scholars share this line of thought.
3) The positive impact of church attendance on social networks results mostly from favourable recruitment opportunities through churches, from the opportunity to gain civic skills through religious involvement, and from religiously driven motivation reinforced by church attendance. Some

authors claim that religious involvement also encourages secular involvement. The positive effects of church affiliation appear to have a limited influence in devout societies such as Poland.

The findings and explanations concerning the patterns of relationships between religion and social capital provide a theoretical framework for my further analyses of religious influences on social capital in Poland in a comparative perspective. Do we find similar relationships between cultural and structural aspects of religion and social capital in Poland? What are the "resulting effects" of religious influence on social capital in Poland? Are patterns of relationships between religion and social capital similar in Poland to those in other countries? Can Poland's exceptionally low endowment with social capital be explained by a unique religious impact on social capital? The next chapter aims to address these questions in order to deepen the understanding of Polish exceptionality.

5 Catholicism and social capital in Poland in a comparative perspective – empirical evidence

5.1 Introduction

An empirical assessment of the impact of religion on social capital in Poland is the main objective of this chapter. Principally, as shown in chapter 4, we need to address two kinds of religious influences on social capital building, which pull in two distinct directions. On the one hand we deal with the hampering "denomination effects" of Catholicism on social networks and trust (though only at the macro level); on the other hand we observe enhancing "affiliation effects," which affect mainly social networks and norms and values. In this chapter I analyse the impact of both types of effects on social capital in Poland in a comparative perspective.

The first section addresses the question: what is the impact of Catholicism on social capital? As discussed in the previous chapter, we can explain the mostly low church-based participation by describing the structural features of the Catholic Church, while the influence of specific value orientations imprinted through Catholic dogma explains the low social capital in a wider, also secular, context. Therefore this chapter focuses on the impact of Catholicism on value orientations, when exploring the "denomination effects" of Catholicism, since we are interested in social capital that is not restricted to religious engagement. The analysis is pursued in three steps. First I develop a concept of Catholic influence on value orientations. Secondly follows an empirical comparative analysis of the strength of Catholic influences across societies. Since the focus is on the particular relevance of the Catholic tradition, the reference group for Poland is restricted to Catholic countries. Therefore the country reference group contains Catholic countries from Central Eastern Europe and Western Catholic countries, in order to counterbalance the potential influence of communist legacies. Thirdly, empirical analyses of the relationship between this Catholic influence and social capital endowment across societies is pursued. In particular the relationships between the Catholic influence and social capital in Poland compared to other Catholic societies are explored.

The second section is devoted to the structural kind of religious influence: "affiliation effects." Conceptually this analysis is less complicated, because church affiliation is measured by the frequency of church attendance. Specifically the objective of the second section of this chapter is to address the question: can a positive influence of church affiliation on social capital, as claimed in the literature, be found in Poland? Societies from Central Eastern Europe are taken as a reference group in this case.

5.2 "Denomination effects" across Catholic societies

In order to assess the importance of the "denomination effects" of Catholicism on social capital I first need to develop a conceptual construct that refers to the specific value orientations espoused by the Catholic tenets. In other words I need to address the question: *what* are the specific "Catholic values" that allegedly appeared in societies dominated by this tradition? Or even more generally *whether* there are consistent value orientations, the origins of which could be traced back to Catholic tenets? To address these questions a concept of *"Religiously Rooted Conservatism"* is developed and subsequently verified empirically (section 5.2.1.). Once the Catholic impact across societies is measured, the relationship between the strength of Catholic influence and social capital is scrutinised (section 5.2.2).

5.2.1 *The concept of "Religiously Rooted Conservatism"*

Assessing the impact of religion in a society is a difficult and challenging matter, since religious influence is the result of continuing and lasting processes, interacting through hundreds of years with complex historical, cultural and social changes. Michelat and Simon stress that religion is "a system of beliefs and practices relating to the sacred; beliefs and practices that also influence the conduct of secular life and unite individual believers into a single community" (Michelat/Simon 1997, 161). In my study religion is seen as a system of beliefs, rites and behavioural codes that constitute a guideline and spiritual force for the believers, influencing their mentality and value orientations. How can we discern these "typical Catholic values" that shape the value orientations of Catholics today? One way is to figure out in which respects value orientations in European Catholic societies differ from those in other European societies. A study conducted by Inglehart and Baker reveals that Catholic societies are marked by more traditional value orientations than other European societies (2000, 29); whereby under these traditional value orientations the scholars understand principally the importance of religion; family; respect for authority; high national pride; and a pro-life stance on abortion, euthanasia and suicide issues (2000, 24-25). Other empirical studies show that Catholics are more likely to practice their religion in terms of church attendance and prayer than Protestants, for instance (Norris/Inglehart 2005, 74). As far as moral issues are concerned, Catholic countries such as Spain, Portugal, Ireland and Poland have the strictest regulations on abortion in Europe.[40] Fukuyama underlines the salience of family bonds in all Catholic societies, not only European (1995, 56); an empirical study confirms these claims (Alesina/Giuliano 2009, 6).

Do these similarities across Catholic societies – emphasis on family bonds, moral values and religious devotion – have common religious roots? Lets us consider religious devotion as a starting point. As mentioned in section 4.2.1.2.2, Catholic tradition stresses the collective nature of the Church and emphasises the importance of the regular practice of religious rites by the faithful. The intensity of religious devotion amplifies the effect of exposure to the social and moral teachings of the Church, i.e. a churchgoer is more likely to internalise traditional values than somebody who is not attending mass regularly or who is not exposed to religious teachings in another way. Furthermore, people raised in a Catholic country might regard themselves as particularly religious and might consider religion to be important in their lives. Moreover, Catholic social teachings highlight moral values as pivotal guidelines in the lives of the faithful, and the role of the family as a basic social institution: "the family is inseparable from the moral and religious values" (Michelat/Simon 1997, 166). Therefore traditionalism and an emphasis on family, moral values and religious devotion can be regarded as reflections of the Catholic influence on value orientations in Catholic societies.

We can generalise by saying that the people in Catholic countries are likely to represent *conservative values and attitudes,* which are *religiously rooted.* Conservatism can be defined as "the tendency to prefer an existing or traditional situation to change."[41] So conservatives dislike changes and new ideas, and cherish tradition; whereby the specific religiously rooted aspects of conservatism are the effects of Catholicism dominating a society. I use the concept of Religiously Rooted Conservatism (RRC) as an indicator of the power of the influence of the Catholic tradition on people's value orientations in predominantly Catholic societies. I expect some societies to be more influenced by Catholicism (more conservative societies) and some less (less conservative societies), due to their different historical paths and present religious behaviours. For instance, in devout Catholic societies with high percentages of people belonging to the church and practising religious rites – for instance Poland, Italy, Spain, and Portugal[42] – we should witness substantial levels of conservatism. In contrast, societies with a legacy of multi-confessional traditions, such as Czech Republic and Hungary,[43] should display less support for RRC.

We need to specify the criteria against which RRC can be empirically measured across societies. Aspects of value orientations that are widespread across Catholic

---

[40] Source: BBC website: http://news.bbc.co.uk/2/hi/6235557.stm; visited on 10.02.2010.
[41] Source: Encyclopaedia Britannica online, reference: conservatism
http://www.britannica.com/EBchecked/topic/133435/conservatism, visited on 13.06.2011.
[42] For classification, see: (Madeley 2003, 31)
[43] Ibid., p. 33.

societies, such as **(1) a traditional concept of family, (2) the relevance of religion, and (3) the salience of moral values** become the main components of the RRC conceptualised here. The list of the components is not exhaustive and could be expanded. My goal, however, is to have a construct that can be operationalised for empirical purposes and that allows me to scrutinise the differences in the power of the Catholic influence on value orientations across societies. Therefore the three aspects (religiosity, morality and concept of family) that cover three realms of life in which religion is potentially a guideline are sufficient to achieve the objective of assessing the differences across societies.

In the following section I first empirically examine the levels of three aspects of RRC across Catholic societies separately. Second, I analyse whether we can find a systematic pattern of all three aspects/components of RRC across Catholic publics. In this second step I investigate whether RRC, as defined by these three aspects, is a single construct.[44] If this is the case, an RRC Index could serve as a measure of the Catholic impact on peoples' value orientations in Catholic countries. Polish society is one of the most religiously devoted societies in Europe, and one of the most traditional ones (Inglehart/Baker 2000, 29), hence I expect especially RRC high scores among the Polish public compared to other Catholic countries.

5.2.1.1 First component: "Traditional concept of the family"

The family is one of the pivotal social institutions in the Catholic tenets. One of the occasions to emphasise the importance of the family and to transmit teachings about family is a special feast of the Holy Family,[45] which serves as a model and guideline for Catholics. To set a family and to be respectful, subordinated and obedient to their parents, just as the biblical figure of the Virgin Mary obeyed God, are some of the highest obligations for a pious Catholic. As a result of these religious imperatives, a devoted faithful should be more likely to support hierarchical structures within a family and rigid, traditional child-rearing principles.

Direct indices that measure whether one shares a traditional concept of the family are difficult to find in survey data, as most of the questions consider this a personal situation and fail to embrace the family in a wider perspective. Hence the

---

[44] A first conceptualisation of RRC was presented at the ECPR Joint Session Workshop, in Lisbon, in April 2009 (Lasinska 2009). In this book I improved the composition of items compiling two components of RRC: "traditional concept of the family" and "relevance of religion." In the "traditional concept of the family" component I deleted one item (referring to support for determination and perseverance in child-rearing), in order to stick strictly to traditional child-rearing methods. In the component concerning the "relevance of religion" I deleted the item referring to church attendance, in order to make clear the distance between the structural and cultural impacts of religion.

[45] The Holy Family consists of Jesus, the Virgin Mary and St. Joseph. The feast of the Holy Family is held on the Sunday within the Octave of Christmas.

support for certain children's qualifications gained at home can serve as a proxy for favouring a traditional concept of the family in general. Specifically, conservatism in family issues can be understood as support for the dependence and subordination of a child, with less attention given to the development of his personality and individualism (see also section 4.2.1.2.2, which discusses the lack of support for individualism in Catholicism). Moreover, conservative people are expected to endorse rigorous child-rearing principles, like the requirement of unconditional respect for parents. Three items in the WVS refer directly to these issues. The first one constitutes a choice between the two following statements:

> "Regardless of what the qualities and faults of one's parents are, we must always love and respect them; or"
> "One does not have the duty to respect and love parents who have not earned it by their behaviour and attitudes."

The answers to both questions are mutually exclusive, and consist of one item in my analysis. The item is scored as "1" when the first possibility – respecting parents is seen an imperative for children - is selected. When respondent chooses the second possibility – respect should be earned – the item is scored as "0" in my analysis (recoded from "2"); in this way a higher value indicates support for a traditional concept of family.
The second item concerns the child's qualities. An introductory question is as follows:

> "Here is a list of qualities which children can be encouraged to learn at home. Which, if any, do you consider to be especially important?"

A respondent chooses five out of 11 qualities. The following two answers are considered for the measurement of the acceptance of a traditional concept of the family:

-"independence"
-"imagination"

Both items are recoded, and both are scored as "0" if selected or "1" if the item is not selected by the respondent. In this way, in the case of all three items, a value of "1" corresponds to support of the traditional concept of the family, while "0" indicates the opposite.

The question of whether we can find a systematic pattern of support for a traditional concept of the family based on these three items is addressed by the use of principle component analysis (PCA). An extracted factor seems to be one dimensional, though only 43 percent of the variance are explained (Cronbach's alpha is very low, α=0.31). As presented in Table 5.1, all loadings of the extracted factor lie between 0.5 and 0.8, which represents an acceptable level. Instead of using these three items separately to further explore RRC, I use an indicator for the acceptance of a traditional concept of family (traditional concept of family indicator, TCFI) resulting from the factor analysis.

Table 5.1 Extraction of a one-dimensional indicator for "traditional concept of family" (factor loadings)

Items	One component extracted (traditional concept of family)
Respect parents unconditionally	0.549
It is not important for a child to have independence	0.699
It is not important for a child to have imagination	0.711
R^2	0.430
Cronbach's alpha	0.309
N	19,831

Notes: extraction method: Principal Component Analysis, missing values deleted listwise.
Source: WVS 1999.

The mean values of the indicator[46] for TCFI across European Catholic countries are displayed in Figure 5.1; Western countries are presented in the left-hand section of the graph, with Central Eastern countries to the right. Low values of TCFI represent a low acceptance of a traditional concept of family in a society, while values close to "1" demonstrate a high acceptance. In general, cross-national differences in the mean values of TCFI are not considerably high, though they are statistically significant (Kruskal-Wallis, p<0.05). East-West discrepancies are also modest (mean values in both groups of societies are 0.02). People in Poland, Portugal, Italy and France seem to show the highest levels of acceptance of the traditional family concept (the mean value of TCFI is above 0.9), whereas Croatia is an outlier on the opposite pole.[47] Among Western countries, Austrian society appears to favour the least traditional concept of the family. In Poland the mean value of TCFI is the highest of all considered countries, meaning that Poles are exceptionally supportive of the traditional concept of the family, which was expected.

---

[46] The indicator for the acceptance of TCFI results from the factor scores after being rescaled to values from 0 to 1.
[47] In the case of Croatia, the distribution of one particular item ("it is important for a child to have imagination") is different in comparison to other analysed societies. Croats support the development of imagination by children more than the publics in other countries. Other items are distributed in a similar way.

Figure 5.1 Support for a traditional concept of family (mean factor scores by country; rescaled – TCFI takes values from 0 to 1)

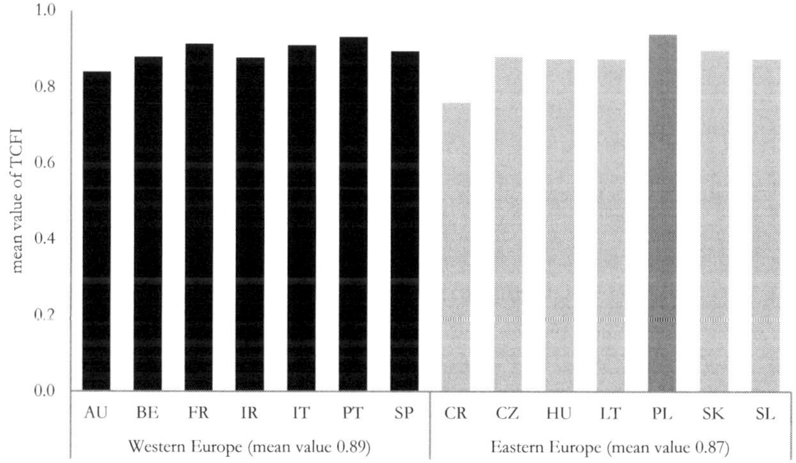

[Bar chart showing mean value of TCFI from 0.0 to 1.0 for Western Europe countries (AU, BE, FR, IR, IT, PT, SP) with mean value 0.89, and Eastern Europe countries (CR, CZ, HU, LT, PL, SK, SL) with mean value 0.87]

Source: WVS 1999.

5.2.1.2 Second component: "Relevance of religion"

The second component of RRC refers to the relevance of religion in one's life. The extent to which one treasures religion is a measure of the impact of religious teachings on one's value orientations. The first item considered deals with a subjective perception whether an individual is religious. The question is worded as follows:

"Independently of whether you go to church or not, would you say you are..."
"a religious person" (coded as 3),
"not a religious person" (coded as 2),
"a convinced atheist" (coded as 1)

The item coding remains unchanged, since the highest value ("3") corresponds to a higher relevance of religion in one's life. Furthermore, several authors investigating the changing religiosity within European societies over the last few decades point to a drift from institutional religiosity to a more individualised version (Jagodzinski/Dobbelaere 1995a, 78-79). Scholars show that with declining church affiliation the beliefs change, too. For instance instead of believing in a personal God – which has biblical roots – beliefs become a more abstract notion (Jagodzinski/Dobbelaere 1995a, 80). Hence, as my objective is to measure the relevance of religion in a traditional sense, in the case of Catholicism, it is indispensable to add items relating to traditional beliefs. Two items refer to the belief in God and the importance of God in one's life. The questions are worded as follows:

"Which, if any, of the following do you believe in?" And the first option is "God;" ("1" if selected, "0" if not);
"And how important is God in your life?" (scaled from 1 "not at all" to 10 "very").

The items' coding remains unchanged, since in both cases a higher value indicates stronger traditional religious beliefs. The question I address now is whether these three items could systematically measure the relevance of religion in one's life. PCA reveals a relatively consistent structure of the three items (almost 80 percent of explained variance, Table 5.2). The values of all three factor loadings are above 0.7, pointing to the high consistency of the latent factor. The value of Cronbach's alpha is relatively low ($\alpha=0.449$). In order to reduce the data, an indicator resulting from PCA (factor scores rescaled to values from 0 to 1) is used to measure the relevance of religion (relevance of religion indicator, RRI) as the second component of RRC.

Table 5.2 Extraction of a one-dimensional indicator for "relevance of religion" (factor loadings)

Items	One component extracted (relevance of religion)
Religious person	0.779
God important	0.789
Believe in God	0.817
R²	**0.795**
Cronbach's alpha	**0.449**
N	**17, 580**

Notes: extraction method: Principal Component Analysis, missing values deleted listwise.
Source: WVS 1999.

Once a measure for the relevance of religion is developed, we can find out whether there are cross-national differences in this regard between European Catholic publics. Figure 5.2 presents the mean scores of RRI across the group of countries studied. The differences between individual societies are substantial; the mean value of RRI ranges from 0.48 in Czech Republic to 0.92 in Poland. The variances differ considerably and are statistically significant (Kruskal-Wallis test significant at p<0.05), pointing to systematic differences between individual societies. East-West discrepancies are in contrast modest (the difference in the mean values between both groups is only 0.03). Religion seems to be an especially important element of life for people in Poland, Portugal, Ireland and Italy, while in Czech Republic and

France religion seems to be the least relevant. Poland takes a leading position, with the highest mean value of RRI of all Catholic countries, which confirms the expectations.

Figure 5.2 Relevance of religion (mean factor scores by country; rescaled – RRI takes values from 0 to 1)

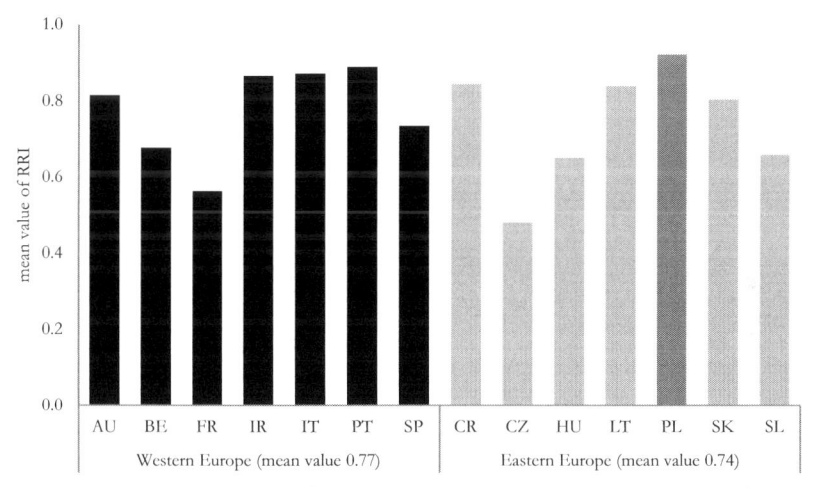

[Bar chart showing mean value of RRI for Western Europe countries: AU, BE, FR, IR, IT, PT, SP (mean value 0.77) and Eastern Europe countries: CR, CZ, HU, LT, PL, SK, SL (mean value 0.74)]

Source: WVS 1999

5.2.1.3 Third component: "Morality"

Morality is, generally speaking, a system of beliefs and values accepted by a person concerning how people should behave. It is a complex issue, embracing a wide range of realms of life, yet for the sake of simplicity, morality is analysed here through one's attitudes concerning four issues: two referring to marriage (adultery and divorce), one referring to abortion, and the last one related to sexual orientations. These issues show the strength of the Catholic impact on one's morality, since in reference to these particular issues the Catholic Church takes an unchanged position, irrespective of a contemporary shift in value orientations within the wider publics of the Western world. Morality is part of the conservative worldview and should be related to religiosity: "religious beliefs still unify positions on broadly defined moral issues" (Jagodzinski/Dobbelaere 1995b, 246). The WVS contains four items referring to the above mentioned issues. The introducing sentence is as follows:

"Please tell me for each of the following statements, whether you think it can always be justified, never be justified, or something in between"

Respondents assess the level of their justification in a scale from 1 "never" to 10 "always." An interviewee has, among others, the following four issues to justify:

- "married man/woman having an affair"
- "homosexuality"
- "abortion"
- "divorce"

All items are rescaled in a reverse direction; higher values indicate a stricter morality. The results of PCA are satisfactory. The degree to which divorce, abortion, homosexuality and adultery are justified by an individual seems to display a systematic pattern, and 60 percent of variance is explained by one latent factor (Table 5.3). The values of the factor loadings are considerable for all four items, providing evidence for a one-dimensional construct. The value of Cronbach's alpha is acceptable, too ($\alpha=0.77$). Therefore all four items can be summarised into a single morality indicator (MI – factor scores rescaled to values from 0 to 1), which is used in the further exploration of conservatism.

Table 5.3 Extraction of a one-dimensional indicator for "morality" (factor loadings)

Items	One component extracted (morality)
Homosexuality justifiable	0.760
Abortion justifiable	0.837
Divorce justifiable	0.856
Adultery justifiable	0.615
R^2	**0.597**
Cronbach's alpha	**0.770**
N	**16,915**

Notes: extraction method: Principal Component Analysis, missing values deleted listwise.
Source: WVS 1999.

As in the case of the two previous components of conservatism, the levels of acceptance of moral values differ moderately across Catholic countries (Figure 5.3). The differences of variances are significant (Kruskal-Wallis; $p<0,05$), and the relative differences in the levels of the mean values are considerable. The lowest score is 0.52 (Slovenia), while the highest is 0.77 (Hungary). East-West differences are modest (differences in mean values of MI are 0.4). The most morally rigid societies were found to be Hungary, Poland, Lithuania and Ireland, while the opposite was found

"Denomination effects" across Catholic societies 131

for Slovenia, France and Czech Republic. The Polish public ranks second after Hungary in morality.

Figure 5.3 Morality (mean factor scores by country; rescaled – MI takes values from 0 to 1)

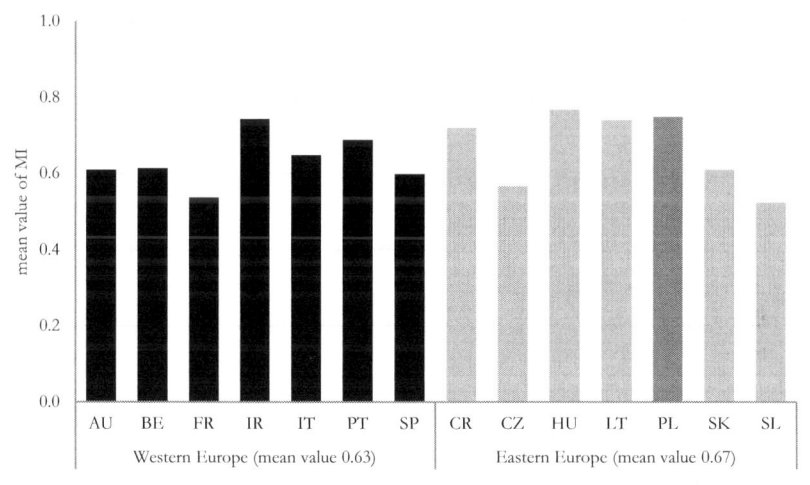

[Bar chart showing mean value of MI by country. Western Europe (mean value 0.63): AU, BE, FR, IR, IT, PT, SP. Eastern Europe (mean value 0.67): CR, CZ, HU, LT, PL, SK, SL.]

Source: WVS 1999.

Summarising the findings, we found three components of RRC – support of a traditional concept of family, relevance of religion and morality – across Catholic countries. Polish society is indeed very conservative, since Poles supported the most traditional concepts of the family and found religion to be more salient in their lives than other Catholic societies. As far as moral issues are concerned, Poles are one of the most rigid among Catholic publics, too. Now we turn to the question of whether the three components of RRC demonstrate a systematic pattern and whether we can say that Poles are the most conservative among Catholic societies in Europe.

5.2.1.4 Religiously Rooted Conservatism

How strong is the Catholic influence on the value orientations of Poles compared to other Catholic societies? Is Polish society the most conservative in Europe? In order to answer this question I proceed with the calculation of an RRC index that is based on three components: traditional concept of the family, relevance of religion and morality. First, I need to examine the dimensionality of RRCI, taking the three components as a basis. The second-order factor analysis PCA provides evidence for the one-dimensionality of RRCI, with 51 percent of explained variances (Table 5.4). The component "traditional concept of the family" turns out to be the least related to the latent factor, while the other two scores have considerable values above 0.7. All coefficients have substantial value, pointing to the consistency of the RRC, and Cronbach's alpha is at a moderate level, $\alpha=0.485$. For further analysis I use RRCI (factor scores rescaled to values from 0 to 1) as a measure of the Catholic influence on value orientations across societies.

Table 5.4 Extraction of a one-dimensional indicator for "Religiously Rooted Conservatism" (factor loadings)

Items	One component extracted (religiously rooted conservatism)
Traditional concept of family	0.579
Relevance of religion	0.755
Morality	0.787
R^2	0.508
Cronbach's alpha	0.485
N	15,116

Notes: extraction method: Principal Component Analysis, missing values deleted listwise.
Source: WVS 1999.

Once RRCI is constructed, we are able to analyse the distribution of conservatism across Catholic countries (Figure 5.4). In general, RRCI mean scores differ considerably between countries, and the mean RRCI values range from 0.64 in Czech Republic to 0.86 in Poland; differences of the variances are significant (Kruskal-Wallis test; $p<0.05$). Again, East-West mean values are almost equal (mean value in Western Europe is 0.76 and 0.75 in Eastern Europe). The least conservative is Czech Republic, followed by Slovenia and France. The most conservative are the Poles, followed by Portugal and Ireland. In other words, Poland has an exceptionally high level of RRC compared to other Catholic countries. So the influence of Catholicism is indeed the strongest in Poland, as expected.

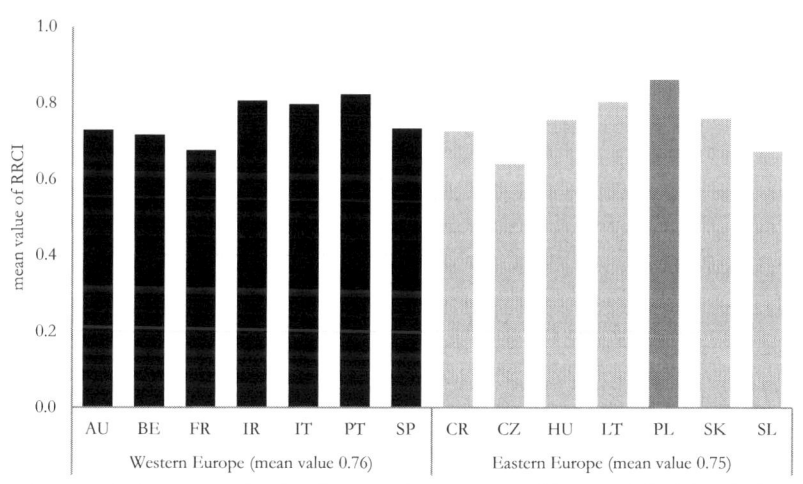

Figure 5.4 Religiously Rooted Conservatism (mean factor scores by country; rescaled – RRCI takes values from 0 to 1)

[Bar chart showing mean value of RRCI from 0.0 to 1.0 for countries: AU, BE, FR, IR, IT, PT, SP (Western Europe, mean value 0.76) and CR, CZ, HU, LT, PL, SK, SL (Eastern Europe, mean value 0.75)]

Source: WVS 1999.

5.2.1.5 Explaining cross-country differences in Religiously Rooted Conservatism

What might be a *rationale* for the differences in levels of conservatism between Catholic countries? If RRC is a measure of the Catholic influence on value orientations, it means that some societies, despite being Catholic, did not inherit the tenets of this tradition to the same extent as other societies. Why is that so? How can we explain why Poland has the most conservative society? Can we find a plausible explanation of the differences in levels of conservatism in the historical legacy of societies?

In most cases, the legacy of church-state relations could partly provide a plausible explanation of distinct cross-national patterns of conservatism. Madeley, when analysing contemporary church-state relations in Europe, proposed a typology based on Rokkan's work on nation building and cleavage formation (2003, 23-50). Madeley divided European Catholic societies into three types according to their legacy of state-church relations. One group, mostly Western societies, is made up of historically mono-confessional Catholic societies such as Italy, Spain, Portugal, France, Belgium, Austria and Slovenia (Madeley 2003, 31). A second group of societies represents a historically multi-confessional (Catholic and diverse Protestant denominations) culture belt; the Czech Republic and Hungary, among others, belong to this group. A third group consists of "newly" mono-confessional societies with a multi-confessional legacy, Poland and Ireland: "the twentieth century re-creation of the Polish and Irish states actually led to historically unprecedented levels of religious homogeneity" (Madeley 2003, 32). In both societies:

> "effective mono-confessionalism has occasionally been the product not of long histories of church establishment, but rather of successful resistance to neighbouring, alternative power centres which have attempted to impose other, alien creeds (...) In each case, attachment to Catholicism was associated with the successful assertion of claims to national autonomy against powerful neighbours."   (Madeley 2003, 38)

In other words, we can partly explain high levels of RRC in Ireland and Poland by the recent amalgamation of attachment to Catholicism with national identity. At first sight it seems a very plausible explanation, since both Poland and Ireland rank at the top in RRC (Figure 5.4). However, this argument reveals only part of the truth, since it fails to explain the high conservatism in Portugal (Figure 5.4). Furthermore, across historically mono-confessional societies conservatism seems to be at a moderate level (with the exception of France[48]), while the least conservative turn to be historically multi-confessional societies, such as Czech Republic (though not Hungary).

When explaining the highest score on the RRC Index in Poland, we should, on the one hand, note historical circumstances from the 19th century that created favourable conditions for the strong relationship between Catholicism and national identity:

> "the Catholic Church and its moral education projects helped to shape the nature of national consciousness in the nineteenth century and at the beginning of the twentieth century (...) Without the Church it would not have been possible for a strong nation to survive in the years of lost sovereignty."
> (Kurczewska 2005, 332-333; see also Grabowska/Szawiel 2001, 38-39; Borowik 2002, 240)[49]

On the other hand, enforcement of the communist ideology strongly reinforced this specific amalgamation of national identity with Catholicism in Poland later on (Luks 1993, 161; see also Marody/Mandes 2007, 404-407, 413). Especially since the 1970s,

---

[48] RRC in France is at one of the lowest levels among Catholic publics. Religious cleavages in France follow a less denominational dimension, but more an anticlerical/pro-clerical dimension, arising out of the French Revolution (Madeley 2003, 24). So in the case of French society the presence of anticlerical movements could successfully diminish the impact of Catholicism on value orientations.

[49] This support differed across parts of divided Polish territory. While Church activity has been the most effective in the Prussian part, in the remaining parts the situation seems to be more complex (Bartkowski 2003, 13, 137-138, 161, 170, 175-176; Kamiński 2008, 13-14).

public expression of religiosity came to be associated with political opposition to communist ideology and with efforts to maintain Polish traditions and culture (Słodkowska 2006, 99; see also Ekiert/Kubik 1999, 32). In addition, two Polish charismatic Church leaders – primate Wyszynski and Pope John Paul II – contributed considerably to the perception of the Catholic Church as an advocate of Polish traditions and culture and a supporter of the struggle against the communist regime (Borowik 2002, 241). In Poland especially during communism, attending Catholic rites was not only a religious act, but to a certain degree also a political act – a demonstration of anti-regime sentiments (Borowik 2002, 241; Słodkowska 2006, 96-98). At the same time, religious symbols became symbols of opposition against communist authorities, especially in the 1980s (Słodkowska 2006, 170-171). While during the 20th century secularisation took place in many societies in Europe, the importance of religion in people's lives diminished and changes in value orientations took place (Jagodzinski/Dobbelaere 1995a, 80-81; Norris/Inglehart 2005, 73-74). In Poland religious acts were an instrument for striving for political (and personal) freedoms (Borowik 2002, 241). Under these specific circumstances, Poles remained religious in the sense of attending religious rites, but also religious in the sense of the salience of the values related to Catholicism (Marody/Mandes 2007, 407).[50] Therefore it is plausible that RRC is relatively high in Poland compared to other Catholic societies. Now we need to address the question: what are the consequences of a stronger Catholic influence on value orientations in Poland for its social capital endowment?

5.2.2 Religiously Rooted Conservatism and social capital

Does it matter for social capital that Poles are particularly conservative? Is there evidence of negative "denomination effects" of Catholicism on social capital in Poland? In order to address these questions I proceed with the empirical analysis of relations between levels of RRC and endowment with social capital in Catholic societies, including Poland. What are the general expectations about the relationship between RRC and social capital? As discussed in chapter 4, negative "denomination effects" should mostly refer to social networks at both the macro and micro levels. Furthermore, at the macro level we expect to find a negative relationship between social trust and levels of RRC. In contrast, norms and values should remain unrelated to RRC.

---

[50] The Catholic Church supported oppositional activities in other communist countries, too, for instance in Czechoslovakia; however this support was strongest in Poland compared to other Catholic communist countries (Krizek 2003, 154).

5.2.2.1 Religiously Rooted Conservatism and social networks

What is the relationship between RRC level and social networks? Are social networks indeed weaker in more conservative societies? Do relationships in Poland fit the general patterns? Can weak social networks in Poland be explained by a relatively high level of RRC? In order to address these questions the analyses are pursued first at the macro level, then at the micro level. Social networks are operationalised in three ways: as membership in voluntary organisations, as volunteering in organisations and as informal ties (for details see section 2.4.1).
The relationship between levels of RRC and aggregated membership in voluntary organisations is depicted in Figure 5.5.

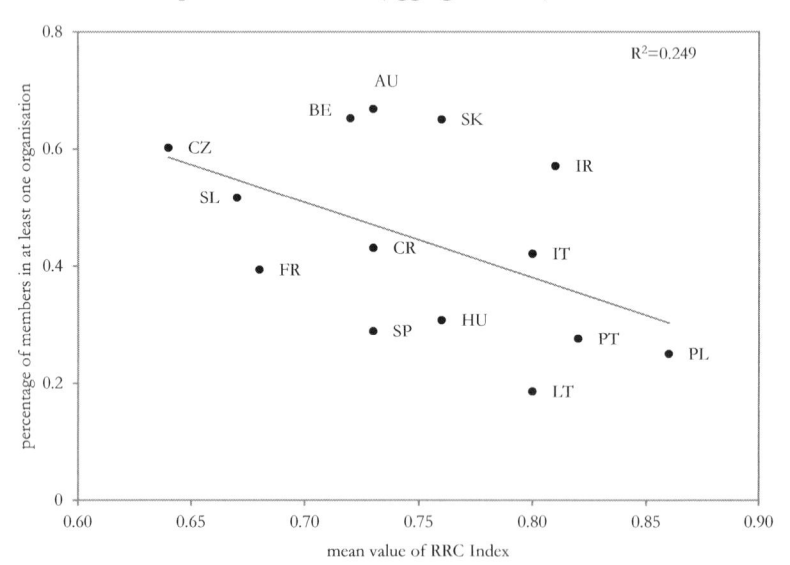

Figure 5.5 Membership and conservatism (aggregate levels)

<chart: scatter plot with x-axis "mean value of RRC Index" from 0.60 to 0.90 and y-axis "percentage of members in at least one organisation" from 0 to 0.8; $R^2=0.249$; points labeled AU, BE, SK, CZ, IR, SL, CR, IT, FR, SP, HU, PT, PL, LT>

Source: WVS 1999.

As expected, membership in voluntary organisations is negatively correlated with conservatism at the macro level, since fewer respondents in more conservative societies declare membership in at least one organisation than in less conservative societies. The level of explained variance is modest (approximately one-quarter). A number of countries are located far from the regression line, for instance Ireland, Slovakia and Austria, and Lithuania, Spain and France are on the other side of the regression line. Poland, Portugal and Lithuania, are found in the right-hand bottom section of the graph with low levels of membership and a high level of RRC. By contrast, another conservative society, Ireland, is situated in the upper section, distant from conservative Poland, Portugal and Lithuania, and high above the regression line. In other words, the level of associational membership in Ireland is relatively high despite relatively strong conservatism. In general we can say that Poland fits rather well in the general pattern of relations between conservatism and membership at the aggregate level. And the expectations are fulfilled – Poland's low level of membership in organisations can partly be explained by the relatively high level of RRC in Polish society. Let us turn to volunteering.

Another way to explore social networks is to examine the levels of volunteering across countries. Like membership, volunteering is negatively related to aggregate levels of conservatism, though in this case the relationship is much weaker (Figure 5.6). The level of explained variance remains low (15 percent). The position of Poland and Portugal is similar to the previous Figure, in the bottom right-hand corner, which indicates a low level of volunteering combined with a high level of RRC. Slovakia[51] is a heavy outlier, located far up on the graph above the regression line. When the relationship between RRC and volunteering is recalculated without Slovakia, the percentage of explained variances raises considerably to 35 percent, which is even higher than in the case of membership. The relationship in Poland fits in to the general pattern: a high level of RRC is combined with a low propensity to volunteer. So we can conclude that, as expected, weak engagement in volunteering in Poland can be explained by relatively high RRC in this society.

---

[51] As discussed in chapter 2 (section 2.4.1) the levels of volunteering in Slovakia reported in the WVS might be too high, since other comparable surveys report relatively lower levels of volunteering in this society.

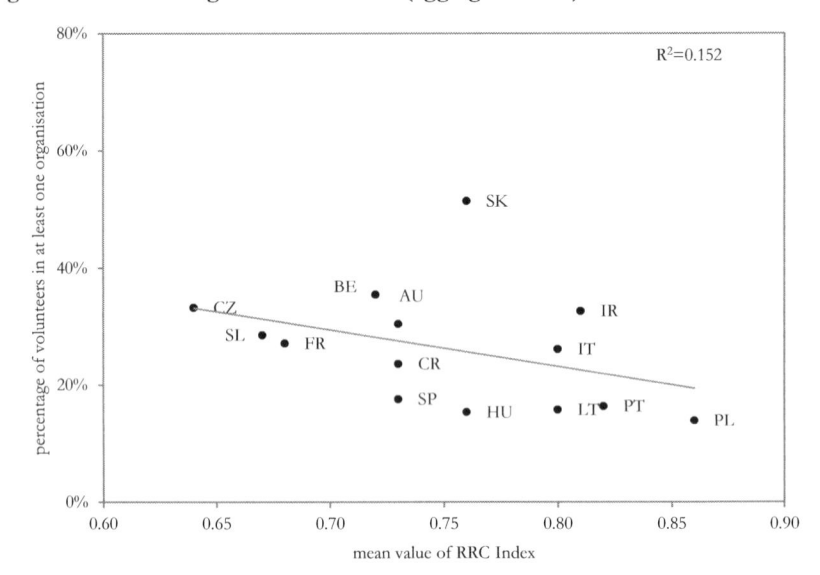

Figure 5.6 Volunteering and conservatism (aggregate levels)

[Scatter plot: x-axis "mean value of RRC Index" from 0.60 to 0.90; y-axis "percentage of volunteers in at least one organisation" from 0% to 80%. $R^2=0.152$. Points labeled: CZ, SL, FR, BE, AU, SK, CR, SP, HU, IR, IT, LT, PT, PL.]

Source: WVS 1999.

As discussed in section 2.4.1, informal networks are supposed to be a relevant type of social network in post-communist societies. Therefore I expect a negative relationship between RRC and informal ties, for the same reasons that we expected a negative relationship between conservatism and formal ties.

At the aggregate level the informal ties, conforming to expectations, are moderately related to RRC (Figure 5.7). The level of explained variance is modest (20 percent). There are two outliers – Hungary and Poland – that bias these results by "pulling" the regression line downwards. A recalculation of the relationship between RRC and informal ties excluding Poland and Hungary reveals that informal networks and RRC remain unrelated to each other. In the model excluding Hungary and Poland, R^2 drops to a very low level of 5 percent. Returning to my question concerning the impact of RRC on social networks, we cannot explain Poland's weak informal ties by a relatively high level of RRC, at least not at the aggregate level.

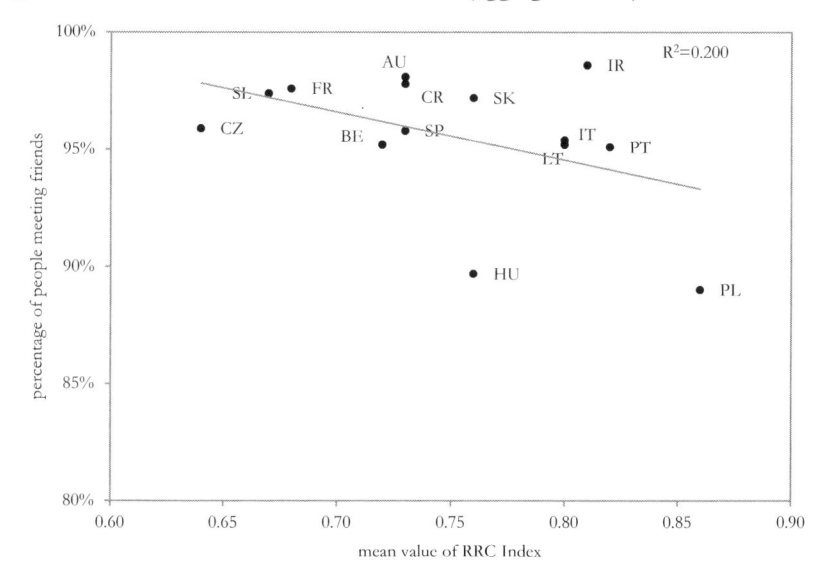

"Denomination effects" across Catholic societies 139

Figure 5.7 Informal networks and conservatism (aggregate levels)

[Scatter plot with x-axis "mean value of RRC Index" from 0.60 to 0.90 and y-axis "percentage of people meeting friends" from 80% to 100%. Data points labeled: AU, IR, SL, FR, CR, SK, CZ, BE, SP, IT, PT, LT, HU, PL. R²=0.200]

Source: WVS 1999.

So far we have examined the relationship between RRC and social networks at the aggregate level, and the findings show that the levels of associational membership and volunteering are systematically lower in conservative societies. What about relationships at the individual level? Are more conservative individuals less likely to participate as members or volunteers in diverse organisations? Does an individual's level of RRC matter for meeting friends, or is it unrelated, as we have seen at the aggregate level? The following section analyses the relationship between individuals' RRC and social networks at the individual level.

Since the RRC Index is a continuous variable with values from 0 to 1, a graphic presentation of the relationship between individual levels of RRC and membership in individual countries would be complicated. A more efficient way is to group individuals according to their relative level of RRC, for instance in four quartiles, and then compare the propensity for network building between the most and the least conservative persons. In this way we can compare the likelihood of belonging to social networks between individuals with a relatively high RRC and those with relatively low conservatism.

Starting with membership, Figure 5.8 displays the percentage of members in at least one organisation within a quarter of the least conservative and a quarter of the most conservative individuals in each society. We can see that in most of the countries – ten out of 14 – the percentage of members in the group of least conservative respondents is higher than that among the most conservative people, whereby in Lithuania and Poland these differences are marginal. Only in Belgium, Czech Republic, Hungary and Slovakia do the least conservative people seem to be more engaged, though the relative differences are very modest. In general it seems that at the individual level, the relationship between RRC and membership is different from that at the macro level. Individual conservatism is positively related to membership in most of the societies, though in Poland RRC seems to be hardly related to the propensity to belong to an organisation.

Figure 5.8 Membership across the most and the least conservative people (percentages)

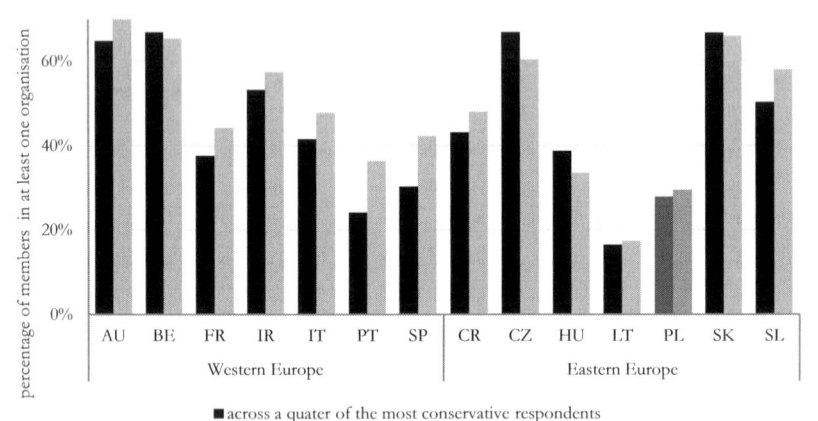

■ across a quater of the most conservative respondents
■ across a quater of the least conservative respondents

Source: WVS 1999.

To get a more precise picture of the relationship between individual conservatism and membership, I calculated the correlations using Pearson's correlation coefficient on the pooled sample and within each individual society. I calculated the correlations between the quarter of the most (or least) conservative individuals in a society and membership in at least one voluntary organisation. The results are presented in Table 5.5; positive correlations indicate that the most conservative individuals are likely to be a member in an organisation. While in the pooled sample the correlation between individual RRC and membership is very weak, negative and statistically significant, in most of the societies RRC and membership are unrelated to each other. Weak negative and significant correlations can be found only in Portugal and Spain; in contrast, results for Hungary and Czech Republic point to the opposite relationships: in these countries the most conservative individuals are more likely to be members in organisations. In Poland individual conservatism shows no relationship to the propensity to join an organisation.

Table 5.5 Relations between membership and conservatism by country (Pearson's correlation coefficient)

Pooled sample	AU	BE	FR	IR	IT	PT	SP	CR	CZ	HU	LT	PL	SK	SL
-0.02*	n.s.	n.s.	n.s.	n.s.	n.s.	-0.11*	-0.10*	n.s.	0.08*	0.13*	n.s.	n.s.	n.s.	n.s.

Notes: * significant, $p<0.05$; n.s.- not significant; N=7,042.
Source: WVS 1999.

Turning to volunteering, the same analysis is pursued in each society in order to assess the relationship between individual RRC and the likelihood to volunteer. Results are presented in Figure 5.9. In the case of volunteering, the relative differences between the percentage of membership within the most conservative and least conservative quarters of each society are very modest. Furthermore, only in Austria and Slovakia are levels of membership slightly higher among the most conservative individuals; in the remaining societies the membership levels between both groups are equal or the least conservative individuals show a slightly higher propensity to volunteer. In Poland there are slightly more volunteers among the least conservative individuals. It seems that, in contrast to the aggregate level, there is no negative relationship between RRC and volunteering at the individual level.

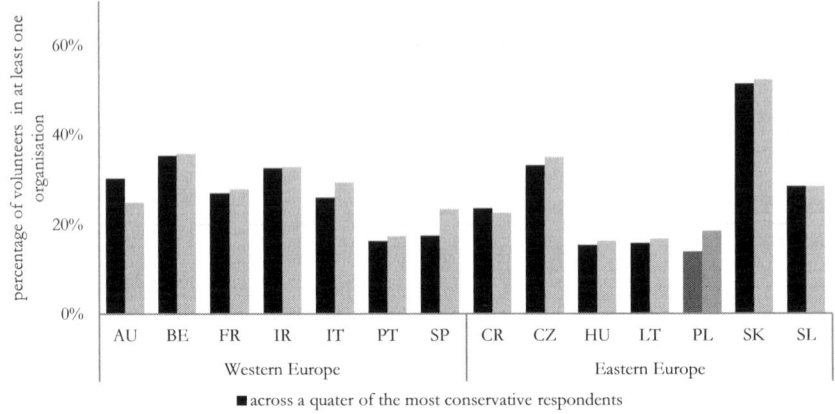

Figure 5.9 Volunteering among the most and least conservative people (percentages)

[Bar chart showing percentage of volunteers in at least one organisation, by country, for Western Europe (AU, BE, FR, IR, IT, PT, SP) and Eastern Europe (CR, CZ, HU, LT, PL, SK, SL), comparing the most conservative quarter (black) and least conservative quarter (grey) of respondents.]

■ across a quater of the most conservative respondents

■ across a quater of the least conservative respondents

Source: WVS 1999.

The results of the Pearson's correlation test between volunteering and individual conservatism presented in Table 5.6 confirm the observations drawn from Figure 5.9. In the pooled sample there is no correlation between individual RRC and the likelihood to be a volunteer. The same results apply to all countries except Austria. Conservative individuals in Austria are more prone to get engaged in volunteer activity. Similar to other societies, individual RRC does not matter in Poland for the likelihood of being a volunteer. In other words the low level of volunteer engagement in Poland cannot be explained by individual RRC.

Table 5.6 Relations between volunteering and conservatism by country (Pearson's correlation coefficient)

Pooled sample	AU	BE	FR	IR	IT	PT	SP	CR	CZ	HU	LT	PL	SK	SL
n.s.	0.11*	n.s.	n.s.	n.s.	n.s.	n.s.	n.s.	n.s.	n.s.	n.s.	n.s.	n.s.	n.s.	n.s.

Notes: * significant, p<0.05; n.s.- not significant; N=7,554
Source: WVS 1999.

At last we turn to the analysis of the relationship between informal networks and individual RRC. At the aggregate level we do not find any relationship between RRC and informal networks. Is individual RRC also unrelated to informal ties? Figure 5.10 demonstrates the percentages of individuals meeting friends among the most and least conservative respondents in each society. In most societies, more conservative individuals declare less frequently meeting friends, though the differences between the groups of individuals are very modest. In Slovakia, Croatia and Ireland there is hardly a difference in the percentage of people reporting meeting friends regularly. In Poland this difference is more considerable. Indeed, conservative Poles report less frequently meeting with friends when compared to the least conservative individuals in this society. So we can say that in contrast to the findings at the macro level, individual RRC seems to matter for the propensity of building informal ties. Individual RRC appears to hamper informal networks, and this relationship applies to Poland, too.

Figure 5.10 Informal networks among the most and the least conservative people (percentages)

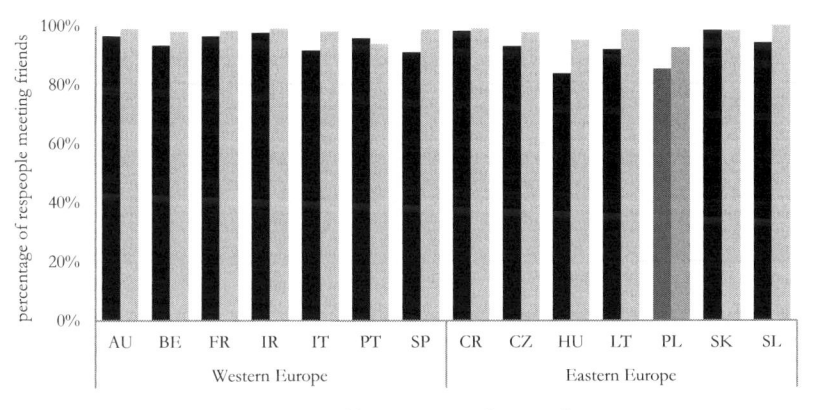

Source: WVS 1999.

Turning to the analysis of correlations between individual levels of RRC and informal networks, the results presented in Table 5.7 confirm the evidence found in Figure 5.10. In the pooled sample individual RRC is negatively and significantly correlated with informal networks, though the correlation is moderate. Negative correlations are found in most societies, too – in nine out of 14 societies, more conservative individuals are less likely to meet friends. In Spain, Hungary and Slovenia the correlation is the highest, and r reaches nearly 0.2. In Poland, similar to most other societies, conservative individuals are less prone to cultivating friendships compared to their relatively less conservative fellow countrymen. So, we can conclude that weak informal ties in Poland can be partly explained by the relatively high individual RRC of those reluctant to build such networks.

Table 5.7 Relations between meeting friends and conservatism by country (Pearson's correlation coefficient)

Pooled sample	AU	BE	FR	IR	IT	PT	SP	CR	CZ	HU	LT	PL	SK	SL
-0.10*	-0.09*	-0.12*	n.s.	n.s.	-0.15*	n.s.	-0.18*	n.s.	-0.11*	-0.19*	-0.16*	-0.12*	n.s.	-0.17*

Notes: * significant, p<0.05; n.s.- not significant; N=7,497
Source: WVS 1999.

Summing up the results of the analyses of relations between RRC and social networks, we can draw several conclusions:
(1) As expected, RRC is negatively related to formal social networks at the macro level. In contrast, informal networks and RRC remain unrelated. Relationships between RRC and social networks in Poland fit the general patterns with the exception of informal networks, where Poland is an outlier.
(2) At the individual level the situation is different. In contrast to expectations, we found no relationship between individual levels of RRC and formal networks. In the case of informal networks, it seems that individual RRC hampers the likelihood of forging informal bonds. In Poland, too, conservative people are less prone to have informal contacts.
(3) What conclusions can be drawn for social capital in Poland? In general the relationship between RRC and social networks in Poland show similar patterns to those in other societies. Weak formal social networks in Poland can be explained by a relatively high level of RRC in this country, though individual levels of RRC are irrelevant. In contrast, individual RRC does matter for the reluctance to build informal networks. In this sense, we come to the conclusion that the high level of RRC in Poland could partly explain the low level of engagement in formal networks in this country, though mainly as a context factor at the macro level. And low informal networks can be explained by Poles' relatively high levels of individual RRC.

5.2.2.2   Religiously Rooted Conservatism and social trust

As presented in chapter 4, Catholicism is negatively related to social trust at the macro level. The evidence at the individual level is inconsistent; while some studies provide evidence of lower trust among Catholics, others do not confirm these findings (for details, see section 4.2.1.1). Some authors argue that the lack of support for egalitarian values in Catholicism could lead to low social trust among Catholics (section 4.2.1.2.2). Therefore we expect negative relationships between RRC and social trust at the aggregate level, and possibly also at the individual level.

The relationship between macro levels of RRC and social trust in Catholic countries is displayed in Figure 5.11. There is no correlation between social trust and RRC. The level of explained variance remains very low (less than one percent). Spain, Austria, Ireland and Italy have a relatively high percentage of trusting people, and the levels of RRC rank from moderate in Spain and Austria to quite high in Ireland and Italy. On the other hand, societies with relatively low levels of RRC, such as Czech Republic, Slovenia and France, are characterised by moderate levels of social trust. Poland is situated at the right-hand side of the graph with the highest level of RRC and the third lowest level of trust. In general, the initial expectations concerning the negative relationship between RRC and social trust are not confirmed. The relatively high level of RRC in Poland does not explain its relatively low social trust. Let us turn to the analysis at the individual level.

Figure 5.11 Trust and conservatism (aggregate levels)

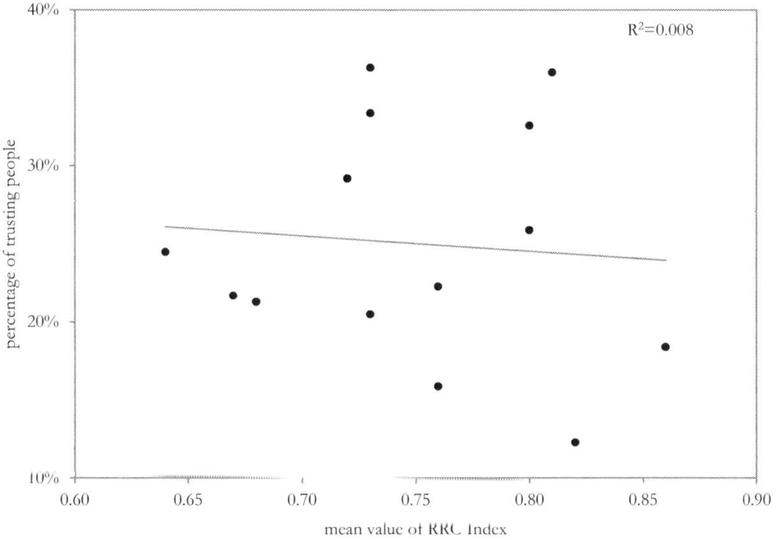

Source: WVS 1999.

A similar method to the one used in the case of social networks was used to examine the relationship between RRC and trust at the micro level. Respondents in each society were divided into four quartiles according to their individual level of RRC. The percentages of respondents declaring trust in the groups of the most and least conservative people in each society were then compared. In this way we assessed whether individual RRC systematically matters across societies for the levels of trust. The results of this examination are demonstrated in Figure 5.12. It seems that there is a systematic pattern – in most of the societies the least conservative individuals tend to declare trust in others more often. The relative differences in the levels of trust between the two groups of people are considerable across societies. While in Portugal the percentage of trusting people is five times higher among the least conservative than among the most conservative individuals, in Lithuania, Poland and Slovakia the relative differences in trust between the two groups are very modest. In contrast, in Croatia and Czech Republic the opposite is true – more conservative individuals display a slightly higher propensity to trust compared to their less conservative countrymen. In Poland, as in most societies, more conservative individuals seem to be less trusting, though the relative difference in the percentages of trusting people is moderate. In general, in contrast to the macro level, it seems that at the individual level we found evidence of a negative relationship between RRC and trust. Let us verify these findings by a statistical analysis of correlations.

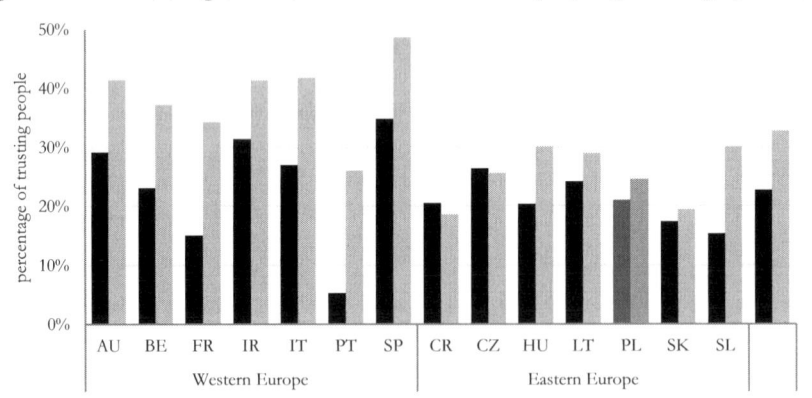

Figure 5.12 Trust among the most and least conservative people (percentages)

■ across a quater of the most conservative respondents
■ across a quater of the least conservative respondents

Source: WVS 1999.

Correlations (Pearson's) between the individual level of RRC and social trust in the pooled sample are negative and statistically significant (p<0.05; see Table 5.8). In most of the societies – nine out of 14 – individual RRC is negatively and significantly correlated with social trust. Only in Croatia, Czech Republic, Lithuania, Poland and Slovakia are correlations between RRC and trust not significant. There is quite a clear West-East division – while in Western Catholic societies RRC matters for trust, in post-communist Catholic societies such patterns are only present in Hungary and Slovenia. Turning to Poland, it seems that individual RRC is irrelevant for explaining the relatively low levels of social trust. So, despite the fact that we found evidence of a negative relationship between RRC and trust, the relatively high individual RRC does not explain the low trust among Poles.

Table 5.8 Relations between trust and conservatism by country (Pearson's correlation coefficient)

Pooled sample	AU	BE	FR	IR	IT	PT	SP	CR	CZ	HU	LT	PL	SK	SL
-0.11*	-0.13*	-0.15*	-0.22*	-0.10*	-0.16*	-0.29*	-0.14*	n.s.	n.s.	-0.11*	n.s.	n.s.	n.s.	-0.18*

* significant, p<0.05; n.s.- not significant; N=7,310.
Source: WVS 1999.

Summarising the findings concerning the relationship between RRC and trust, we can say that the expectations concerning the macro level relations were not confirmed: RRC is not negatively related to social trust. At the individual level, we found the expected negative relationship between RRC and trust, however this pattern was not found in Polish society.

5.2.2.3 Religiously Rooted Conservatism and norms and values

Finally I turn to the analysis of the relationship between RRC and the last component of social capital: norms and values. As discussed in chapter 4, previous studies did not find any relationship between Catholicism and norms and values. Therefore I expect to find no relationship between RRC and norms and values at both the macro and micro levels.

Before presenting the results of the empirical analyses I will recall the operationalisation of norms and values used in this study. Support for norms has been clustered into two groups (see section 2.4.3 for details), one referring to the civil sphere of life ("norms of civil behaviour," NCB) and the other one related to the social sphere ("norms of social behaviour," NSB). Let us pursue the examination at the macro level, starting with an analysis of the relationship between RRC and level of support for NCB.

As expected, aggregate levels of RRC remain unrelated to the levels of acceptance of NCB in all societies. The level of explained variance does not exceed four percent (Figure 5.13). Countries with low levels of RRC, such as Slovenia and France, are characterised by relatively modest levels of acceptance of NCB, as are more conservative countries like Portugal and Ireland. Poland lies at the bottom right-hand corner of the graph with a high level of RRC and a relatively high level of acceptance of NCB. In other words, the relatively high RRC in Poland does not explain the relatively high level of support for NCB.

Figure 5.13 Norms of civil behaviour (NCB) and conservatism (aggregate levels)

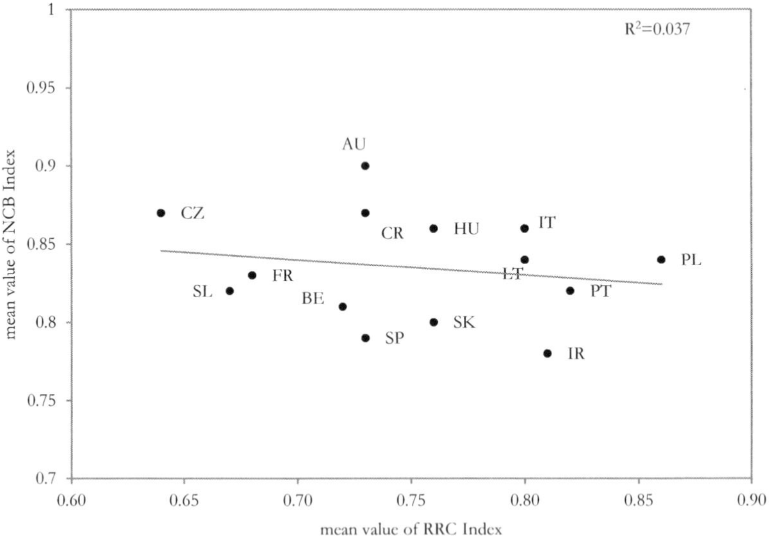

[Scatter plot with $R^2=0.037$; x-axis: mean value of RRC Index (0.60 to 0.90); y-axis: mean value of NCB Index (0.7 to 1). Countries plotted: AU, CZ, CR, HU, IT, SL, FR, BE, LT, PL, SP, SK, PT, IR.]

Source: WVS 1999.

Turning to the macro-level relationship between support for NSB and RRC, we have a similar situation. Levels of acceptance of NSB do not seem to be related to the aggregate level of RRC (Figure 5.14). The level of explained variance slightly exceeds eight percent. However, this time there is a heavy outlier, Slovakia, located far away from the remaining countries. If we recalculate the relationship between support for NSB and RRC without taking Slovakia into consideration, the value of R^2 rises to 28 percent. In other words, in contrast to expectations, there is a positive relationship between the level of RRC in a society and the level of acceptance of NSB, except for Slovakia. Poland is situated in the upper right-hand corner pointing to the high level of RRC and the relatively high acceptance of NSB. So we can conclude that the relatively high level of support for social behaviour in Poland can partly be explained by the relatively high level of RRC in this society.

Figure 5.14 Norms of social behaviour (NSB) and conservatism (aggregate levels)

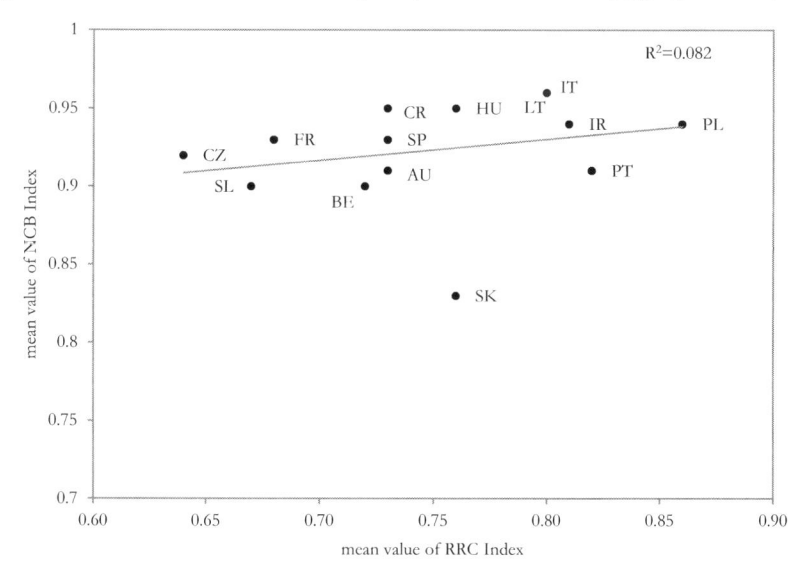

Source: WVS 1999.

Let us turn to the analysis of the relationship between support for norms and RRC at the individual level. Similar to the examinations presented in previous sections of this chapter, we compare the acceptance of norms among the most and least conservative individuals. In particular we address the question of whether the mean levels of support for both types of norm differ between the most and least conservative people.

Figure 5.15 displays levels of support for NCB and individual RRC in Catholic societies. We can see that the relative differences in support for norms between the two groups of respondents are marginal in virtually all societies. So, as expected, there is no general pattern of relationships between support for norms among the most and least conservative individuals. In Poland the levels of support for both groups are equal.

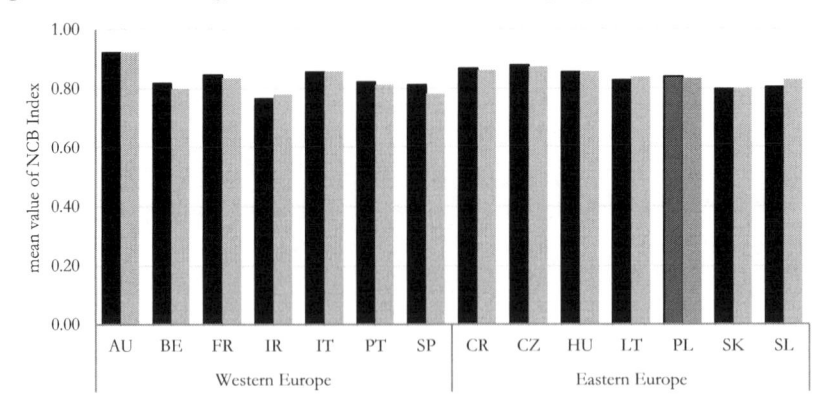

Figure 5.15 NCB among the most and least conservative people (mean values)

[Bar chart showing mean value of NCB Index across Western Europe (AU, BE, FR, IR, IT, PT, SP) and Eastern Europe (CR, CZ, HU, LT, PL, SK, SL) countries, comparing the most conservative quarter with the least conservative quarter of respondents.]

■ across a quater of the most conservative respondents
■ across a quater of the least conservative respondents

Source: WVS 1999.

Turning to the analysis of the relationship between support of NSB and individual RRC, we found a similar situation in all of the analysed countries (Figure 5.16). The relative differences in levels of support for NSB are marginal between the most and least conservative people in virtually every society. A systematic pattern of support for norms in both groups of respondents is also difficult to find. So the expectations are confirmed: RRC is irrelevant for support of NSB; this applies to Poland, too.

Figure 5.16 NSB among the most and least conservative people (mean values)

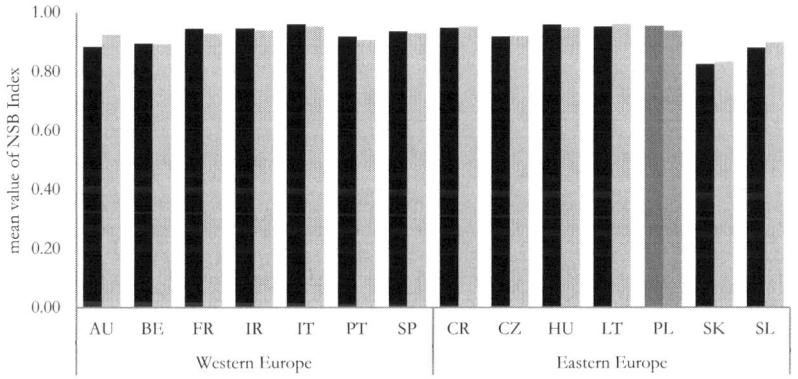

[Bar chart showing mean value of NSB Index from 0.00 to 1.00 for Western Europe (AU, BE, FR, IR, IT, PT, SP) and Eastern Europe (CR, CZ, HU, LT, PL, SK, SL), with bars for "across a quater of the most conservative respondents" and "across a quater of the least conservative respondents"]

Source: WVS 1999.

At last we examine the correlations between support for norms of civil and social behaviour and RRC at the individual level. As presented in Table 5.9, in most countries support for norms and individual RRC remain unrelated to each other. The only exception is the positive correlation between support for social norms and individual RRC in France. In Poland and other societies, individual RRC is not correlated with support for norms.

Table 5.9 Relations between support for norms of civil and social behaviour and conservatism by country (Pearson's correlation coefficient)

	Pooled sample	AU	BE	FR	IR	IT	PT	SP	CR	CZ	HU	LT	PL	SK	SL
NCB[a]	n.s.	n.s.	n.s.	n.s.	n.s.	n.s.	n.s.	n.s.	n.s.	n.s.	n.s.	n.s.	n.s.	n.s.	n.s.
NSB[b]	n.s.	n.s.	n.s.	n.s.	.08*	n.s.	n.s.	n.s.	n.s.	n.s.	n.s.	n.s.	n.s.	n.s.	n.s.

* significant, p<0.05; n.s.- not significant; [a] N=6171, [b] N=6740
Source: WVS 1999.

Summarising the results of the analyses of the relationship between RRC and norms, in general, as expected, RRC remains unrelated to norms. The only exception is a positive relationship between support for social norms and RRC at the macro level. In Poland, no relationship between RRC and support for norms was found. In other words, the relatively high RRC in Poland can only explain the relatively high support for social norms at the macro level.

5.2.3 *"Denomination effects" – concluding remarks*

In this section I empirically explored the accuracy of the claim that Catholicism has a negative impact on social capital, labelled as "denomination effects," which has been raised by several authors (see section 4.2). RRC, which measures the influence of the Catholic tradition on value orientations, is to a certain degree related to a number of components of social capital such as formal networks and NSB. These relationships could, however, only be seen at the aggregate level. In contrast informal networks, trust and acceptance of NCB remain indifferent to RRC at the macro level. On the other hand, only individual RRC matters for weak informal networks and low social trust; the latter relationship was not found in Poland.

Poland is the most conservative of all European Catholic countries; in other words it is the most heavily influenced by the Catholic tradition. Therefore the weak social engagement of Polish people might be partly explained by its overwhelming RRC, although only in the sense of a Catholic influence at the macro level. Similarly, a relatively high acceptance of NSB can be partly seen as a consequence of dominant conservative attitudes in society. Nevertheless, we learned that individual RRC does not explain the low levels of individual social capital. In this sense we can conclude that Polish people are reluctant to get involved in social networks because they live in a conservative country, but not because of their individual RRC.

5.3 "Affiliation effects" in Central Eastern Europe

We turn now to the analysis of the second (structural) aspect of religious influences on social capital, the "affiliation effects." The aim is to verify claims concerning the positive influences of churchgoing on social capital. These relationships were examined in several studies, though positive evidence concerns mostly the individual level of analysis (see section 4.2.2.1). Before we empirically explore the effects of churchgoing on social capital we need to discuss potential problems we might face when comparing church affiliation in Central Eastern European countries.

Does it matter for our analysis that the group of post-communist countries is religiously heterogeneous – they belong to four different religious traditions? On the one hand, frequency of churchgoing depends on denomination. While some denominations, such as Catholicism or Islam, oblige their faithful to attend religious services at least once a week, other denominations, like Protestantism or the Orthodox tradition, are not as strict in this regard. Most Central Eastern European countries are Catholic and Orthodox, while two Baltic countries are Protestant, and Bosnia and Herzegovina is Muslim. On the other hand, it is less important *how often* one attends church than whether it happens *on a regular basis*. Only regular contacts with the religious community result in building social networks (see section 4.2.2.2). So even if church attendance is less frequent, we should observe similar positive effects from being a member of a church community on social network building, if these contacts are regular.

I consider four types of churchgoers when analysing "affiliation effects" in Central Eastern European countries[52] – very frequent churchgoers (attending religious services once a week or more), frequent churchgoers (once a month), occasional churchgoers (less than once a month) to non-churchgoers (never attending religious services).

5.3.1 Church affiliation and social capital

Can we find a positive effect of churchgoing on social capital in Central Eastern Europe? Does widespread church affiliation in Poland have a positive effect on social capital, too? As presented in section 4.2.2.1, churchgoers are generally more connected to social networks and more likely to support NSB. On the other hand, the macro-level relationship with trust is negative – more devout societies are characterised by lower levels of social trust. Furthermore, in religiously devout societies churchgoing seems to be a less powerful indicator of social engagement. Polish society is one of the most devout in Europe, therefore the national context can matter in the Polish case (see section 4.2.2.2). In the following sections I investigate the relationship between church affiliation and three components of social capital: social networks, social trust and norms and values.

5.3.1.1   Church affiliation and social networks

The main reason why church attendance is important for social capital is that through churches the faithful are connected to social networks. The question arises: are churchgoers connected to wider social networks, or only to those related to

---

[52] Question wording in the WVS is as follows: "Apart from weddings, funerals and christenings how often do you attend religious services these days?" The item is coded on a 6-point scale: 1="more than once a week," 2="once a week," 3="once a month," 4="Christmas/Easter Day, other specific holidays, once a year", 5="less often", 6="never, practically never." The item is recoded into a 4-point scale, from the highest frequency of church attendance to the lowest (4 = "more than once a week" & "once a week"; 3 ="once a month", 2= Christmas/Easter Day, other specific holidays, once a year" & "less often", 1="never, practically never").

churches? As we saw in chapter 4, church affiliation is positively related mostly to involvement in church-related social activities. Some studies also provide evidence of a positive relationship with involvement in social activities outside the church, though this claim is not commonly shared. Other scholars claim that there is a spillover effect of religious engagement into secular engagement – meaning that those engaged in religious networks are more ready to engage in secular organisations, too (see section 4.2.2.2). Furthermore, a high level of religious devotion in a country could weaken the positive impact of church attendance on social networks. Can we find similar patterns across Central Eastern European societies? Is Poland an exception in this regard, or are "affiliation effects" in Poland similar to those in other countries in the region?

In order to address these questions, we need to consider three types of networks separately: church-based networks, secular networks and informal networks. At the aggregate level we might find a negative effect of church affiliation on social trust; otherwise levels of church attendance should remain unrelated to networks and norms and values (see section 4.2.2.1). At the individual level the situation is more complex. For the first two types of networks (church-based and secular) the expectations are actually different. I expect a positive relationship between church affiliation and engagement in church-based networks, while I predict that churchgoing and secular networks are unrelated (for details see 4.2.2.2). Furthermore, I address the question of whether we find spillover effects of religious engagement into secular engagement in post-communist societies, and whether it matters that Poland is a devout country. As far as informal networks are concerned, we can also expect positive effects of church affiliation (Becker/Dhingra 2001, 329).

5.3.1.1.1   Church affiliation and church-based networks

Aggregate levels of church affiliation and church-based networks

Relationships between church affiliation and social networks were discovered mainly at the individual level, therefore I do not expect any relationship between churchgoing and social networks at the macro level. Before proceeding to the examination of relationships, we first need to examine the distribution of both variables – church attendance and engagement in religious organisations – in post-communist countries. Both distributions are relevant for further examining the spillover effects of religious engagement and for assessing the relevance of the national context, especially in reference to Poland (see the next subsection).

Churchgoing in post-communist countries is considered in Figure 5.17. Poland is the only country in which a majority – almost 60 percent of respondents – declare very frequent church attendance (once a week or more). In Slovakia, very frequent churchgoers are also the largest group of the populace. In addition among Croats, Bosnians and Romanians more than 20 percent of the population declared very frequent church attendance; in the remaining countries this group does not exceed 17 percent. The most secularised countries were the Czech Republic, Hungary and Russia, where the most numerous are those who never attended religious services. In contrast, in **Poland** and **Romania** less than 10 percent of the population declared that they never attended any religious service, so these **are the most devout countries in the region**. In most of the countries occasional churchgoers (less than once a month) represented the largest portions of the populations: between 37 percent in Croatia and about 50 percent in Bulgaria, Lithuania and Ukraine.

Figure 5.17 Frequency of church attendance in Central Eastern Europe (percentages)

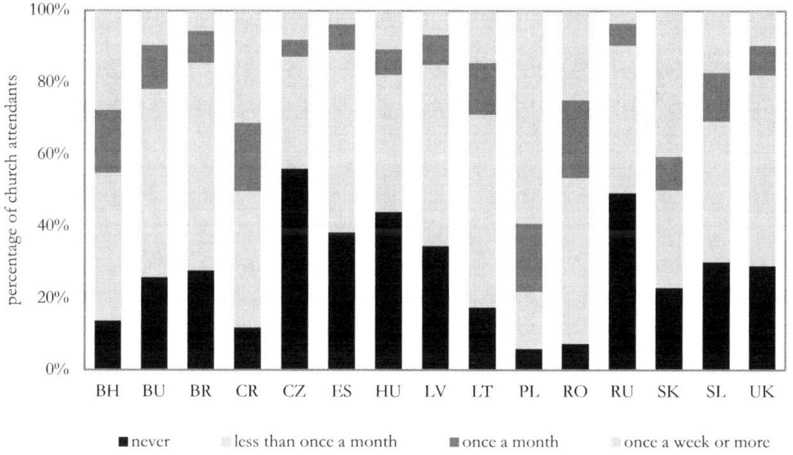

Source: WVS 1999.

Next I considered the levels of engagement in church-related organisations in Central Eastern European countries (Figure 5.18). Patterns of religious engagement were similar between countries – in every country there were more respondents declaring membership in an organisation than volunteering (with the exception of Belarus); the average proportion of people who volunteered (4.1 percent) was lower than the average percent of people who were members of organisations (6.8 percent). This is plausible since volunteering, in general, requires more time and personal involvement than being a member in an organisation (one can also be a passive member). In Croatia, the Czech Republic, Estonia and Hungary the number of volunteers was more than twice the number of members; in the remaining countries the relative differences were smaller. In Russia the level of volunteering was extremely low (less than one percent); in this case the level of membership was much higher than volunteering. In a cross-national comparison, Russians, Bulgarians, Belarusians and Ukrainians were the least religiously engaged people. In contrast, the most engaged (both as members and volunteers) were Slovaks, Hungarians and Croats. In Poland the levels of membership and volunteering were below the average levels in the region. So, even if we find spillover effects of religious engagement in Poland, this would concern only 5.4 percent of the population (the level of religious membership).

Figure 5.18 Membership and volunteering in religious organisations in Central Eastern Europe (percentages)

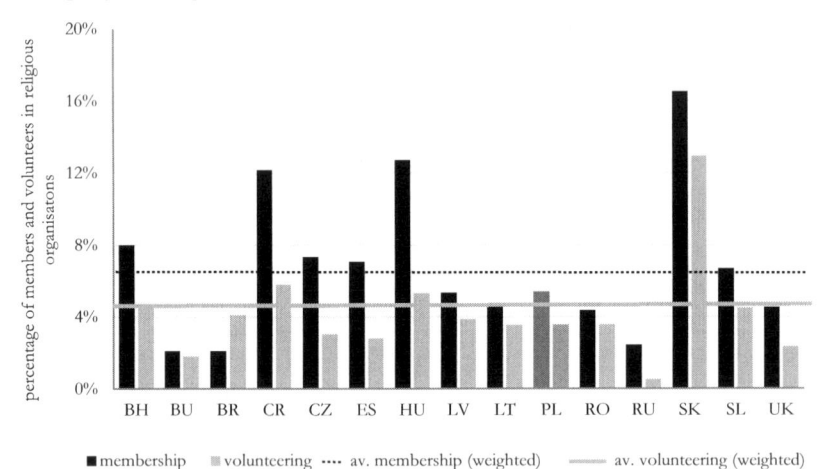

Source: WVS 1999.

Finally, the relations between churchgoing and religious engagement (membership and volunteering) at the macro level are depicted in Figure 5.19 and 5.20. It seems that, as expected, there is no relationship between churchgoing and membership in religious organisations at the macro level (Figure 5.19). Slovakia is an outlier with a particularly high percentage of membership and a moderate level of church affiliation. As far as volunteering is concerned, the situation seems to be slightly different. A very modest positive relationship appears between levels of church-related volunteering and levels of churchgoing (Figure 5.20). The more secularised a society is, the lower its level of church-related volunteering. Poland, with high rates of church attendance and a level of volunteerism slightly beneath the trend line, follows the general pattern. Slovakia is again an outlier, with especially high rates of volunteering and moderate rates of churchgoing. Removing Slovakia from the analysis doubles the level of explained variance to 13.5 percent. This evidence demonstrates that, contrary to expectations, levels of church attendance are positively related to religious volunteering in Central and Eastern Europe at the macro level. In other words, a high level of church affiliation in Poland is positively related to church-based volunteering at the aggregate level.

Figure 5.19 Membership in religious organisations and churchgoing (aggregate levels)

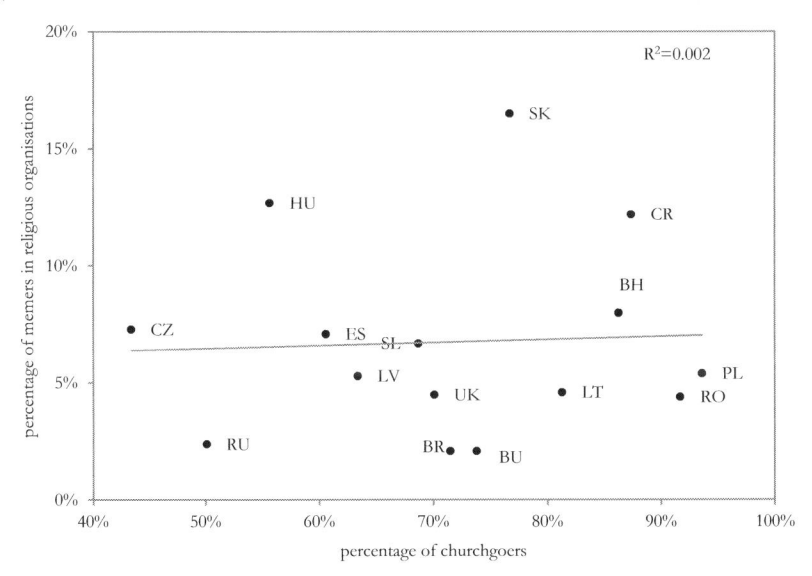

Source: WVS 1999.

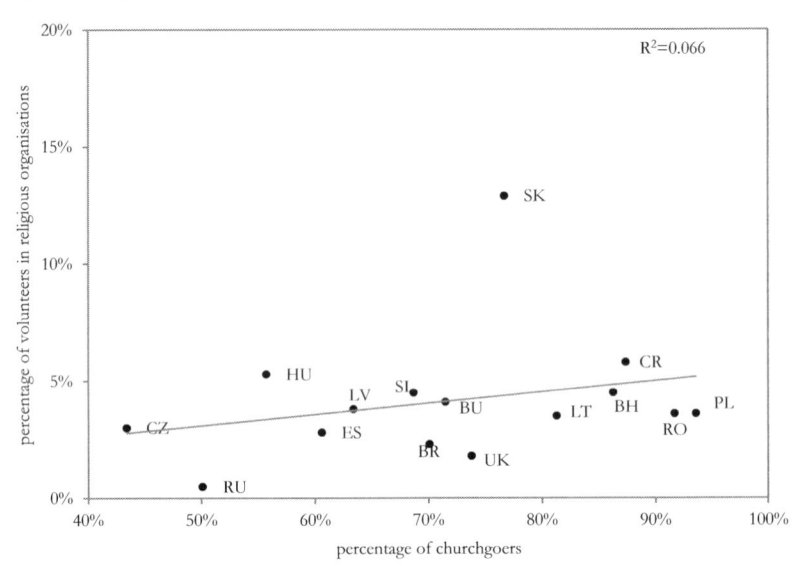

Figure 5.20 Volunteering in religious organisations and churchgoing (aggregate levels)

Source: WVS 1999.

Are churchgoers more likely to get involved in church-based networks?

Let us turn to the individual-level exploration of "affiliation effects" within individual societies. I expect to find that churchgoing positively affects religious engagement.

In all countries in the region, "affiliation effects" are found at the micro level, as expected. In every single country churchgoers declare membership in church-related organisations considerably more often than non-affiliated respondents (Figure 5.21). Moreover, the chance of being a member in a church-related organisation rises systematically in every society (with the exception of Bosnia and Herzegovina) with the frequency of churchgoing – very frequent churchgoers (attending religious services once a week or more) have a higher chance of being religiously engaged than less devoted people and non-attendants. Furthermore, with the exception of Russia, those declaring church attendance once a month are also more active in church-based groups compared to their less devout fellow countrymen, though here the relative differences are much more modest.

"Affiliation effects" in Central Eastern Europe 159

Figure 5.21 Membership in religious organisations and church attendance (percentage of members by type of churchgoers)

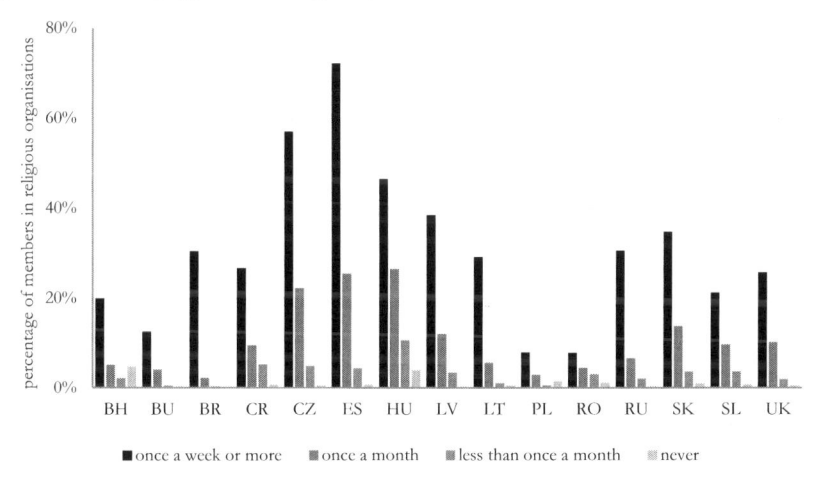

[Bar chart showing percentage of members in religious organisations for countries: BH, BU, BR, CR, CZ, ES, HU, LV, LT, PL, RO, RU, SK, SL, UK. Legend: once a week or more, once a month, less than once a month, never]

Source: WVS 1999.

Correlation coefficients between individual church attendance and religious membership in the pooled sample are statistically significant (p<0.05) and relatively strong (r=0.307, see Table 5.10). Correlations between churchgoing and religious membership are significant in every single country, though they reveal a distinct power of "affiliation effects" in post-communist societies. The impact of attending religious services on the propensity to be involved in a church-related organisation seems to be the strongest in Estonia and Slovakia (r value around 0.4), while the same effects in Poland and Romania are the weakest among the considered countries (r values around 0.1). Different effects of church attendance on religious membership are shown in Figure 5.21. While in the Czech Republic and Estonia over 50 percent of frequent churchgoers declare membership in a religious organisation, in Poland and Romania only 8 percent do so.

Table 5.10 Correlation between membership in religious organisations and church attendance (Pearson's coefficients)

Pooled sample	BH	BU	BR	CR	CZ	ES	HU	LV	LT	PL	RO	RU	SK	SL	UK
0.31*	0.23*	0.22*	0.34*	0.29*	0.53*	0.45*	0.38*	0.36*	0.30*	0.13*	0.10*	0.28*	0.40*	0.28*	0.32*

Notes: *level of significance p<0.05; N=18,326.
Source: WVS 1999.

One explanation for the low "affiliation effects" in Poland and Romania could lie in the substantial levels of religious devotion in these countries, according to the claims of Ruiter and de Graaf (2006) (see section 4.2.2.2). These countries have the lowest percentage of people that never attend religious services (6 percent in Poland and 7 percent in Romania, see Figure 5.22), which means that virtually all individuals are to a certain degree integrated into a church community, even if some go to church only occasionally. Quite different situations are found in Slovakia and Croatia, where the percentages of very frequent churchgoers reach high levels (around 30-40 percent), however the percentage of non-attendants is higher than in Poland and Romania: 12 percent and 20 percent, respectively. In other words, "affiliation effects" in Poland are the same "in kind" though different "in degree," so Poland in this sense is an exception among the studied countries.

"Affiliation effects" are also observed in the levels of volunteer engagement (Figure 5.22). Bars representing the percentage of volunteers among frequent churchgoers are consistently higher in every country compared to bars that depict the percentage of volunteers among less religiously devoted people. Again, there are noteworthy country differences – while about 30 percent of frequent churchgoers declare volunteering in Czech Republic, Estonia, Latvia and Slovakia, in Poland and Romania there are only 5 percent. In Poland the patterns are similar – the most frequent churchgoers also seem to be more frequently engaged as volunteers in church-related organisations.

Figure 5.22 Volunteering in religious organisations and church attendance (percentage of volunteers by type of churchgoers)

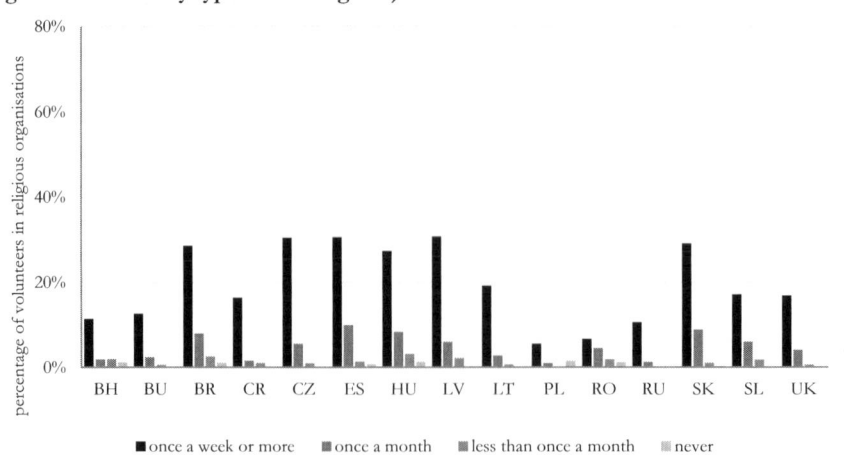

Source: WVS 1999.

Pearson's correlation coefficient of religious volunteering and churchgoing in the pooled sample is significant (p<0.5) and reaches a considerable value (r=0.27), however it indicates less powerful effects of churchgoing on volunteering than on membership (Table 5.11). The values of Pearson's correlation coefficients confirm the distinct power of "affiliation effects" across countries. The strongest effects of church affiliation can be seen in the Czech Republic and Slovakia (r=0.41 and r=0.38, respectively), whereas in Poland and Romania the correlation is much weaker (r=0.11). So, as in the case of religious volunteering, "affiliation effects" seem to be far more modest when the country's population is devoted.

Table 5.11 Correlation between volunteering in religious organisations and church attendance (Pearson's coefficients)

Pooled sample	BH	BU	BR	CR	CZ	ES	HU	LV	LT	PL	RO	RU	SK	SL	UK
0.27*	0.18*	0.23*	0.26*	0.27*	0.41*	0.27*	0.31*	0.33*	0.30*	0.11*	0.11*	0.18*	0.38*	0.27*	0.28*

Notes: *level of significance p<0.05; N=18,326.
Source: WVS 1999.

In sum, affiliation effects on church-based engagement in Poland are the same "in kind" though different "in degree." It seems that it matters that Poland is a devout country, so the macro-level context hampers effects at the individual level. In this sense Poland is an exception in Central Eastern Europe.

5.3.1.1.2   Church affiliation and secular networks

I have now analysed engagement in church-related organisations. What about the wider spectrum of social activity? Does church attendance also matter for non-religious involvement? Investigations of other scholars' cross-country studies brought mixed results (see section 4.2.2.2).

Aggregate levels of church affiliation and secular networks

Let us analyse relationships at the macro level first. Aggregate levels of church affiliation and membership in secular organisations are depicted in Figure 5.23. Countries are scattered across the whole graph, though Slovakia is the most distant from the regression line. The Czech Republic, Slovenia, Hungary and Lithuania also lie far away from the regression line. In general four countries (the Czech Republic, Slovakia, Slovenia and Belarus) appear to have relatively high levels of membership – more than 40 percent of the population – while in the remaining countries these rates are between 15 and 30 percent; Croatia is in the middle. The level of explained variance is very low: around 10 percent. The relationship seems to be negative, since among countries with higher aggregate levels of church affiliation, membership in secular organisations is relatively low. Poland is situated in the bottom right-hand corner of the graph with the highest rates of church affiliation and one of the lowest percentages of secular membership. In sum, the situation in Poland fits the general pattern across Central European countries.

Figure 5.23 Membership in non-religious organisations and churchgoing (aggregate levels)

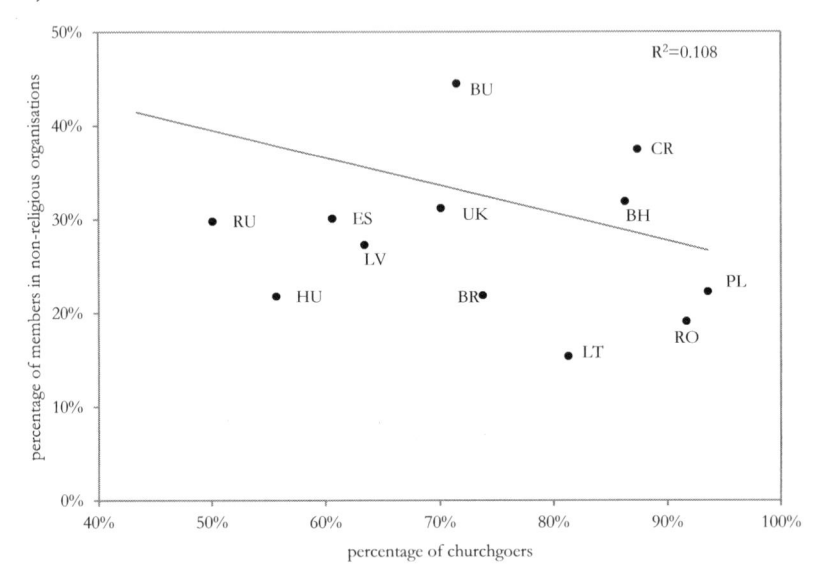

<chart: scatter plot with x-axis "percentage of churchgoers" from 40% to 100% and y-axis "percentage of members in non-religious organisations" from 0% to 50%. $R^2=0.108$. Points: BU, CR, RU, ES, UK, BH, LV, HU, BR, PL, LT, RO.>

Source: WVS 1999.

In contrast, aggregate levels of church affiliation and secular volunteering seem to be unrelated to each other (Figure 5.24). Two countries are placed a considerable distance from the majority: the Czech Republic and Slovakia. Both are characterised by much higher percentages of secular volunteers compared to other countries in the region, though their aggregate levels of church affiliation differ. After excluding Slovakia and the Czech Republic from the analysis, the level of explained variance rises, though still remains at a very low level (8 percent). In other words, secular volunteering is very weakly and positively related to aggregate levels of church attendance in Central Eastern Europe, contrary to expectations. In Poland secular volunteering remains at one of the lowest levels, despite high rates of church attendance.

Figure 5.24 Volunteering in non-religious organisations and churchgoing (aggregate levels)

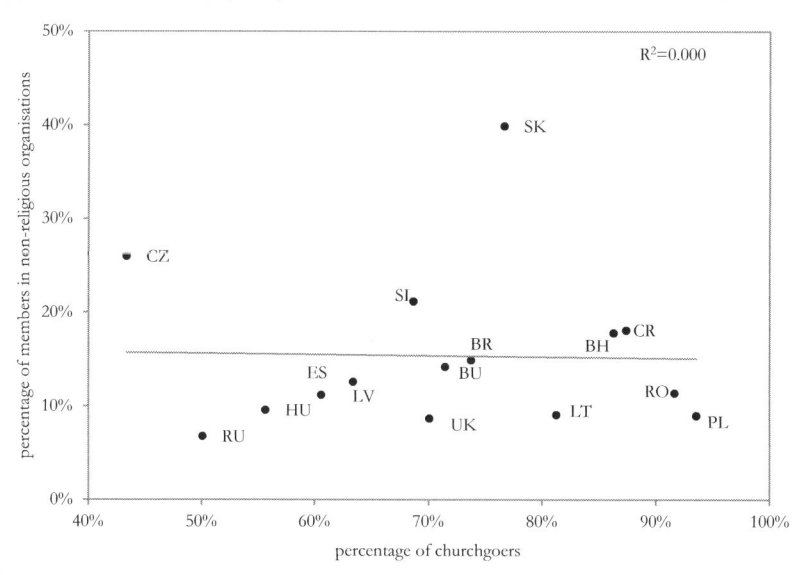

[Scatter plot: x-axis "percentage of churchgoers" (40%–100%), y-axis "percentage of members in non-religious organisations" (0%–50%). $R^2=0.000$. Data points: CZ, SK, SI, BR, BH, CR, ES, BU, LV, HU, UK, LT, RO, PL, RU.]

Source: WVS 1999.

Are churchgoers more likely to get involved in secular networks?

What about the relationship between secular engagement and churchgoing at the individual level? Secular engagement in Central Eastern European countries by frequency of churchgoing is depicted in Figure 5.25. It seems that very frequent churchgoers are not more ready to get involved outside the church than non-churchgoers. The differences in percentage of members by type of churchgoers are in general modest, with the exception of a few countries – Bulgaria, Estonia, Poland and Ukraine. Only in Estonia and Bulgaria do very frequent churchgoers remain the most engaged group of society, in non-religious types of activities as well. In addition, Poland is the only country where the percentage of membership is higher among non-churchgoers than among very frequent churchgoers. We will find out whether this observation is statistically significant with the analysis of correlations.

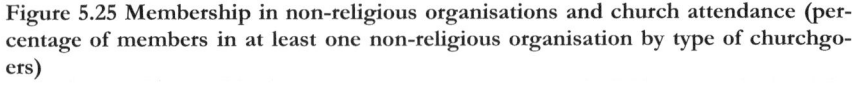

Figure 5.25 Membership in non-religious organisations and church attendance (percentage of members in at least one non-religious organisation by type of churchgoers)

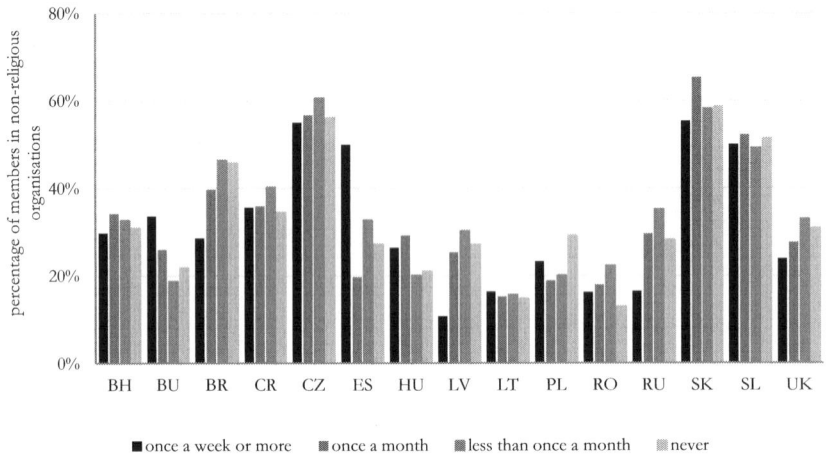

[Bar chart showing percentages for countries BH, BU, BR, CR, CZ, ES, HU, LV, LT, PL, RO, RU, SK, SL, UK with four categories: once a week or more, once a month, less than once a month, never]

Source: WVS 1999.

To calculate correlations I use Pearson's test to check for a linear correlation, and Gamma to test for symmetrical correlations and abnormal distribution (Table 5.12). Analysis of the pooled sample provides evidence of a very weak positive relationship between church attendance and non-religious social involvement (r=0.025; γ =0.045, both statistically significant, p<0.01). At the country level, however, there is no evidence of a significant relationship except for two countries. In Bulgaria churchgoing is weakly positively related to secular engagement, while in Belarus this relationship is negative. In Polish society, churchgoing has no significant effect on secular engagement, as is the case in most of the other countries in the region.

Table 5.12 Correlation between membership in non-religious organisations and church attendance (Pearson's and Gamma coefficients)

	Pooled sample	BH	BU	BR	CR	CZ	ES	HU	LV	LT	PL	RO	RU	SK	SL	UK
r	0.03*	n.s.	0.08*	-0.07*	n.s.	n.s.	n.s.	n.s.	n.s.	n.s.	n.s.	n.s.	n.s.	n.s.	n.s.	n.s.
γ	0.05*	n.s	n.s	n.s	n.s	n.s	n.s	n.s	n.s	n.s	n.s	n.s	n.s	n.s	n.s	n.s

Notes: *level of significance p<0.05; n.s.- not significant; N=18,326.
Source: WVS 1999.

Spillover or crowding out effects?

Finally I explore the relationship between religious and non-religious social involvement: whether there is a spillover effect of religious engagement on non-church-related social activities. As presented in chapter 4, there is mixed evidence in this regard: while in some societies religiously engaged people get involved in secular activity; in other societies, religiously engaged people are reluctant to extend their social activity into the secular realm. Before directly addressing the issue of the spillover effect of religious engagement, I first analyse the popularity of religious organisations compared to other types of organisations in Central Eastern Europe. In this fashion we learn the extent to which a spillover effect may concern social networks in post-communist societies in general. Distributions of four of the most popular types of organisations are considered in Figure 5.26.

Figure 5.26 Membership in the four most popular types of organisations in Central Eastern European countries (percentages)

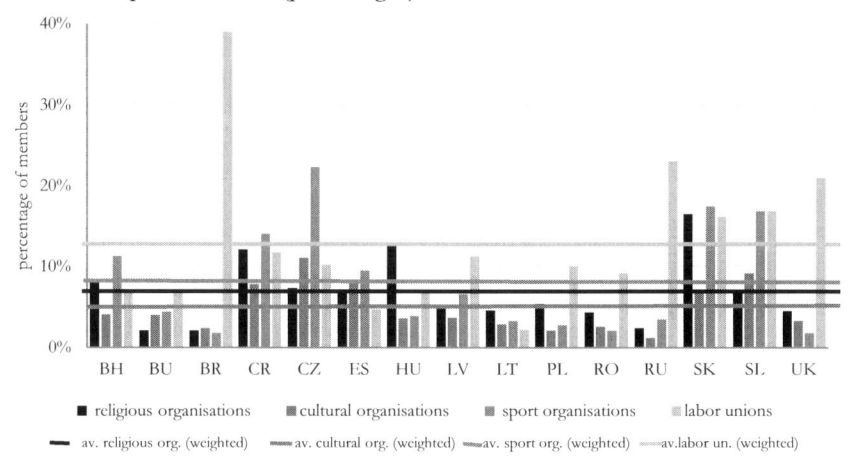

Source: WVS 1999.

Labour unions are by far the most frequently joined organisation in most of the countries under consideration[53] (on average 13.1 percent of the populations belong

---

[53] Labour unions rank highest in Belarus, Bulgaria, Latvia, Poland, Romania, Russia and Ukraine; in Slovenia they rank highest together with sport organisations. Howard explains this unusually high inclination for participation in labour unions in countries from this region by the communist legacy. Labour unions have been highly politicised and their membership mandatory, furthermore these organisations were not dissolved after the collapse of communism (Howard 2003, 67).

to labour unions), sport organisations take second place (8.1 percentage on average), religious organisations third place (on average 6.8 percent), and cultural associations come in fourth (on average 4.9 percent). In Bosnia and Herzegovina, Croatia, Estonia and Slovakia membership in sport organisations is the most popular mode of social participation. Hungary and Lithuania are the only countries in which church organisations are the most frequently joined, otherwise this mode of engagement ranks second position in Bosnia and Herzegovina, Croatia, Poland, Romania, Slovakia and Ukraine. In Poland, membership in all four types of organisations ranks below the averages in the region. In general across this region, religious engagement, ranked third, is a relatively popular mode of engagement. In Poland the popularity of religious organisations is even higher (second place). Still, in absolute terms religious engagement, similar to secular engagement, remains at a very modest level.

Turning to the question of whether religious engagement enhances secular engagement, we need to explore the situation in each country, since spillover effects seem to differ between distinct social contexts (see section 4.2.2.2). The presence of a spillover effect of religious involvement is difficult to assess directly, since there is no specific question in the survey about whether a person was first religiously involved and then got engaged in other secular organisations. However when we calculate the percentage of members in non-religious organisations among those religiously engaged, we will learn how many religiously active people do not limit their engagement to church-related organisations. When we compare this number with the percentage of members in non-religious organisations among those who are *not* religiously active, we learn whether non-religious engagement is *relatively* higher among church-related members.

This examination brings mixed results. In Figure 5.27 the bars represent membership in secular organisations of two groups of respondents in each country – religiously engaged and not engaged. In most countries membership in non-religious organisations is higher among these religiously involved, for instance in Bosnia and Herzegovina, Bulgaria, Croatia, Czech Republic, Estonia, Hungary, Lithuania, Poland, Romania and Slovenia. In other countries this is not the case (Belarus, Latvia, Russia, Slovakia and Ukraine). This would indicate that in most of these countries there is a spillover effect.

Figure 5.27 Non-religious involvement of members and non-members of religious organisations (percent of members in at least one non-religious organisation from two groups – members and non-members of religious organisations)

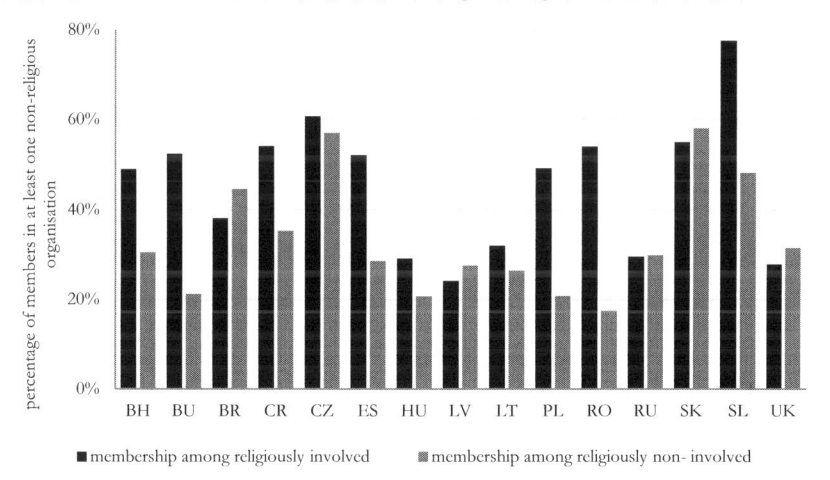

[Bar chart showing percentages for countries: BH, BU, BR, CR, CZ, ES, HU, LV, LT, PL, RO, RU, SK, SL, UK, comparing membership among religiously involved vs membership among religiously non-involved]

Source: WVS 1999.

In order to get clearer evidence, a relative measure of spillover effect on secular involvement in both groups of respondents is calculated. I label this relative measure "S," which is calculated in the following way: the percentage of members of at least one non-religious organisation among religiously involved people is divided by the percentage of members in at least one non-religious organisation among not religiously involved respondents. Values of "S" above 1 indicate a spillover effect, while less than 1 indicates no spillover effect (a "crowding out"[54] effect).

Table 5.13 Spillover effect of religious engagement on secular engagement

	BH	BU	BR	CR	CZ	ES	HU	LV	LT	PL	RO	RU	SK	SL	UK
S	1.6	**2.5**	0.9	1.5	1.1	1.8	1.4	0.9	1.2	**2.4**	**3.1**	1.0	0.9	1.6	0.9

Source: WVS 1999.

We can see in Table 5.13 that the spillover effect occurs in most of the countries except Belarus, Russia, Latvia, Slovakia and Ukraine. The strongest spillover effect is found in Romania – here we are three times more likely to meet a member of a

---

[54] A "crowding out" effect means that involvement in one type of organisation impedes involvement in other types of organisations. In this case, people engaged in religious organisations are not likely to participate in other types of organisations.

secular organisation among those religiously engaged than among those non-religiously engaged. Furthermore, in Poland and Bulgaria spillover effects seem to be quite strong, too; this relationship is 2.5 times to 1. On the other hand, spillover effects are relatively moderate in Croatia and Hungary ("S" around 1.5), since every second member of religious organisations also declares membership in at least one other non-religious organisation. In Belarus, Latvia, Slovakia and Ukraine in contrast, there is a "crowding out" effect ("S"<1). Furthermore, in three countries with high spillover effects, the absolute levels of religious involvement remain relatively low – 6 percent or lower (Figure 5.26). This means that these effects are relevant for small portions of the populace only. These findings also apply to Poland – here the spillover effects are relatively strong, though in absolute terms they concern only about five percent of the population.

5.3.1.1.3 Church affiliation and informal networks

Informal networks are particularly important for Central Eastern Europe (chapter 3). Similar to relations between churchgoing and formal networks, we expect a positive influence of churchgoing on informal network building. Churchgoers might be organised not only in church-based organisations, but also might find friends and acquaintances through their connection to the church community. A study on American parishes confirms such a positive relationship: "We find support for the idea that much of the 'church effect' on volunteering operates through friendship networks" (Becker/Dhingra 2001, 326). Let us examine whether we can find positive relationships between church attendance and informal ties in Central Eastern European societies, too. And how does the situation look in Poland? First I analyse aggregate levels of church affiliation and friendship ties, then examine the individual level.

Aggregate levels of church affiliation and informal networks

At the aggregate level, informal networks seem to be unrelated to church affiliation, since less than one percent of the variance is explained (Figure 5.28). There are two outliers – Poland and Romania – situated at a considerable distance from the remaining countries in the bottom right-hand corner that represent high levels of church attendance and low levels of informal networks. When Romania and Poland are excluded from the analysis the level of explained variances rises considerably to over 36 percent. This exceptional situation in both countries could be explained by an extraordinarily high percentage of churchgoers. In a country where virtually all people attend religious services, church is not a different place from the workplace or neighbourhood, where one could find friends or acquaintances. In other words, informal networks do not seem to depend as much on levels of churchgoing in devout countries.

Figure 5.28 Informal networks and churchgoing (aggregate levels)

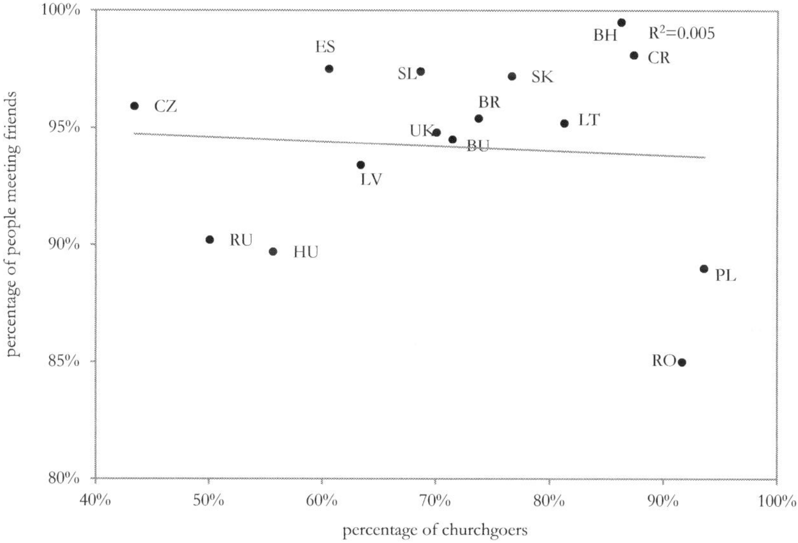

[Scatter plot: x-axis "percentage of churchgoers" (40%–100%), y-axis "percentage of people meeting friends" (80%–100%). Data points: BH, ES, SL, SK, CR, R²=0.005, CZ, BR, UK, BU, LT, LV, RU, HU, PL, RO.]

Source: WVS 1999.

Are churchgoers more likely to get involved in informal networks?

Can we find a similar positive relationship between churchgoing and informal networks at the individual level? Is Poland also in this case an exception? Bars representing percentages of respondents meeting with friends seem to differ only slightly by frequency of church attendance (Figure 5.29). There is hardly a general pattern to observe. Relative differences in informal networks between churchgoers and non-attendants are exceptionally high only in Russia and Romania – around 15 percentage points. In Russia these findings are contrary to expectations: the most frequent churchgoers report meeting friends the least often. In Romania by contrast, findings conform to the expectations: churchgoers declare meeting with friends the most often. In Poland, too, those never attending religious services meet the least often with friends. Moreover the relationship between the frequency of churchgoing and informal networks is difficult to assess, since those who go to church once a month or less are the most likely to meet friends, while the most frequent churchgoers and non-attendants meet with friends less often.

Figure 5.29 Informal networks and church attendance (percentage of people meeting with friends by type of churchgoers)

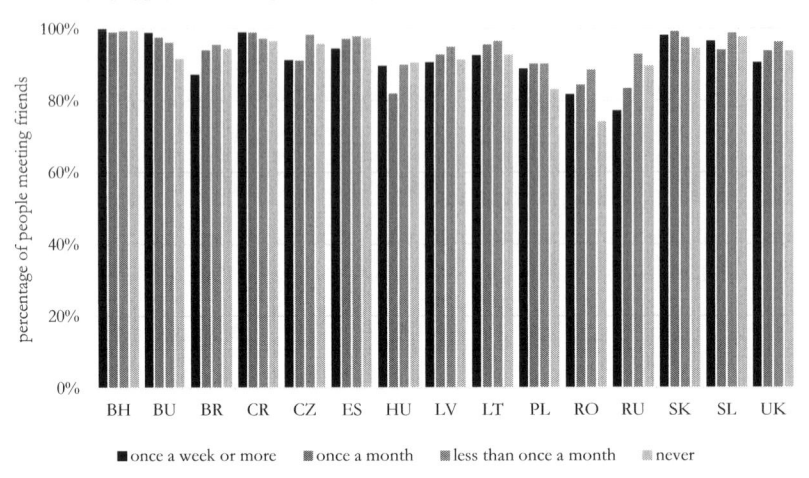

[Bar chart showing percentages (0%–100%) on vertical axis labeled "percentage of people meeting friends" and countries on horizontal axis: BH, BU, BR, CR, CZ, ES, HU, LV, LT, PL, RO, RU, SK, SL, UK. Legend: ■ once a week or more ■ once a month ■ less than once a month ■ never]

Source: WVS 1999.

Correlations between churchgoing and meeting with friends are not significant (p<0.05) in the pooled sample for both Pearson's and Gamma correlations. Correlations are significant in one-third of individual countries: Bulgaria, Croatia, the Czech Republic, Russia and Slovakia (Table 5.14). Surprisingly, in Russia and the Czech Republic meeting with friends is negatively correlated with churchgoing, though only one of the applied tests has significant results. In Slovakia and Bulgaria the correlations are positive, though weak. In Croatia the Pearson's coefficient shows a strong correlation, though the Gamma coefficient shows a weaker correlation. In Poland, the individual frequency of churchgoing is unrelated to meeting with friends. In this case patterns in Polish society are neither exceptional nor regular, since there is no regularity.

Table 5.14 Correlation between informal networks and church attendance (Pearson's and Gamma coefficients)

	Pooled sample	BH	BU	BR	CR	CZ	ES	HU	LV	LT	PL	RO	RU	SK	SL	UK
r	n.s.	n.s.	0.10*	n.s.	0.38*	-0.05*	n.s.	n.s.	n.s.	n.s.	n.s.	n.s.	-0.05*	0.08*	n.s.	n.s.
γ	n.s.	n.s	0.44*	n.s	0.07*	n.s	n.s	n.s	n.s	n.s	n.s	n.s	0.36*	n.s	n.s

Notes: *level of significance p<0.05; n.s.- not significant; N=17,923
Source: WVS 1999.

5.3.1.1.4 Concluding "affiliation effects" on social networks

Summarising the results of our analyses of "affiliation effects" on social networks in Central Eastern Europe and Poland, the following conclusions can be drawn:

1. Contrary to expectations, there are relationships between the levels of church attendance and participation in social networks at the macro level in Central Eastern Europe. Surprisingly, the level of churchgoing is positively related to volunteering in religious organisations, and to informal networks; in contrast, the relationship to secular membership is negative. Poland is an exception with regard to informal networks – a positive relationship with church attendance was not found. In other words in Poland, despite a high level of church attendance, informal networks are not strong. Similarly in Poland, the level of secular volunteering is not high despite a high level of church affiliation. Therefore we can conclude that the positive effects of high levels of church attendance are not found in Poland to the same extent as in other societies.
2. In general, the positive effects of church attendance at the macro level are much weaker in devout countries like Poland or Romania. In other words, national levels of religious devotion matter for the power of "affiliation effects" by making them weaker than in non-devout countries, which confirms the findings in the literature.
3. At the micro level, as expected, churchgoers are more likely to be engaged in religious organisations, and the inclination to participate in church-related activities rises with the frequency of churchgoing. The evidence for a relationship between individual church attendance and secular engagement is much less convincing and was found only in the pooled sample.
4. Spillover effects of religious engagement onto secular engagement are found in most countries, including Poland. Poland has one of the strongest spillover effects; however this impact is limited, because religious en-

gagement is quite modest in absolute terms and does not exceed 6 percent of the population.

It turns out that the situation in Poland is, to a certain extent, different when compared to other countries: even if church affiliation shows a positive influence on participation in general, strong religious devotion does not enhance these effects. Neither a high frequency of churchgoing nor a higher percentage of churchgoers among the populace reinforce the "affiliation effects." Moreover, the spillover effects of religious engagement onto secular engagement, though quite strong in Poland, concern only a small part of the population.

5.3.1.2   Church affiliation and social trust

As presented in section 4.2.2.1, the empirical findings concerning the relationship between churchgoing and social trust are not consistent. At the macro level church affiliation is negatively related to social trust, since the most trusting societies are also the most secularised. On the other hand, micro-level analyses bring mixed results: it seems that in some countries churchgoers are more likely to trust than non-churchgoers, while in other countries this is not the case. The question I address in this section is whether similar evidence of the relationship between trust and churchgoing can be found in Central Eastern Europe, and whether Polish society is an exception when compared to other countries from the region.

5.3.1.2.1   Church affiliation and social trust at the macro level

Can we say that societies with lower levels of church affiliation are more trusting? As demonstrated in Figure 5.30, churchgoing is negatively related to social trust at the macro level, as expected. With one outlier (Belarus), levels of social trust drop with rising levels of church affiliation. Belarus has an extraordinarily high level of social trust compared to other societies in the region and is situated far above the trend line. After withdrawing Belarus from the analysis the level of explained variance rises to 26 percent. The relationship between levels of churchgoing and social trust is negative, with the exception of Belarus. Furthermore, Polish society is situated in the bottom right-hand corner of the graph with a high level of church attendance and one of the lowest levels of social trust, so the situation in Poland fits the general pattern. Similarly, other devout societies such as Romania, Bosnia and Herzegovina and Croatia – with nearly 90 percent of the population reporting church attendance – appear to have the lowest percentages of trusting people.

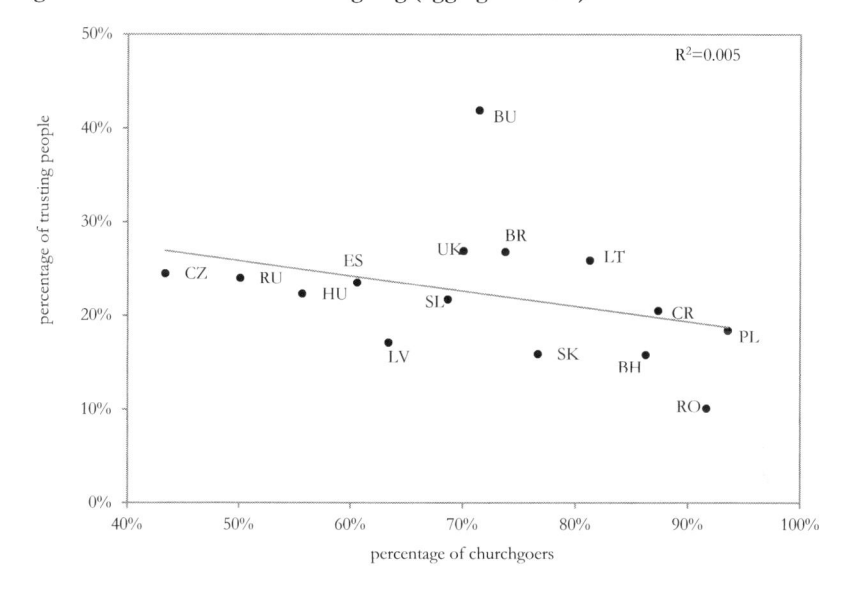

Figure 5.30 Social trust and churchgoing (aggregate levels)

[Scatter plot: x-axis "percentage of churchgoers" from 40% to 100%; y-axis "percentage of trusting people" from 0% to 50%. $R^2=0.005$. Data points labeled: CZ, RU, ES, HU, UK, BR, LT, SL, LV, SK, CR, BH, RO, PL, BU.]

Source: WVS 1999.

So in general, "affiliation effects" on social trust in Central Eastern Europe are similar to those observed in the wider spectrum of societies. Relationships in Poland follow the general pattern. In the following micro-level perspective I look closer at the influence of the frequency of churchgoing on trust in each society separately.

5.3.1.2.2   Are churchgoers more likely to trust others?

At the micro level, patterns of relations between trust and churchgoing are mixed among Central Eastern European societies and we can distinguish at least three kinds of similarities (Figure 5.31). In one group of countries (Bosnia and Herzegovina, Croatia, Estonia, Russia and Ukraine) the highest percentage of trusting persons can be found among those who attend church services very frequently (at least once a week). In contrast, in three other countries (Poland, Romania and Slovenia) the highest percentage of trusting people are among non-attendants. Whereas in Poland and Romania the group of non-attendants is relatively small (6 percent and 7 percent, respectively, see Figure 5.17), in Slovenia non-attendants are more numerous and represent almost one-third of the population. In the case of trust we cannot say that a country's religious devoutness is a factor diminishing the impact of "affiliation effects," as in the case of social networks. In the remaining countries (Bulgaria, Belarus, the Czech Republic, Hungary, Latvia, Lithuania, Poland and Slovenia) it is difficult to assess whether there is a relationship between churchgoing and trust. To get a clearer picture we turn to statistical tests.

Figure 5.31 Social trust by frequency of churchgoing (percentage of trusting people by type of churchgoers)

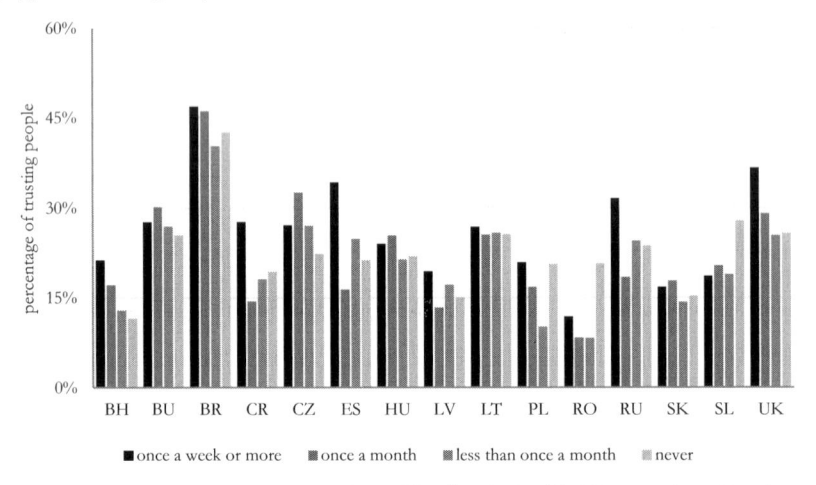

■ once a week or more ■ once a month ■ less than once a month ■ never

Source: WVS 1999.

A statistical analysis of the correlations between churchgoing and trust (Pearson's and Gamma) brings clearer results (Table 5.15). In the pooled sample, churchgoing is related significantly and positively to social trust (r= 0.016; γ = 0.029; significance level p<0.05), meaning that the likelihood of meeting a trusting person increases with the rise in frequency of churchgoing among analysed individuals. In individual countries this positive correlation between churchgoing and trust seems to be confirmed in the cases of Bosnia and Herzegovina, Croatia, the Czech Republic and Poland (r and γ statistically significant, p<0.05). So the results in Poland are similar to those in the pooled data – churchgoers are more likely to trust. In contrast in Bulgaria, Belarus, Estonia, Hungary, Lithuania, Russia, Slovakia and Ukraine the frequency of church attendance does not appear to be related to the propensity to trust. In the remaining three countries (Latvia, Romania and Slovenia), the results of both tests differ from each other. In Latvia and Romania, only r is statistically significant and indicates a negative correlation, while γ is insignificant. In Slovenia by contrast, Gamma points to a negative and significant correlation between trust and churchgoing, while the results of Pearson's test remain insignificant.

Table 5.15 Correlation between trust and church attendance (Pearson's and Gamma coefficients)

	Pooled sample	BH	BU	BR	CR	CZ	ES	HU	LV	LT	PL	RO	RU	SK	SL	UK
r	0.02*	0.10*	n.s.	n.s.	0.08*	0.05*	n.s.	n.s.	-0.06*	n.s.	0.07*	-0.07*	n.s.	n.s.	n.s.	n.s.
γ	0.03*	0.21*	n.s	n.s	0.15*	0.13*	n.s	n.s	n.s	n.s	0.18*	n.s	n.s	n.s	-0.14*	n.s

Notes: *level of significance p<0.05; n.s.- not significant; N=17,766.
Source: WVS 1999.

Summing up, we do not observe a general pattern of relationships between churchgoing and trust in post-communist countries at the micro level. In this regard the situation in Poland is neither exceptional nor follows the mainstream. It is worth noting that in Poland the strength of the positive correlation between church attendance and trust is one of the highest in the region.

5.3.1.3 Church affiliation and norms and values

Are "affiliation effects" on norms and values visible across Central Eastern Europe? I use the operationalisation of norms and values presented in chapter 2.[55] If the patterns in Central Eastern Europe are to be same as those in Western Europe, we would expect that acceptance of social and civil norms is barely related to churchgoing at the macro level and could be positively related at the micro level[56] (see section 4.2.2.1).

5.3.1.3.1 Aggregate levels of church affiliation and acceptance of norms of civil and social behaviour

Analyses of aggregate data point partly in the expected direction. There is no correlation between the percentage of churchgoers in a country and the level of accep-

---

[55] The NCB-Index and NSB-Index cannot be computed for Bosnia and Herzegovina, because some questions that are part of these indices were not asked in this country (see chapter 2 for the details), so Bosnia and Herzegovina is excluded from the analyses.
[56] Church affiliation is negatively correlated with pro-social child-rearing objectives (Gabriel et al. 2002, 126-130), however my operationalisation of norms differs in this respect, so these findings are irrelevant for my expectations here.

tance of NCB. In Figure 5.32 we can see that in countries where the percentage of churchgoers does not exceed 80 percent of the population, the means of the NCB-Index are higher than in countries with a lower percentage of churchgoers. Belarus and Bulgaria are outliers; Belarus has a considerably low mean score on the NCB-Index, while in Bulgaria the mean of the NCB-Index is the highest, and in both countries the percentage of churchgoers is about 70 percent. Poland, Croatia and Romania, with the highest rates of church attendance (around 90 percent) display relatively high levels of acceptance of NCB, but similarly in the Czech Republic, with a low level of church attendance, the acceptance of NCB is also relatively high. In other words, it seems that, in general, in line with expectations, church attendance is not related to the acceptance of NCB at the macro level.

Figure 5.32 Norms of civil behaviour (NCB) and churchgoing (aggregate levels)

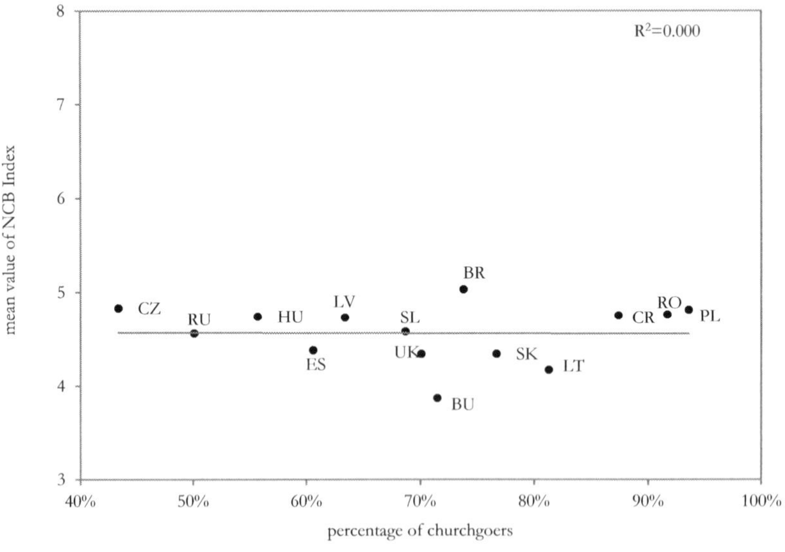

Source: WVS 1999.

In turn, patterns of relations between church attendance and acceptance of NSB are more systematic in Central Eastern Europe, though the level of explained variance is very modest, only 13 percent (Figure 5.33). In most countries a lower percentage of churchgoing is related to a low acceptance of NSB, and with a rise in the level of church attendance, the mean NSB-Index also rises in the observed countries. The two outliers are Belarus and Slovakia. The level of explained variances rises with the withdrawal of both countries from the analysis to a moderate 28 percent. Poland, with one of the highest means of NSB-Index and one of the highest rates of churchgoing, fits the pattern of the majority of countries.

Figure 5.33 Norms of social behaviour (NSB) and churchgoing (aggregate levels)

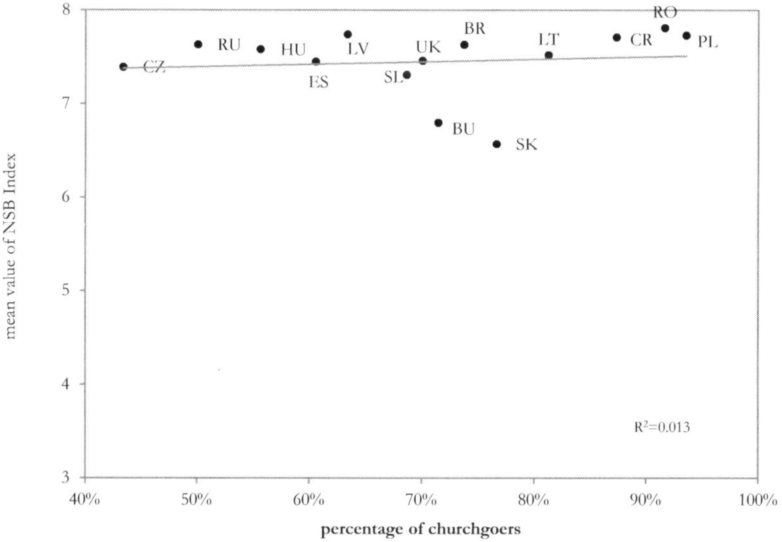

[Scatter plot: x-axis "percentage of churchgoers" from 40% to 100%; y-axis "mean value of NSB Index" from 3 to 8. Points labeled CZ, RU, HU, LV, ES, SL, UK, BR, LT, BU, SK, RO, CR, PL. $R^2=0.013$.]

Source: WVS 1999.

To summarise findings at the aggregate level, the patterns found in Eastern Central Europe only partly conform to expectations. Aggregate levels of churchgoing are positively related to levels of acceptance of NSB, with the exception of two countries (Belarus and Slovakia). As far as the acceptance of civil norms is concerned, there is no relationship with levels of church affiliation, as expected. Poland fits the general trends. It seems that widespread churchgoing is positively related to the high acceptance of social norms. In other words, a high frequency of church attendance could partly explain the high acceptance of social norms in Poland.

5.3.1.3.2 Are churchgoers more likely to accept norms of civil and social behaviour?

Turning to the relationship at the individual level, do we find systematic patterns between church attendance and the acceptance of norms? Churchgoing seems to be positively related to a higher acceptance of NCB, since in most of countries (except

Bulgaria and Ukraine) very frequent churchgoers most often declare their acceptance of NCB (Figure 5.34). However the differences among the means of the NCB-Index between different types of churchgoers are very modest in each society, so we need to analyse these relationships with statistical tests. In Poland very frequent churchgoers tend to support NCB slightly more than less frequent churchgoers and non-attendants, though the differences are minor. It could indicate a positive correlation between churchgoing and support of NCB. Let us explore these relationships with a statistical test.

Figure 5.34 Norms of civil behaviour (NCB) by frequency of churchgoing (mean value of NCB Index by type of churchgoers by country)

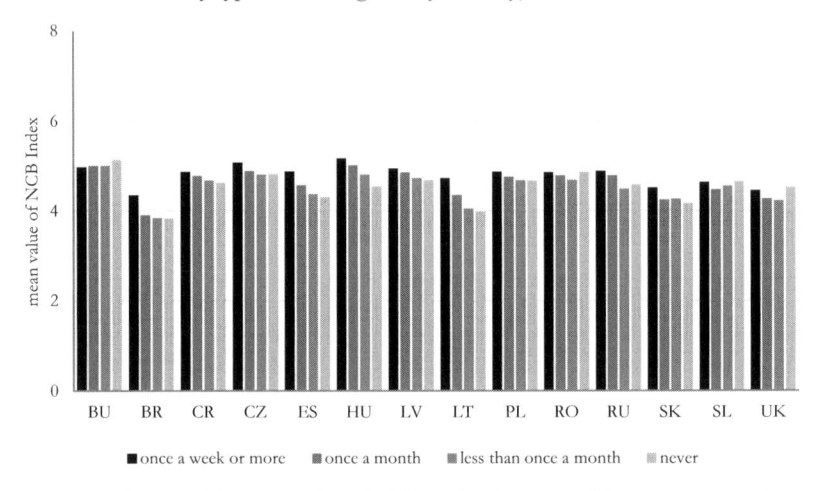

Source: WVS 1999.

Analysis of variances (ANOVA and Kruskal-Wallis test[57]) of means of NCB-Index scores among different types of churchgoers in the pooled sample has a statistically significant result, meaning that the acceptance of NCB varies systematically between different types of churchgoers (Table 5.16). However the analysis of the situation in individual societies turns out to be less satisfactory – the differences are significant in only six of them – the Czech Republic, Estonia, Hungary, Lithuania, Poland and Slovakia (when ANOVA and Kruskal-Wallis tests are used) – while in Croatia, Latvia, Romania, Russia and Ukraine the results of the analysis of variances are not consistent (the tests have contradictory results). Moreover, in Bulgaria, Belarus and

---

[57] Since the NCB-Index is not normally distributed across countries' populations, I calculated both ANOVA and Kruskal-Wallis tests.

Slovenia the differences in NCB means between different types of churchgoing are not statistically significant. In other words, in Central Eastern Europe we partly find the expected positive effects of church affiliation on acceptance of NCB, though this pattern does not seem to be universal in all countries under consideration. In Poland the frequency of churchgoing is significantly related to the acceptance of NCB.

Table 5.16 Analysis of variances of NCB-Index (Kruskal-Wallis tests and ANOVA)

	Pooled sample	BU	BR	CR	CZ	ES	HU	LV	LT	PL	RO	RU	SK	SL	UK
H**	s.	n.s.	n.s.	n.s.	s.	s.	s.	n.s.	s.	s.	s.	s.	s.	n.s.	s.
A***	0.07*	n.s	n.s	0.09*	0.08*	0.09*	0.21*	0.08*	0.20*	0.11*	n.s	n.s	0.14*	n.s.	n.s

Notes: *level of significance p<0.05, **p-values of Kruskal Wallis test, *** ANOVA results. s.- significant, n.s.- not significant; N=15,046.
Source: WVS 1999.

Turning to NSB, we find similar results. Acceptance of NSB does not vary considerably between different types of churchgoers in every country (Figure 5.35). As expected, in most of the societies – 11 out of 14 – very frequent churchgoers show a higher acceptance of social norms (except Bulgaria, Slovenia and Ukraine) than less frequent churchgoers and non-attendants. In Poland very frequent churchgoers also declared a higher acceptance of social norms, so the relationships in Poland fit the general pattern.

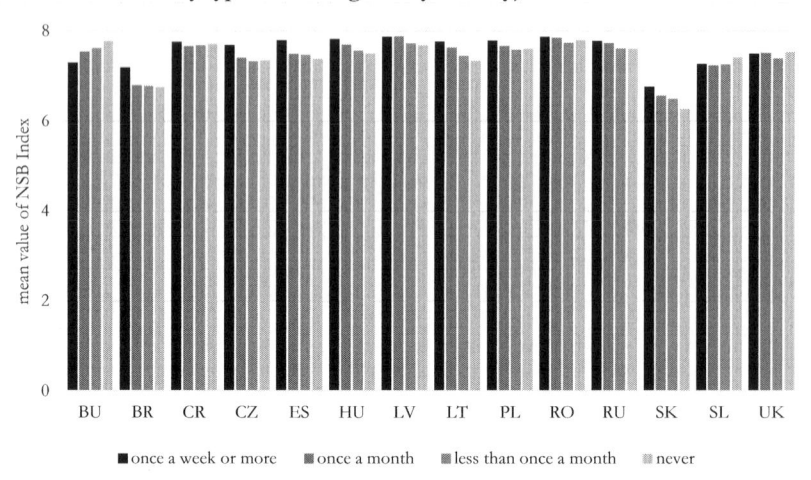

Figure 5.35 Norms of social behaviour (NSB) by frequency of churchgoing (mean value of NSB-Index by type of churchgoers by country)

[Bar chart showing mean value of NSB Index (0 to 8) by country: BU, BR, CR, CZ, ES, HU, LV, LT, PL, RO, RU, SK, SL, UK. Legend: once a week or more, once a month, less than once a month, never.]

Source: WVS 1999.

Statistical analysis of the means confirms the observations (Table 5.17). As expected, differences in variances of NSB between the four types of churchgoers are significant in the pooled sample. Likewise, differences among variances of acceptance of social norms within individual countries are significant except for Belarus, Croatia, Russia and Ukraine. In Poland, church affiliation also matters for acceptance of social norms. So we can explain the relatively high support for social norms in Polish society by the high frequency of church attendance.

Table 5.17 Analysis of variances of NSB-Index (p-values of Kruskal-Wallis test)

	Pooled sample	BU	BR	CR	CZ	ES	HU	LV	LT	PL	RO	RU	SK	SN	UK
H*	s.	s.	n.s.	n.s.	s.	s.	s.	s.	s.	s.	s.	n.s.	s.	s.	n.s.

Notes: * p-values of Kruskal Wallis test: s.-significant, n.s.- not significant; N=16,474.
Source: WVS 1999.

Summing up the micro-level findings presented in this section, churchgoing positively influences the acceptance of civil and social norms, though the effects are not found in every country. In Poland, church attendance matters for the acceptance of social and civil norms. In this regard the patterns found in Polish society follow general trends.

5.3.2 *"Affiliation effects"* – *concluding remarks*

What did we find out about the effects of church attendance on social capital in post-communist societies? Do the results conform to expectations? Is the situation in Poland similar to those in other countries in the region?

In general, many unexpected relationships were found at the aggregate level. In contrast to the findings in the literature, we found weak positive relationships in the post-communist societies between levels of church attendance and two kinds of networks – religious (though only in reference to volunteering) and informal. Also surprising were the positive macro-level relationships between church affiliation and acceptance of social norms. Further unexpected results concern a weak negative relationship between macro-level churchgoing and membership in secular organisations. Other findings – a negative relationship to social trust and no relationship with civil norms – conformed to expectations.

The findings in the micro-level analyses were far less remarkable. In Central Eastern Europe, churchgoing is a relevant source of social capital at the individual level in some respects. We found a positive relationship between church attendance and social networks (though only religious networks), and norms and values. In contrast for social trust, secular networks and informal networks, church affiliation was not related to individual church attendance, as expected.

Are there differences in patterns of relations between churchgoing and social capital in Poland compared to other post-communist societies? In general four dissimilarities were discovered. First, the high level of church attendance in Poland seems to be a factor hampering the positive effects of churchgoing on social networks that are found in other post-communist publics – churchgoers in Poland get less involved in social networks than religious people in other countries. Second, the spillover effect (the idea that those who get involved in religious organisations are also more likely to join secular associations) is particularly high in Poland compared to other societies. The third dissimilarity concerns social trust. While in post-communist societies the relationship between social trust and churchgoing at the individual level shows no unique pattern, in Poland it is positive and significant. Finally, the fourth dissimilarity concerns informal networks at the macro level. In other societies, high levels of religious devotion are positively related to informal networks, however not in Poland.

In summary, church affiliation in Poland is a relevant factor for social capital building *but its power is weaker than in other societies*, especially when social networks are concerned. In Poland the mobilising effect of church attendance is weakest for informal networks at the macro level and formal social networks at the individual level. One could say, as Ruiter and de Graaf do, that the mobilising potential of ready-made networks of churchgoers is "saturated" in Poland. Furthermore, although we find a spillover effect of religious engagement in Poland into secular networks, this is a very modest effect at the national level, since the percentage of religiously involved people does not exceed six percent of the population. In other words, high religious devotion weakens the positive "affiliation effects" in Poland.

5.4 The impact of religion on social capital in Poland – conclusions

The main objective of this chapter was to compare the impact of religion on social capital in Poland with that of other countries in the region. It turns out that relationships between religion and social capital are complex, and differ not only in their direction – positive or negative – but also at the macro and micro levels. While at the macro level religious effects point in different directions, findings at the individual level are more consistent. The impact of Catholicism at the micro level is mainly negative, whereas the impact of church affiliation is mostly positive. So, results at the individual level generally conform to the claims in the literature, in contrast to the results at the macro level. At the macro level a negative effect of Catholicism finds empirical confirmation only in social (formal) networks.

Table 5.18 presents an overview of the results of the analyses pursued in this chapter. The effects of Catholicism and affiliation are depicted separately, as are results at the macro and micro levels. For both kinds of religious impacts and both levels, the findings (located in the column labelled "found effects"), are compared to the prior expectations based on the literature (column labelled "expected effects"). Results for Poland are displayed in the third column ("evidence for Poland"), so that dissimilarities in the religious impacts on social capital between Poland and other countries can be easily seen. Dissimilar results found in Polish society are marked by a blue-coloured background.

Table 5.18 Overview of findings concerning "denomination effects" and "affiliation effects" in all countries and in Poland

COMPONENTS OF SOCIAL CAPITAL	MACRO LEVEL			MICRO LEVEL		
	"Denomination effects"					
	expected effects	found effects	evidence for Poland	expected effects	found effects	evidence for Poland
Formal social networks	-	-	-	-	0	0
Informal social networks	-	0	0	-	-	-
Trust	-	0	0	+ & -*	-	0
Norms and values (civil)	0	0	0	0	0	0
Norms and values (social)	0	+	+	0	0	0
	"Affiliation effects"					
	expected effects	found effects	evidence for Poland	expected effects	found effects	evidence for Poland
Formal religious networks	0	0/+**	0/+**	+	+	+
Formal secular networks	0	-/0**	-/0**	0	-	-
Informal social networks	0	+	0	0	0	0
Trust	-	-	-	- & +*	0	+
Norms and values (civil)	0	0	0	- & +*	+	+
Norms and values (social)	0	+	+	- & +*	+	+

Notes: "+" – positive effect, "-" – negative effect, "0" – no effect;
   * both directions of relationship are reported in the literature;
   ** the first sign refers to membership, the second to volunteering

The majority of the findings concerning the relationships between religion and social capital conform to the expectations, though there are quite a few exceptions. The most surprising results concern the "**denomination effects.**" At the macro level, the expected negative relationships between Catholicism and informal networks and trust did not find empirical support. Dominant Catholicism in a society seems to be unrelated to the level of social trust and to informal networks. In contrast the acceptance of social norms was found to be positively influenced by the Catholic tradition, which was unexpected. Another finding that was contrary to expectations was at the individual level: individuals who were more influenced by Catholicism were not more reluctant to join social (formal) networks. This negative influence was found only for trust and informal networks.

The findings concerning **church affiliation** were surprising mostly at the macro level. With the exception of social trust, the level of religious devotion in societies was expected to be unrelated to other components of social capital. The analyses, however, revealed several contradictory relationships. In societies with a high percentage of churchgoers there was more voluntary engagement in religious networks, more informal networks, and a higher level of acceptance of social norms. Another unexpected finding concerns the lower level of secular membership in religiously devout societies. Turning to the micro level, the findings are much less surprising. Churchgoers were more reluctant to join secular organisations. In contrast, the expected relationships between attending church and trust were absent.

What can we say about the religious impact in Poland? Is it similar to other societies, or did we find dissimilarities in religious influence that were specific to Poland? In general, both kinds of religious influences – cultural and structural – seem to be similar in Poland, with three exceptions. First, religious devotion is generally positive for informal networks, however not in Poland. Second, in Poland stronger individual conservatism, rooted in the Catholic tradition, does not seem to have a negative effect on trust, as in other societies. Third, churchgoers in Poland are more trusting, which is not the general pattern among churchgoers in other societies.

Does it matter for social capital building that Polish society is especially religiously devoted? In general, the high level of religious devotion in Poland makes the religious impact weaker. While churchgoers in Poland, as in other societies, tend to be more engaged socially, this effect is weaker in Poland. Another difference is the relatively high spillover effect of religious engagement into secular engagement.

Returning to the question concerning the "resulting effects" of Catholicism on social capital: can we assess whether the impact of religion is positive or negative in Poland? To what extent can religion be an explanatory factor for the low endowment with social capital in Poland? It depends on the component of social capital that is considered. The cultural impacts of Catholicism on social networks are mostly negative, while the effects of churchgoing are mostly positive, though weaker than in other societies (at the individual level). So in the case of social networks we can say that *the resulting effect of religion might be negative, or at least less positive compared to other societies*. As far as trust is concerned, only church affiliation seemed to be related to trust – negatively at the aggregate level, and positive at the individual level. So in the case of trust, we can conclude that *Polish society is not as trusting due in part to its high level of religious devotion*. As far as norms and values are concerned, the impact of religion on the acceptance of norms is definitely positive, which means that we can partly explain the high acceptance of norms in Poland by its high levels of religious devotion.

With this chapter the comparison of conditions for social capital building between Polish and other societies is accomplished. In the following chapter I turn to the comparative analysis of the mechanisms of social capital building between Poland and other societies.

6 Is social capital building different in Poland?

6.1 Introduction

Studying dissimilarities in the mechanisms of social capital building in Poland compared to other countries is the main objective of this chapter. The investigation of conditions that are crucial for social capital, pursued in chapters 3 and 5, revealed a number of dissimilarities between Poland and other post-communist, Catholic countries. While a couple of aspects are related to (1) the communist legacy or (2) the systemic transition and its consequences such as income inequalities or disillusionment, other factors have their source in (3) Catholicism as a tradition that influences value orientations in strong religiously devoted Polish people.

So far we have explored the influence of single factors on social capital building in Poland. This chapter goes one step further and investigates the impact of the relevant aspects using multivariate models, allowing the exploration of relative powers and directions of single factors in relation to each other. This approach helps understand the characteristics of social capital building in Poland. It might be that not only the conditions, but also the mechanisms of its accumulation, differ in the case of Poland. In this chapter we focus on relationships at the individual level. The first section explains the research methods used and provides technical information on operationalisations of key factors; the second section compares the mechanisms of social capital building in Poland using multivariate regression analyses.

6.2 A comprehensive picture of social capital building in Poland

Before analysing which factors matter for the individual level of social capital in Poland, we first need to address some technical questions: which reference group of societies should be used, how should the variables be operationalised, which independent variables should be included in the models, and how should the research be designed?

6.2.1 Reference group

A group of countries is needed to serve as a reference for Poland when analysing social capital building: those related to the communist legacy and the systemic transition and those associated with religion. To assess the impact of Catholicism in Poland, other countries shaped by this tradition need to be considered on a comparative basis, while evaluating the relevance of the communist legacy requires including prior communist countries in the analyses. Two possible combinations of countries meet these requirements: either all European Catholic countries (post-communist and non post-communist) or all post-communist countries (irrespective of denomination). Since the second option includes non-Catholic countries, RRC – meant as a measure of Catholic influence – would not apply to some of the sample. As shown in chapter 5, Catholicism matters not only as a context variable but, as in the case of informal networks, is also relevant as an individual factor. Therefore incorporating uniquely Catholic countries in the sample allows an assessment of the impact of Catholicism in Poland in reference to societies influenced by the same denomination. The inclusion of societies with and without prior experience of communism allows us to study possible combined influences of Catholicism and post-communism on the one hand, and Catholicism and lack of communist legacy on the other. Thus in this chapter the reference for Poland is the group of European Catholic countries with and without prior communist experience.

6.2.2 Explaining social capital

6.2.2.1 Communist legacy

Communist legacy refers to a number of societal features that are consequences of prior communist experiences. On the one hand, several similar societal patterns of attitudes and behaviours such as a distrust syndrome, persistence of informal networks, "*homo sovieticus*" phenomenon, etc. were found across prior communist societies (for details see Table 3.2, chapter 3). They are claimed to be generally detrimental to social capital building. On the other hand, as discussed in section 3.3, communist regimes differed in some respects. In Poland we found substantial differences, such as a somewhat higher degree of pluralism and autonomy that was tolerated by the authorities, protest actions steadily challenging the system and the supportive and relatively independent role of the Catholic Church. Whether these differences, in particular the anti-systemic character of the opposition activities (see section 3.4), left an imprint on the propensity to build social capital in Poland is an empirical question addressed in this chapter.

In the following empirical investigation the similarities in attitudes and behaviours between citizenries in post-communist societies resulting from prior communist experiences are captured by the dummy variable "**post-communism**" at the macro level, which has a value of "1" if an individual lives in a post-communist country and "0" for others. Likewise, the dummy variable "**Poland**" ("1" for a person living in Poland and "0" for others) captures the specific impact of the communist legacy in Poland. According to the argument presented in chapter 3, a negative impact of prior communist system experience on all components of social capital is expected (with the exception of informal ties). These mechanisms should also apply to the Polish public; the anti-systemic character of oppositional activity in Poland may have resulted in a stronger reluctance to join diverse organisations after the collapse of communism.

6.2.2.2 Systemic transition

The difficult times during systemic transitions – deteriorating living conditions, rising prices, numerous bankruptcies related to unemployment, political instability and so on – that followed the collapse of communism are usually claimed as further reasons for the low stock of social capital in post-communist societies. Since some post-communist conditions in Poland deviate from those in other societies, their impact on social capital needs to be examined separately. In section 3.5.2 three conditions were disentangled, in which the systemic transition in Poland seems to have been more difficult compared to other countries in the region.

The first dissimilarity is the particularly soaring social costs of the economic transformation, and a deepening gap between rich and poor in Poland (see sections 3.5.2.2 and 3.5.2.4). The level of income inequalities can be measured by the GINI coefficient for income inequality[58] for each country; the value of the GINI coefficient for each country is included in the analyses as the context variable "**income inequality**." As argued in chapter 3, it is expected that individuals from countries with higher income inequalities are less likely to trust and more reluctant to get socially engaged.

Second, we turn to individual features as possible determinants of social capital. Many authors stress a widespread disappointment within post-communist societies concerning the political and economic situation after the collapse of communism as a reason for lacking social engagement: "people who are disappointed are less likely to participate in voluntary organisations, and their disenchantment or frustration will be associated with increased passivity and withdrawal" (Howard 2003, 109; see also Dalton/Klingemann 2007, 16). Disappointment may concern

---

[58] Source: the World Bank, for details see section 3.5.2.2.

the material conditions of living and especially a deepening gap between rich and poor during the transition period, since the value of equality becomes particularly relevant in the advanced phase of transformation (Koralewicz/Ziółkowski 2007, 214-223; Wnuk-Lipiński/Fuchs 2005, 54-60; for details see section 3.5.2.1). Again, it seems that Poles are more disappointed than people from other countries (section 3.5.2.4), so we need to analyse whether disappointment hampers the production of social capital.

The operationalisation of **disappointment** is difficult with the WVS, because there is no question that refers directly to the subjective assessment of one's general situation after the collapse of communism. Hence, we need to compensate this omission by including a more general question, which concerns a general subjective state of happiness or unhappiness. The question is worded as follows:

"Taking all things together, would you say you are..."
"very happy,"
"quite happy,"
"not very happy,"
"not at all happy."

Items were scaled from 1 to 4, whereby the first option has a value of "1" and the last "4." The second question refers to concerns about the material situation of the family:

"To what extent do you feel concerned about the living conditions of your immediate family?"

The answers are scaled from "very much" ("1") to "not at all" ("5"). Neither item refers to the actual material situation of the respondent, but rather a subjective evaluation of actual conditions, which is what we need, because disappointment is basically a subjective assessment of one's situation (the "objective" measure of economic status of respondents — income level — is also considered: see section 6.2.3.4).

In chapter 3 we discussed the relevance of disappointment for social capital. The WVS data allow us to compare the disappointment in Poland to that of citizens in other countries, and we saw that in Poland dissatisfaction was reported to be larger than in other post-communist societies. Are people in Central Eastern Europe unhappier than those in Western Europe? Can we say on the basis of the two WVS questions that Poles are more disappointed than other Central Eastern Europeans? The subjective state of unhappiness between countries is demonstrated in Figure 6.1. In general Westerners indeed appear to be less unhappy than their Eastern counterparts. The weighted average percentage of "not very happy" responses is twice as high in the group of Eastern societies (about 19 percent) compared to that of Western societies (9 percent); "not at all happy" responses were 3.4 percent and 1.6 percent in Eastern and Western Europe, respectively. People in Poland are, as expected, among the unhappiest in the region. In Poland 4.7 percent of people declared being "not at all happy," and 21 percent reported they were "not very happy," which ranks Poland as the third unhappiest country after Hungary (5.8 and 22 percent, respectively) and Slovakia (4.8 and 25 percent, respectively).

Figure 6.1 Subjective state of unhappiness (percentage of people reporting being "not very happy" or "not at all happy")

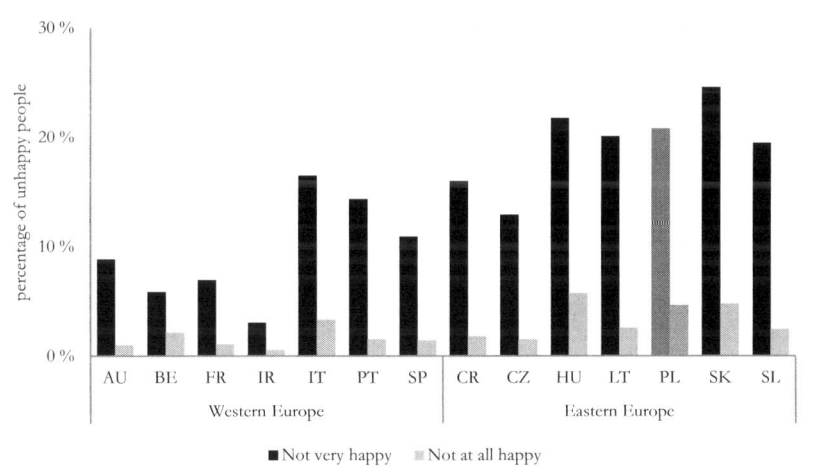

■ Not very happy   ■ Not at all happy

Source: WVS 1999.

Concern about the family (Figure 6.2) seems to be less related to the consequences of the systemic transition. On average, Westerners are slightly more concerned about family than Easterners: 64 vs. 59 percent are "very much concerned," 22 vs. 21 percent are "much concerned" and 32 vs. 31 percent are "to a certain extent concerned." The picture in Poland does not correspond to expectations: 72 percent of the Polish people declared they were "very much concerned" about family. This places Polish society in the fifth position out of 14 countries, after Hungary (88 percent), Lithuania (81 percent), Belgium (76 percent) and Portugal (76 percent). These statistics show that discontent among Poles might be indeed rather high, though it is not the highest of the societies considered. Besides, the relatively high rankings of Belgium and Portugal indicate that much concern about the family is also reported by people in societies that are not undergoing systemic transitions. Still, concern about the family reflects an individual's subjective evaluation of the well-being of himself/herself and his/her family, so it can be an explanatory factor of low social engagement in countries undergoing transition, including Poland. Therefore the disappointment resulting from the systemic transition is measured by both items in further analyses,[59] whereby negative effects of both variables on the propensity to build social capital are expected.

Figure 6.2 Concern about the living conditions of the immediate family (percentage of people being "very much," "much," or "to a certain extent" concerned)

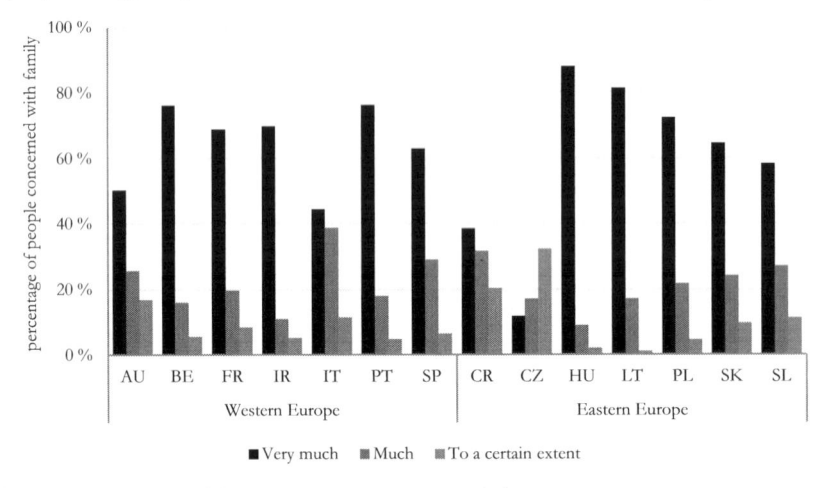

Source: WVS 1999.

The third condition, in which Poland apparently differs from other post-communist countries, is the **high level of protest activity** (Ekiert/Kubik 1999, 112; for details see section 3.5.2.5), which could also be negatively related to low organisational engagement (Dekker et al. 1997, 229; for details see section 3.5.2.5). The WVS contains a battery of questions referring to unconventional political participation, and three items concern attending different protest activities: (1) occupying buildings or factories, (2) attending lawful demonstrations, and (3) joining unofficial strikes. Are Poles indeed more "rebellious" than other societies, as Ekiert and Kubik claim? Figure 6.3 depicts the levels of these three types of protest activities across societies. In general, lawful demonstrations are the most popular form of protest activity (in the pooled sample, 23 percent of respondents declared having taken part in this form of protest), joining strikes was the second most popular (6 percent of respondents), and the least popular was occupying buildings or factories (3.3 percent). Polish respondents reportedly occupied buildings or factories more than other post-communist citizens, though the level remains very low – only 3 percent of Polish respondents declared taking part in these activities. Among Western societies, en-

---

[59] Missing values are dropped from the analyses.

gagement in such activities is higher in Belgium, France and Italy (6, 9, and 8 percent, respectively). As far attending demonstrations is considered, Poland ranks in one of the lowest position of all countries studied (8.8 percent), while France and Belgium take the lead (39 percent) and Italy is second (35 percent). Among East European countries, taking part in a demonstration is lower than in Poland only in Croatia and Hungary (7.7 and 4.9 percent, respectively). Taking part in strikes is more popular in Poland than in all other post-communist societies (4.6 percent) except the Czech Republic, where 10.4 percent of respondents declared taking part in this form of protest activity. A higher percentage of respondents reported taking part in strikes in France, Belgium, Spain, Ireland and Italy than in Poland.

Figure 6.3 Taking part in protest activities (percentage of people attending a protest action)

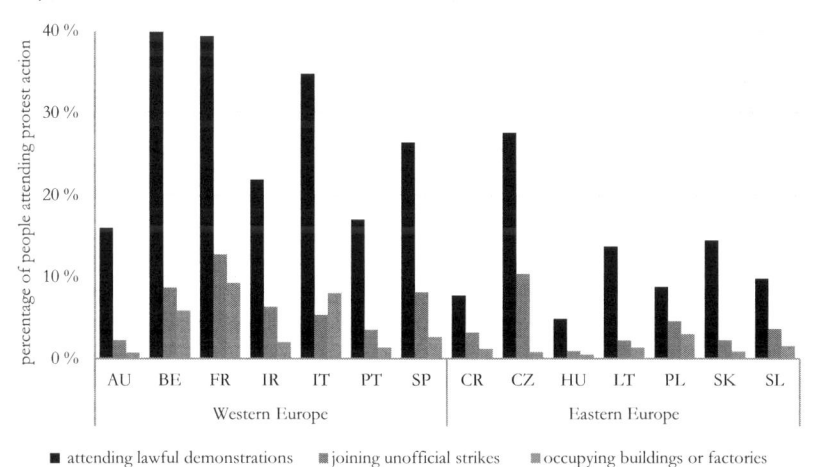

■ attending lawful demonstrations   ■ joining unofficial strikes   ■ occupying buildings or factories

Source: WVS 1999.

In summary, participation in occupying buildings and strikes is relatively higher in Poland compared to other societies. In contrast, taking part in demonstrations is at one of the lowest levels in Europe. This finding does not support the claim of Ekiert and Kubik about the "rebellious" nature of Polish society. However, their study is based on press reports and measures the number of protest actions from 1989-1993, rather than the level of participation. Despite the differences in the evidence found, I include the three items concerning protest actions in the analyses. All three items are dummy variables; a value of "1" was assigned to respondents who declared participation in a protest action and "0" to those who did not.[60]

6.2.2.3 Catholicism

Religion apparently matters for social capital. As discussed and examined in chapter 5, we are examining two kinds of religious influences on social capital. First, religion matters for social capital as a structural component of society: the role of churches and church affiliation in social capital building is in general positive, though mostly at the individual level. Second, Catholicism, through its emphasis on value orientations, affects social networks and trust in a negative way (for details see Table 5.16). By implication, when analysing the determinants of social capital we need to include **church attendance** and **RRC** as two variables in this examination.

The operalionalisation of "church attendance" is presented in section 5.3.1.1.1. I expect positive effects of affiliation on all components of social capital except formal secular networks and informal networks (see Table 5.16). In Poland, the influence of churchgoing on engagement in formal networks could be weaker due to the high level of religious devotion, which seems to hamper the positive effects of churchgoing (see section 5.3.1).

The RRC-Index (RRCI) is constructed in section 5.2.1; it is a continuous variable with a value from 0-1. Two problems should be addressed before including this variable in the regression analyses: its asymmetrical distribution within individual societies and the high percentage of missing values in some countries.[61]

First, the distribution differs considerably from country to country (see Table 6.1). In most of the countries, with exception of the Czech Republic, the distribution of RRCI is asymmetrical and skewed to the right, while in Poland the skewness is exceptionally strong. In Poland both the mean value and the median are the highest of all the countries studied. In addition the kurtosis of the distribution is exceptionally high, meaning that the distribution has a much wider tail when compared to other countries. These cross-national discrepancies in the distribution of the RRCI might have important consequences for the results when we only compare the absolute levels of individual conservatism, without considering distributions within individual societies. For instance, a person with a score close to 0.6 would belong to

---

[60] Missing values are dropped from the analyses.
[61] This problem was not discussed in chapter 5, since we analysed only bivariate relations between RRC and components of social capital, so that the number of missing cases was not impeding validity of the results. The differences in the distributions of RRC across countries were irrelevant, since we analysed the relative individual levels RRC in each society (the quartile of the most and the least conservative people in each society). In case of regression analyses, which are pursued in the pooled sample, the problem of missing values and asymmetrical distributions need to be addressed.

the minority of the population in a conservative country, like Poland or Portugal – so this individual would be less conservative than the majority of his counterparts. In contrast, a person with the same score would be close to the average in a non-conservative country, such as the Czech Republic or Slovenia.

Table 6.1 Characteristics of the country distributions of the Religiously Rooted Conservatism Index

	mean	median	skewness	kurtosis	N
Austria	0.73	0.75	-0.53	-0.19	1,279
Belgium	0.72	0.74	-0.59	-0.15	1,611
France	0.68	0.69	-0.39	-0.42	1,275
Ireland	0.81	0.82	-0.78	0.52	867
Italy	0.80	0.82	-0.92	0.85	1,713
Portugal	0.82	0.84	-0.78	1.05	847
Spain	0.73	0.76	-0.74	0.13	936
Croatia	0.72	0.75	-0.75	-0.83	884
Czech Republic	0.64	0.63	0.20	-0.57	1,466
Hungary	0.76	0.79	-0.67	0.06	837
Lithuania	0.80	0.82	-0.83	0.61	621
Poland	**0.86**	**0.89**	**-1.72**	**1.92**	**924**
Slovakia	0.76	0.78	-0.62	-0.20	1,025
Slovenia	0.67	0.69	-0.31	-0.48	831
Pooled sample	0.74	0.77	-0.62	-0.11	15,116

Source: WVS 1999.

So should we consider the *relative level of conservatism* for further analyses, in order to avoid caveats related to substantial differences in RRC distribution across societies? To address this problem I examine the correlations between the *absolute* RRCI and *relative* individual measures of conservatism within each society. Each society is divided into four groups, each of which covers one-quarter of the respondents (quartiles). In this way we can distinguish how conservative a respondent is *in relation to his compatriots*. We want to know whether this *relative measure of conservatism* (rank within a society) would bring other results in the cross-national analysis than the *absolute measure of conservatism* (RRCI). The results of Pearson's correlation test show that despite the fact that RRCI is asymmetrically distributed within some societies, its absolute measure (RRCI) and the relative measure are highly correlated (r over 0.9, p<0.01). This means that the RRCI brings results that are highly comparable to the relative measures of RRC. For the sake of simplicity, only the absolute measure of conservatism (RRCI) is used in the further analyses.

The second problem is the large number of missing RRCI values that resulted from dropping the missing values of the items included in the course of factor analysis. The percentage of valid scores between countries ranges from a very modest level of 39 percent, in the case of Spain, to over 80 percent in most of the other countries; in Poland 84 percent of the scores in the dataset were valid. Since the amount of missing scores is large (much higher than 5 percent), dropping the missing cases in the analysis of determinants for social capital is not recommended. In order to avoid a bias in results due to insufficient case numbers, the missing data is replaced by the mean value of RRCI for each country. When presenting the results of regression analyses in the following sections of this chapter, both coefficients and odds ratios are considered: for RRCI with and without the replaced missing values.

Principally, I expect the individual level of conservatism to be negatively related to informal networks and to trust, as the results from the bivariate analysis presented in chapter 5 show (see Table 5.18). Otherwise RRC should not be related to formal networks, or the acceptance of NCB and NSB. In Poland I expect a negative effect only on informal ties.

6.2.2.4   Socio-economic demographic determinants

A large body of studies on social participation and social capital provides empirical evidence of several individual features that are positively related to the propensity to get socially involved. In general, people with a high **socio-economic status** are more engaged in social activities (Almond/Verba 1963, 383 ff.; Verba et al. 1995, 281; Gabriel et al. 2002, 98-99) and more trusting (Gabriel et al. 2002, 123; Welch et al. 2004, 331; Newton 1999, 181). Therefore two variables measuring socio-economic status – level of education and income – are introduced to the analyses. The level of education is standardised in the WVS across countries; the variable has values of "1" for elementary level to "8" for a university degree. Income is standardised too, and assigned values from "1" for the lowest relative country income to "10" for the relative highest income. Data concerning income are missing in a number of cases (the percentage of valid cases varies between countries from 70 percent in Slovakia to 98 percent in Poland; unfortunately for Portugal all cases are missing). In order to keep the highest number of cases in the analysis, the missing values are replaced by the mean value for each considered country. For individuals in Portugal I introduced an average income from the pooled sample,[62] therefore the results are probably overestimated. I expect a positive influence of socio-economic status indicators on social formal networks and social trust. Additionally, education should be positively correlated with the propensity to approve NSB (Gabriel et al. 2002, 104).

Furthermore, we know from other studies that men are more engaged than women in general (Gabriel et al. 2002, 98) and that age has a curvilinear relation to social engagement; the most engaged are middle-aged individuals, while younger and older people are principally less ready to get involved (Gabriel et al. 2002, 98-99). Therefore both age and gender are introduced into the analysis: age is operationalised by the item "age"[63] (continuous variable) in the WVS; and gender is a dichotomised variable ("1" for men and "2" for women). Except for the expectations related to participation mentioned above, age should also be positively correlated with the approval of NSB (Gabriel et al. 2002, 104).

6.3 Research strategy

A set of six models is calculated for each of the single components of social capital as dependent variables – social networks, trust, norms and values – that are operationalised as described above. These sets of six models start with the simplest model, which includes only two determinants related to religion and the post-communist legacy. In five steps the models are expanded with an additional set of explanatory variables. Model 6 contains all determinants of social capital and dummy variables for all considered countries. Since we have dichotomised dependent variables, logistic regression models are applied. For the continuous dependent variables – NCB and NSB – linear regression analyses are pursued.

In the first model (**Model 1**), three independent variables of special interest are considered in the pooled sample: both religious factors (RRC and church attendance) and post-communism as a contextual factor. This allows the assessment of the explanatory power of conservatism, church affiliation and prior communist experience on social capital in relation to each other.

---

[62] Portugal is the least developed country in Western Europe (GDP per capita in 2008 reached 73 percent of the average level of the EU-27, source: http://epp.eurostat.ec.europa.eu), therefore the average individual income in this country is likely lower than the EU average.

[63] In the case of the curvilinear relationship, in addition to the variable "age" we should also introduce the variable "age squared" to the analysis. An analysis of bivariate relations between my dependent variables and age shows, however, that we are dealing with linear relationships: positive in the case of membership and volunteering in at least one organisation, and in the case of membership and volunteering in religious organisations. Besides, there is no relationship to secular membership and volunteering. Therefore the variable age squared is not included in the models.

In the next step (**Model 2**), the predictive impact of religious influence and prior communist experiences is controlled for socio-demographic factors: education, income, age and gender. As mentioned earlier, socio-economic status is a common micro-level explanatory factor for the level of social capital, and social engagement in particular.

Model 3 provides information about the impact of the consequences of systemic transitions on social capital building. Disappointment caused by the change in political system is claimed to be an important reason for poor levels of social engagement in post-communist societies. Model 3, in addition to all variables included in Model 2, contains objective and subjective variables related to systemic changes. The objective variable is a context variable: the GINI coefficient of income inequality reflecting countries' levels of income disparities. Two further variables concerning individual subjective well-being, such as state of happiness and concern about the immediate family, are included in Model 3 in order to assess the impact of individual subjective disappointment. Essentially, I expect all three variables to have a negative influence on social capital. They should also diminish the predictive power of the "post-communism" variable, if disappointment is indeed the consequence of the troubles caused by systemic transformation.

Protest actions are claimed to be characteristic of the Polish mode of participation in social and political life; this is why three dummy variables concerning attendance of various types of protest actions are added to **Model 4**, together with all other variables previously considered in the models. All three variables are expected to be negatively associated with formal social networks. Furthermore, protest actions could be especially relevant for explaining the low engagement in formal networks in Poland.

The difference between **Model 5** and the previous one consists of the introduction of Poland as a dummy variable. This allows an assessment of the extent to which Poland is a relevant context for the individual level of social capital. Regression analyses will provide evidence of the importance of the specific Polish characteristics in addition to those considered up to this point – religious factors, the communist experience, individual socio-demographic features, disappointment and protest actions.

Model 6 is a modification of Model 5. Instead of a dummy for Poland, dummies for all other countries are introduced to the analysis, while Poland remains a reference country with a value of "0." Two context variables – GINI coefficient for income inequality and post-communism – are excluded from the model in order to avoid colinearity problems. The goal of Model 6 is to control the impact of the independent variables against the probably high predictive power of the national contexts. As commonly claimed, a large part of the differences in social capital between societies depends on the specific countries' characteristics, so a considerable rise in explained variance of the dependent variables is expected in this case.

6.4 Exploring determinants of Polish social capital

6.4.1 Social networks

The question of why certain people are involved in social networks and some are not, and especially why Polish people are more reluctant to join both formal and informal types of networks compared to other societies, was partly answered in the previous chapters of this study. This section finally gathers all factors that seem to be important for social engagement in Poland and compares them to each other, with other Catholic societies (both with and without prior communist experience) as a background. First, membership and volunteering are analysed irrespective of the type of organisation. In the second step the examination is more specific and concerns church-related groups and secular organisations separately. Finally an inquiry of informal ties follows.

6.4.1.1   Formal networks

Let us begin with the analysis of membership in formal networks. Results of logistic regression analyses with membership as a dependent variable are depicted in Table 6.2 and with volunteering in the Table 6.3.

Table 6.2 Logistic regression analyses of membership in at least one organisation (odds ratio Exp (B), R2 Nagelkerke, and N, unweighted)

Independent variables	Model 1	Model 2	Model 3	Model 4	Model 5	Model 6
	Exp (B)	Exp (B)	Exp (B)	Exp (B)	Exp (B)	Exp (B)
RELIGIOUS FACTORS						
Conservatism (RRCI)	0.353***	0.668**	1.135	1.400**	1.537***	2.099***
Conservatism (missing values replaced)[a]	0.309***	0.566***	1.056	1.318*	1.470*	2.112***
Church attendance (1-never; 4-once a week)	1.084***	1.069***	0.993	0.995	0.991	1.038
POST-COMMUNIST LEGACY						
Post-communism (dummy)	0.863***	0.862***	0.804***	0.879**	0.935	-
SOCIO-DEMOGRAPHIC FEATURES						
Education (1-elementary; 8-university degree)		1.163***	1.163***	1.146***	1.147***	1.196***
Income (1-lowest; 10-highest)		1.108***	1.091***	1.090***	1.088***	1.057***
Age		1.006***	1.005***	1.005***	1.005***	1.003**
Gender (1-male; 2-female)		0.719***	0.701***	0.731***	0.729***	0.706***
SYSTEMIC TRANSITION						
Income inequality (GINI)			0.896***	0.895***	0.900***	-
Happiness (1-happy; 4-not happy)			0.852***	0.847***	0.846***	0.903**
Concerned (1-very; 4-not at all)			1.067**	1.061**	1.056**	1.004
PROTEST ACTIONS						
Demonstrations (1-yes; 0-no)				1.562***	1.565***	1.605***
Strikes (1-yes; 0-no)				1.257*	1.265*	1.195
Occupying buildings (1-yes; 0-no)				1.091	1.106	1.301*
COUNTRY DUMMIES						
Poland					0.677***	Ref.
Austria						6.260***
Belgium						4.116***
France						1.700***
Ireland						3.583***
Italy						1.669***
Portugal						1.115
Spain						1.286*
Croatia						1.786***
Czech Rep.						4.873***
Hungary						1.394**
Lithuania						0.467***
Slovakia						5.720***
Slovenia						3.433***
N	13,188	13,188	13,188	13,188	13,188	13,188
N[a]	15,683	15,683	15,683	15,683	15,683	15,683
Nagelkerke R²	0.013	0.076	0.134	0.145	0.147	0.198
Nagelkerke R²[a]	0.015	0.073	0.133	0.145	0.147	0.197

Notes: Significance levels: *p<0.05, **p<0.01, *** p<0.001
[a] results of logistic regression pursued using the same models with a modification concerning the independent variable "conservatism", which is replaced by "conservatism with replaced missing values by countries' means. In this case the number of cases included in the analysis is higher.
Source: WVS 1999.

Analysis of the odds ratios displayed in Table 6.2 gives us information about how single determinants can explain membership in Catholic European countries with and without prior communist experience. In the last row we can follow the changes in Nagelkerke R^2, which measures the level of explained variance. Explanation of the variance in membership rises stepwise with the introduction of the new variables into the models but remains low (about 20 percent) in Model 6.

Turning to the examination of coefficients, the findings generally conform to expectations, though there are a number of surprising results concerning the predictive power and direction of single independent variables. First, **conservatism** has unexpected effects. A rise in individual conservatism diminishes the likelihood of being a member in an organisation, though this evidence was found only in the first two models. After considering the consequences of systemic transition (Model 3), individual conservatism was irrelevant for predicting membership, as expected. Surprisingly, in the last three models, when protest actions and countries' contextual effects are controlled for, an increase in individual conservatism raises the likelihood of being a member. These mechanisms seem to be similar in Poland and in other countries, since the use of a dummy variable for Poland does not cause substantial changes in the odds ratios of conservatism. The unexpected positive effects of conservatism might be related to the fact that the membership analysed here concerns all types of organisations. Whether the same predictors matter for religious and secular types of organisations is examined in the next section.

A positive predictive impact of **church attendance** occurs only in the two first models (i.e., without control for individual socio-demographic features). Churchgoing ceases to be a significant predictor of membership when factors related to the consequences of systemic transition, protest activity and countries' dummies are included in the model. A plausible explanation, based on the previous bivariate analysis, would be that churchgoing only increases the probability of membership in religious organisations, and not in secular ones. In the next section we explore whether church attendance has a different predictive effect depending on the type of organisation.

Prior **communist experience** seems to be a significant predictor of not being a member, as expected, and – despite the inclusion of individual socio-demographic features, disappointment and protest actions – the predictive power of post-communism remains robust. Yet after the introduction of Poland as a dummy variable to the analysis, communist experience became insignificant. This finding can be interpreted as evidence of an exceptional situation in Poland, meaning that the Polish specific context takes precedence over the predictive power of prior communist experience. In other words, the predictive power of post-communism seen in the first four models actually indicates the relevance of the Polish context.

All variables related to the **systemic transition** are, as expected, significant in predicting the probability of membership. In countries with higher income disparities there is less chance of being a member and subjective happiness increases the probability of membership; in contrast, concern about the living conditions of the immediate family shows the opposite effect. Furthermore, with the introduction of variables related to systemic transition we can observe a minor increase in explained variance and a slight decrease in the level of odds ratio related to post-communism, as expected. This suggests that disappointment and subjective well-being are partly influenced by systemic transitions, but also partly depend on the subjective perception of the situation by individuals in Western countries. Nonetheless, the predictive power of income inequalities and happiness is significant and robust when controlled for other variables. In the case of concern about the immediate family, its significance disappears when countries' specific contexts are controlled for.

As far as individual **socio-demographic** features are concerned, the effects corroborate expectations and are robust in all models – male gender and both socio-economic variables raise the likelihood of being a member. The effects of age are negative – the likelihood of being a member is slightly lower among younger people. Moreover, the inclusion of socio-demographic variables diminishes the predictive power of the factors that were previously included in the model, as expected – especially in regard to conservatism. Surprisingly, attending two forms of **protest actions** – demonstrations and strikes – raises the probability of membership; in contrast, occupying buildings remains insignificant for predicting membership.

Finally, the odds ratio for **Poland** as a dummy variable receives a value less than 1 and is significant, as expected, meaning that being Polish diminishes a respondent's chance of belonging to an organisation. In addition to overtaking the predictive power of prior communist experience, the Polish context does not influence the impact of other factors considerably. The effects of countries' dummies are significant with the exception of Portugal, and in most cases the country's context raises the probability of membership (except for Lithuania), compared to Poland. This finding underlines the unique position of Poland, the context of which decreases chances of membership. Moreover, in the case of Lithuania the odds ratio is less than 1, which means that in Lithuania (as in Poland) there are specific conditions that decrease the chances of membership. The high predictive power of the countries' specific context corroborates the expectations, and it is important that, despite the high predictive power of countries' context, the impact of factors such as conservatism, subjective well-being and attending demonstrations remains significant for the prediction of membership.

Table 6.3 Logistic regression analysis of volunteering in at least one organisation, excluding Slovakia (odds ratio Exp (B), R2 Nagelkerke, and N, unweighted)

Independent variables	Model 1	Model 2	Model 3	Model 4	Model 5	Model 6
	Exp (B)	Exp (B)	Exp (B)	Exp (B)	Exp (B)	Exp (B)
RELIGIOUS FACTORS						
Conservatism (RRCI)	0.560***	1.140	1.435**	1.881***	2.075***	2.852***
Conservatism (missing values replaced)[a]	0.504***	0.964	1.290	1.675***	1.872***	2.707***
Church attendance (1-never; 4-once a week)	1.047*	1.029	1.004	1.006	1.003	1.038
POST-COMMUNIST LEGACY						
Post-communism (dummy)	0.793***	0.787***	0.802***	0.896*	0.962	-
SOCIO-DEMOGRAPHIC FEATURES						
Education (1-elementary; 8-university degree)		1.181***	1.179***	1.159***	1.159***	1.184***
Income (1-lowest; 10-highest)		1.074***	1.060***	1.058***	1.057***	1.044***
Age		1.1004**	1.1004**	1.1004**	1.1004**	1.1002
Gender (1-male; 2-female)		0.702***	0.699***	0.735***	0.799***	0.724***
SYSTEMIC TRANSITION						
Income inequality (GINI)			0.957***	0.956***	0.960***	-
Happiness (1-happy; 4-not happy)			0.807***	0.799***	0.799***	0.843***
Concerned (1-very; 4-not at all)			1.059*	1.052*	1.043	0.974
PROTEST ACTIONS						
Demonstrations (1-yes; 0-no)				1.609***	1.613***	1.583***
Strikes (1-yes; 0-no)				1.275**	1.279**	1.222*
Occupying buildings (1-yes; 0-no)				1.240	1.260	1.351**
COUNTRY DUMMIES						
Poland					0.644***	Ref.
Austria						2.753***
Belgium						2.348***
France						2.056***
Ireland						2.523***
Italy						1.694***
Portugal						1.171
Spain						1.377*
Croatia						1.574**
Czech Rep.						3.312***
Hungary						1.201
Lithuania						0.855
Slovakia						2.794***
Slovenia						2.753***
N	12,400	12,400	12,400	12,400	12,400	12,400
N[a]	14,694	14,694	14,694	14,694	14,694	14,694
Nagelkerke R²	0.007	0.061	0.076	0.090	0.092	0.110
Nagelkerke R²[a]	0.007	0.057	0.074	0.087	0.089	0.106

Notes: Significance levels: *p<0.05, **p<0.01, *** p<0.001
[a] results of logistic regression pursued with the same models, with a modification concerning the independent variable "conservatism", which is replaced by "conservatism with replaced missing values by countries' means. In this case, the number of cases included in the analysis is higher.
Source: WVS 1999.

Let us turn now to the analysis of volunteering, irrespective of the type of organisation (Table 6.3). As discussed in chapter 2, the data in the WVS concerning volunteering in Slovakia are not quite reliable; therefore Slovaks' answers are excluded from the dataset.

As in previous analyses, the degree of explained variance increases stepwise when new predictors are added to the examination; however, the levels of explained variables remain very low in all models and reach only 11 percent in Model 6.

Similar to membership, most of the findings concerning volunteering conform to expectations, though with several surprising results. First of all, the expected negative impact of **conservatism** appears only in Model 1. With the inclusion of further variables in the model, conservatism actually raises the chance of volunteering. In the last model, conservatism remains a strong predictor, whereby a one-unit increase in the level of individual conservatism increases the chance of being a volunteer by almost three times. The results are similar, though slightly weaker, when considering conservatism with replaced missing values; conservatism with replaced values turns irrelevant only in Model 3, which means that other factors are relevant determinants for volunteering.

A second surprising result is the lack of the expected positive effect of **church attendance**. Churchgoing is significant for predicting volunteering only in the first model; after controlling for other factors, the significance of church affiliation disappears. An explanation for this finding may lie in the dependent variable – with church attendance one could probably only predict volunteering in religious, not secular, organisations. This is why we need to distinguish between the types of organisations.

The experience of **communism** diminishes the chance of volunteering, and the significance of the communist legacy disappears with introduction of a dummy for Poland into the analyses. This means that, as in the case of volunteering, the negative effect of prior communist experience indicates the importance of the specific Polish context. **Socio-demographic** variables show moderate, significant and robust influences in all models, which conforms to expectations. Similarly, the impact of two out of three variables related to **systemic transition** remains negative, significant and constant in all models, as expected. A rise in concern about the family slightly increases the chance of volunteering, which was expected. This effect disappears when the Polish context is controlled. In other words, we could interpret this finding by saying that concern about the living conditions of the immediate family raises the chance of volunteering in Poland, which again indicates differences between Poland and other countries.

Among the variables related to **protest actions**, attending demonstrations is a significant predictor for volunteering, which remains robust in all the models. Taking part in strikes also seems to have a significant (though weak) predictive power for volunteering. After the introduction of countries' dummies, the level of significance drops (p<0.1 in Model 5 to p<0.5 in Model 6). On the other hand, taking part in occupying buildings is significant for predicting volunteering only in Model 6 after controlling for countries' context, which contradicts the expectations. So, in general, attending protest actions is a significant determinant for volunteering.

The **Polish** context diminishes the chance of being a volunteer and, as mentioned above, including a Poland dummy in the analysis makes post-communism and concern about family insignificant. Furthermore, the contextual effects of most of the countries are considerable, positive (again, except for Lithuania) and significant (with the exception of Portugal, Hungary and Lithuania). Despite the significant predictive power of country dummies, most of the factors included in the analyses remain robust predictors for volunteering (i.e., conservatism, subjective well-being and attending protest actions). So again, we need to stress that the specific features of the Polish context impede volunteering, when compared to other countries. In Lithuania the conditions are negative for volunteering, similarly to Poland.

The previous analyses (section 5.3.1.1) showed that religious factors have different impacts on religious and secular organisations. In particular we learned that churchgoing is relevant for the propensity to volunteer and membership only in religious organisations. Therefore, we now turn to the analysis of membership in religious and secular organisations separately. The research strategy remains the same and all models include the same independent variables. Both factors related to religion – conservatism and church attendance – are expected to be positively related to church-related networks, and not related to membership in secular organisations. From the results of the regression analyses depicted in Table 6.4 we learn whether these expectations are fulfilled.

Table 6.4 Logistic regression analysis of membership in secular and religious organisations, excluding Slovakia (odds ratio Exp (B), R^2 Nagelkerke, and N, unweighted)

Independent variables	Model 1 Exp (B) S^b	Model 1 Exp (B) R^c	Model 2 Exp (B) S^b	Model 2 Exp (B) R^c	Model 3 Exp (B) S^b	Model 3 Exp (B) R^c	Model 4 Exp (B) S^b	Model 4 Exp (B) R^c	Model 5 Exp (B) S^b	Model 5 Exp (B) R^c	Model 6 Exp (B) S^b	Model 6 Exp (B) R^c
RELIGIOUS FACTORS												
Conservatism (RRCI)	0.630***	104.543***	0.607***	152.736***	0.837	283.789***	0.852	295.291**	0.897	359.809***	1.096	468.817***
Conservatism (missing values replaced)[a]	0.555***	121.302***	0.520***	158.752***	0.750*	321.371***	0.757*	331.369***	0.812	417.094***	1.045	542.471***
Church attendance (1-never; 4-once a week)	0.986	1.132***	0.986	1.131***	0.952**	1.055*	0.952**	1.055*	0.949**	1.045	0.998	1.046
POST-COMMUNIST LEGACY												
Post-communism (dummy)	1.823***	0.824**	1.835***	0.827**	1.739***	0.858*	1.758***	0.879*	1.813***	0.988	-	-
SOCIO-DEMOGRAPHIC FEATURES												
Education (1-elementary; 8-university degree)			1.003	1.135***	1.001	1.130***	0.999	1.122***	1.000	1.122***	1.007	1.181***
Income (1-lowest; 10-highest)			1.011	1.062***	1.004	1.045**	1.004	1.044**	1.003	1.042**	0.999	1.013
Age			1.002	1.008***	1.001	1.008***	1.001	1.008***	1.001	1.007***	1.001	1.007**
Gender (1-male; 2-female)			1.037	1.150**	1.035	1.157**	1.040	1.174**	1.039	1.168**	1.028	1.164**
SYSTEMIC TRANSITION												
Income inequality (GINI)					0.947***	0.901***	0.947***	0.901***	0.950***	0.911***	-	-
Happiness (1-happy; 4-not happy)					0.993	0.855***	0.993	0.853***	0.993	0.849***	0.990	0.910*
Concerned (1-very; 4-not at all)					1.077***	1.032	1.077***	1.032	1.074***	1.019	1.056*	1.013

PROTEST ACTIONS						
Demonstrations (1-yes, 0-no)	1.066	1.245**	1.067	1.245**	1.054	1.434***
Strikes (1-yes; 0-no)	0.961	0.845	0.964	0.857	0.903	0.842
Occupying buildings (`-yes; 0-no)	1.019	0.822	1.026	0.841	1.120	1.066
COUNTRY DUMMIES						
Poland			0.824*	0.425***	Ref.	Ref.
Austria					0.935	12.522***
Belgium					1.161	3.559***
France					0.723**	1.770**
Ireland					0.424***	5.310***
Italy					0.579***	2.426***
Portugal					1.053	1.404
Spain					1.035	1.872**
Croatia					1.495***	4.265***
Czech Rep.					2.260***	3.921***
Hungary					0.782*	4.430***
Lithuania					0.567***	0.832
Slovakia					2.832***	5.986***
Slovenia					1.803***	3.367***

N	13,188	13,188	13,188	13,188	13,188	13,188	13,188	13,188	13,188
N ᵃ	15,683	15,683	15,683	15,683	15,683	15,683	15,683	15,683	15,683
Nagelkerke R²	0.030	0.092	0.030	0.111	0.046	0.142	0.046	0.144	0.047
Nagelkerke R² ᵃ	*0.031*	*0.086*	*0.032*	*0.102*	*0.048*	*0.133*	*0.048*	*0.135*	*0.049*

Notes: Significance levels: *p<0.05, **p<0.01, *** p<0.001

ᵃ results of logistic regression pursued with the same models with a modification concerning the independent variable "conservatism," which is replaced by "conservatism with replaced missing values by countries' means. In this case, the number of cases included in the analysis is higher.

ᵇ membership in secular organisations

ᶜ membership in religious organisations

Source: WVS 1999.

Do religious factors demonstrate distinct predictive powers for membership in secular and religious organisations? Let us start with **conservatism**. The predictive power of conservatism in the cases of religious and secular organisations is indeed different (Table 6.4). Conservatism is a strong predictor of membership in religious organisations: the chance of meeting a member of a religious organisation rises by almost 500 times with a one-unit increase in conservatism. However, with increasing conservatism, membership in secular organisations is less likely, as the two first models show. Eventually the significance of conservatism disappears after other factors relevant for participation are considered. When conservatism is considered with after replacing missing values, its effects are significant in Models 3 and 4, but disappear when the Poland dummy variable is introduced. This finding indicates that the positive effects of conservatism on secular membership apply to Polish respondents, which points to *exceptional mechanisms in Poland* (only when conservatism with the replaced missing values is considered). Furthermore, expectations concerning the positive effects of conservatism on religious organisations are confirmed.

The second religious factor – **church attendance** – also shows a distinct predictive power according to the type of organisation, though the effects are much weaker than in the case of conservatism. An increase in churchgoing slightly raises the chance of membership in religious organisations when Poland is not included in the analysis. With the inclusion of Poland the positive effects of church attendance disappear. This finding indicates, again, *an exceptional situation in Poland – positive effects of church attendance on Polish society*. A rise in the frequency of churchgoing slightly decreases the chances of membership in a secular organisation when other factors – such as social costs of systemic transition, participation in protest actions and Poland – are included in the analysis (Models 3 to 5). Eventually, in Model 6, changes in church attendance become irrelevant for predicting secular membership. So, the expectations are partly confirmed: when all determinants are included in the model, church attendance is irrelevant for predicting secular membership. Surprisingly, however, there is a lack of evidence of positive effects of churchgoing on religious membership when all determinants are considered in the model.

Third, a **post-communist legacy** decreases the likelihood of membership in a religious organisation. With the Polish context controlled, the significance of communist experiences disappears. Surprisingly, having experienced communism almost doubles the probability of being a member in a secular organisation, and this predictive power remains significant and robust in all models. This is an interesting finding that indicates communist regimes probably influenced the patterns of social engagement in Central Eastern societies in such a way that the character of social engagement became mainly secular. A more fine-grained analysis by types of organisations would probably show that post-communism is a good predictor for membership in labour unions (see Table 5.26; and Howard 2003, 67).

Specific characteristics of the **Polish** context decrease the chance of membership in a religious organisation, overtaking the negative effect of communist experience and the positive effect of church attendance. This finding shows that mechanisms of how religious networks are built are different in Poland than other Catholic countries with and without prior communist experiences.

The predictive power of higher education, lower age, higher subjective well-being and attending demonstrations remain significant for membership in religious organisations. In contrast, women are more likely than men to be a member of church-related groups. Interestingly, socio-demographic characteristics and attending protest actions are unrelated to secular membership.

Finally, by splitting the types of organisations into religious and secular, we have different levels of explained variance. In the case of secular membership, the level of explained variance drops to a very low level of 8 percent in Model 6, while in the case of church-related engagement, Negelkerke R^2 remains at the similar level of 19 percent.

Can we find similar dissimilarities when exploring the factors predicting religious and secular types of volunteering? Table 6.5 provides us with this information.

Table 6.5 Logistic regression analysis of volunteering in secular and religious organisations, excluding Slovakia (odds ratio Exp (B), R² Nagelkerke, Hosmer-Lemeshow test and N, unweighted)

Independent variables	Model 1 Exp (B) S[b]	Model 1 Exp (B) R[c]	Model 2 Exp (B) S[b]	Model 2 Exp (B) R[c]	Model 3 Exp (B) S[b]	Model 3 Exp (B) R[c]	Model 4 Exp (B) S[b]	Model 4 Exp (B) R[c]	Model 5 Exp (B) S[b]	Model 5 Exp (B) R[c]	Model 6 Exp (B) S[b]	Model 6 Exp (B) R[c]
RELIGIOUS FACTORS												
Conservatism (RRCI)	0.341***	263.695***	0.707*	612.815***	0.860	726.021***	1.133	816.326**	1.244	1,044.713***	1.580**	1,212.933***
Conservatism (missing values replaced)[a]	0.311***	305.348***	0.616**	640.774***	0.792	813.817***	1.039	896.632***	1.156	1,182.164***	1.535**	1,424.639***
Church attendance (1-never; 4-once a week)	1.045*	1.121**	1.029	1.114***	1.006	1.093*	1.008	1.094*	1.005	1.085*	1.033	1.074
POST-COMMUNIST LEGACY												
Post-communism (dummy)	0.790***	0.761**	0.793***	0.732***	0.809***	0.812*	0.909	0.862	0.974	1.012	-	-
SOCIO-DEMOGRAPHIC FEATURES												
Education (1-elementary; 8-university degree)			1.161***	1.245***	1.159***	1.238***	1.139***	1.221***	1.139***	1.220***	1.161***	1.254***
Income (1-lowest; 10-highest)			1.069***	1.036	1.055***	1.022	1.052***	1.019	1.051***	1.019	1.036**	1.004
Age			1.000	1.006*	1.000	1.006*	1.000	1.006*	1.000	1.006**	1.002	1.006*
Gender (1-male; 2-female)			0.664***	1.083	0.661***	1.095	0.694***	1.136	0.694***	1.130	0.684***	1.135
SYSTEMIC TRANSITION												

	(1)	(2)	(3)	(4)	(5)	(6)	(7)	(8)
Income inequality (GINI)	0.959***	0.963***	0.958***	0.964***	0.963***	0.972**	-	-
Happiness (1-happy; 4-not happy)	0.806***	0.732***	0.798***	0.726***	0.798***	0.725***	0.837***	0.758***
Concerned (1-very; 4-not at all)	1.052*	0.980	1.044	0.980	1.035	0.965	0.943*	0.945
PROTEST ACTIONS								
Demonstrations (1-yes; 0-no)			1.589***	1.483***	1.593***	1.490***	1.548***	1.579***
Strikes (1-yes; 0-no)			1.319**	0.932	1.322**	0.944	1.264*	0.929
Occupying buildings (1-yes; 0-no)			1.243	0.816	1.262	0.838	1.367**	0.907
COUNTRY DUMMIES								
Poland					0.627***	0.484***	Ref.	Ref.
Austria							2.559***	3.977***
Belgium							2.318***	2.136***
France							1.843***	1.983**
Ireland							2.897***	3.148***
Italy							1.882***	2.209***
Portugal							1.150	1.322
Spain							1.434*	2.101**
Croatia							1.658**	2.674***
Czech Rep.							3.639***	2.388***
Hungary							1.056	2.719***
Lithuania							0.678	1.001
Slovenia							2.741***	3.386***
N	12,400	12,400	12,400	12,400	12,400	12,400	12,400	12,400

N^a	14,964	14,964	14,964	14,964	14,964	14,964	14,964	14,964	14,964	14,964
Nagelkerke R^2	0.011	0.090	0.056	0.122	0.068	0.131	0.082	0.134	0.084	0.138	0.103	0.147
Nagelkerke $R^{2\,a}$	0.011	0.086	0.053	0.113	0.066	0.123	0.080	0.125	0.081	0.129	0.100	0.140

Notes: Significance levels: *p<0.05, **p<0.01, *** p<0.001

[a] results of logistic regression pursued with the same models with a modification concerning the independent variable "conservatism," which is replaced by "conservatism with replaced missing values by countries' means. In this case, the number of cases included in the analysis is higher.
[b] membership in secular organisations
[c] membership in religious organisations

Source: WVS 1999

Religious factors, especially conservatism, seem to be a good predictor for volunteering in church-related organisations, though not in secular, which conforms to expectations. **Conservatism** is a powerful predictor for religious volunteering: a one-unit rise in conservatism increases the probability of meeting a religiously engaged volunteer by more than 1,000 times (last two models). Conservatism displays a modest ability to predict secular engagement only in Model 6, while in Model 1 it appears to diminish the likelihood of volunteering. The second religious factor – **church attendance** – turns out to be a very weak and significant predictor for volunteering in church-related organisations, though this effect disappears in Model 6 when countries' dummy variables are included. As far as secular volunteering is concerned, church attendance remains irrelevant, except for Model 1.

A number of variables demonstrate similar effects on volunteering in both types of organisations. **Post-communism** is expected to display significant negative (though weak) effects on volunteering in religious and non-religious organisations. For both types of volunteering, the predictive power of post-communism disappears after the introduction of variables related to attendance at protest actions. Similarly, with higher income disparities and a decrease in subjective well-being, the chance of being a volunteer drops slightly but significantly for both types of organisations. In contrast, among those respondents attending demonstrations there is a higher chance of volunteering. The **Polish context** shows negative effects on both types of volunteering. Furthermore, the introduction of the Polish dummy variable does not considerably change the predictive power of any other variable. This means that the mechanisms for volunteering in Poland are similar to those in other countries. Countries' specific contexts raise the probability of volunteering in religious and secular organisations.

Among the **socio-demographic** variables, only education has the same effect on both types of volunteering. A one-point increase in educational level slightly raises the chance of being a volunteer in both types of organisations. A one-unit rise on a country's income scale increases the likelihood of secular volunteering only; with rising age, the likelihood of volunteering in religious organisations drops, while women are more prone than men to volunteer in church-related groups. Attending strikes raises only the probability of predicting secular volunteering.

In general, variables included in the models are better suited to predict religious volunteering than secular. The levels of explained variance are low for both types of volunteerism, and reach a modest level of almost 15 percent for religious volunteering and 10 percent for its secular counterpart.

Summarising the analyses of formal networks, we can draw two main conclusions. First, as expected, religious factors are more suited to predicting membership and volunteering in religious organisations than secular. Surprisingly, it is not the structural aspects that turn out to be important for predicting religious engagement, but the cultural characteristics – it matters more for the probability of religious engagement whether an individual is conservative (i.e., one's value orientations are more influenced by Catholic tenets than by whether or not one goes to church on a regular basis). This finding shows that the motivation to be engaged is more relevant than the recruitment; or, using Verba and colleagues' phrasing, people get engaged religiously because they want to, rather than because they were asked to.

A second important finding concerns Poland and partly answers the main question of this chapter: are the mechanisms of social capital building distinct in Poland? We found out that the mechanisms of membership in Poland indeed differ from those in other countries. Church attendance is important for predicting religious membership in Poland, in contrast to other countries, where it is irrelevant. Furthermore, conservatism is a relevant determinant for secular membership only in Poland, not in other countries (though this evidence was found only with a modified measure of conservatism that included missing values). However, the mechanisms for volunteering do not differ in Poland compared to other societies.

6.4.1.2 Informal networks

Why do certain individuals meet with friends and some do not? Are the determinants for informal networks the same in the studied societies, or is Poland again an exception? As we learned in chapter 2, friendship ties are weaker in Poland compared to other countries. Furthermore, bivariate analyses showed that conservatism is a negative predictor for meeting friends in most of the societies analysed, including Poland, while churchgoing remains unrelated (see section 5.2.2.1). Is this finding still relevant after considering other potential factors?

What other determinants for informal networks, besides conservatism, can be expected? The influences of post-communism and systemic transitions on informal ties are difficult to specify. On the one hand, many authors stress the importance of informal ties during communism as a counterbalance for the inadequate civil society. Furthermore, acquaintances were indispensable for survival under communist regimes and planned economies (Paldam/Svendsen 2000, 8; Howard 2003; Pichler/Wallace 2007, 425). Howard argues that the societal patterns remained rather unchanged after the collapse of communism (2003, 105). On the other hand, successful transformations made the informal ties less important, so that "provisional" informal ties and connections lost their relevance (Howard 2003, 113). Therefore, two options are plausible – informal networks might be positively related to post-communism, if societal patterns remained unchanged after the collapse of communism; or not at all related, if the patterns changed as the result of the regular provision of goods and services. Furthermore, we should find a positive effect of failed systemic transition on informal networks: in this case economic hardship could force people to stick together and count on friends' networks. Living in a country with higher income inequalities should be prone to the maintenance of informal ties, and the same expectation could be applied to concern about the family (Howard 2003, 113). In addition, the introduction of variables related to systemic transition should diminish the predictive power of post-communism.

Finally, attending diverse forms of protest actions could also be related to informal ties, since some scholars signal there is a positive relationship between interpersonal networks and political participation (van Deth 1997, 9). Socio-economic status should increase the probability of meeting with friends, while men should be more likely to socialise informally than women.[64] Table 6.6 outlines the results of the logistic regression analyses pursued in a similar way as those of the formal networks.

---

[64] Examination of bivariate relations between gender and informal networks shows significant effects of gender: men are slightly more likely to have informal networks than women (Pearson's r 0.046, p<0.01).

Table 6.6 Logistic regression analysis of informal networks (odds ratio Exp (B), R^2 Nagelkerke, and N, unweighted)

Independent variables	Model 1	Model 2	Model 3	Model 4	Model 5	Model 6
	Exp (B)	Exp (B)	Exp (B)	Exp (B)	Exp (B)	Exp (B)
RELIGIOUS FACTORS						
Conservatism (RRCI)	0.032***	0.346**	0.350**	0.420*	0.630	0.655
Conservatism (missing values replaced)[a]	*0.036***	*0.335***	*0.363**	*0.437*	*0.619*	*0.684*
Church attendance (1-never; 4-once a week)	1.020	0.987	0.999	1.002	0.989	0.941
POST-COMMUNIST LEGACY						
Post-communism (dummy)	0.693***	0.626***	0.727**	0.783*	0.992	–
SOCIO-DEMOGRAPHIC FEATURES						
Education (1-elementary; 8-university degree)		1.214***	1.203***	1.183***	1.188***	1.221***
Income (1-lowest; 10-highest)		1.096***	1.074**	1.071**	1.067**	1.053*
Age		0.965***	0.967***	0.965***	0.964***	0.967***
Gender (1-male; 2-female)		0.718***	0.740**	0.785*	0.771**	0.758**
SYSTEMIC TRANSITION						
Income inequality (GINI)			1.004	1.005	1.029*	–
Happiness (1-happy; 4-not happy)			0.623***	0.620***	0.620***	0.627***
Concerned (1-very; 4-not at all)			1.033	1.025	1.010	0.960
PROTEST ACTIONS						
Demonstrations (1-yes; 0-no)				3.040***	3.000***	3.194***
Strikes (1-yes; 0-no)				0.747	0.799	0.809
Occupying buildings (1-yes; 0-no)				0.676	0.684	0.718
COUNTRY DUMMIES						
Poland					0.398***	Ref.
Austria						4.193***
Belgium						1.093
France						3.355***
Ireland						7.130***
Italy						1.834**
Portugal						2.871***
Spain						2.758***
Croatia						4.107***
Czech Rep.						2.090**
Hungary						1.173
Lithuania						2.741**
Slovakia						4.599***
Slovenia						3.093***
N	13,112	13,112	13,112	13,112	13,112	13,112
N[a]	*15,578*	*15,578*	*15,578*	*15,578*	*15,578*	*15,578*
Nagelkerke R^2	0.038	0.134	0.149	0.159	0.167	0.192
Nagelkerke R^{2a}	*0.036*	*0.136*	*0.151*	*0.161*	*0.166*	*0.189*

Notes: Significance levels: *p<0.05, **p<0.01, *** p<0.001
[a] results of logistic regression pursued with the same models with a modification concerning the independent variable "conservatism," which is replaced by "conservatism with replaced missing values by countries' means. In this case, the number of cases included in the analysis is higher. Source: WVS 1999.

The prediction power of the models remains at moderate levels and rises stepwise with the inclusion of the new variables. First, a sharp increase in explained variances from 4 to 13 percent appears after the introduction of socio-demographic factors.

Of the two religious factors, only **conservatism** shows a significant predictive power for meeting friends, as expected, though not when country contexts are considered. With a rise in conservatism, the probability that a person reports meeting friends decreases (Model 4). After the inclusion of Poland as a dummy variable (Model 5), this effect of conservatism becomes insignificant and remains insignificant in Model 6. This indicates *that in Poland the mechanism of building informal ties might be different than in other countries*. Analysing conservatism with the missing values replaced by means brings very similar results. The second religious factor – **church attendance** – does not show any significant relationship with meeting friends, which conforms to expectations.

The **post-communist legacy** decreases the likelihood of sustaining informal networks, which is an expected finding. However, after the introduction of Poland, post-communism becomes an insignificant predictor for meeting friends, which again *points to an exceptional situation in Polish society*. Variables related to **systemic transition** remain insignificant for predicting whether a person meets friends. The only exception is that subjective well-being shows negative effects – unhappy individuals are less likely to meet with friends. An expected positive effect of high income disparities on informal ties appears only in Model 5, when Poland is included in the analysis. Furthermore, **attending demonstrations** is the most powerful predictor for meeting friends, while taking part in other forms of protest actions remains insignificant. All **socio-demographic** variables are significant for predicting informal networks, as expected. A higher economic status and age raise the chance of having informal contacts. The effects of gender are as predicted – men are more likely to meet friends than women.

Conforming to expectations, being Polish lowers a respondent's chance of having informal networks. In addition, as mentioned above, consideration of the Polish context makes conservatism and post-communism insignificant for informal networks. This indicates that there are different mechanisms for building informal networks among Polish individuals.

With the inclusion of the country dummies, the impact of socio-demographic characteristics, subjective well-being and attending demonstrations remain significant. Otherwise, the odds ratios related to all country dummies are significant and over 1.0 (with the exception of Belgium and, again, Lithuania). This confirms that exceptionally weak informal ties are a specific characteristic of Poland.

6.4.1.3 Social networks: conclusions

The results of analyses concerning social networks are complex and – in a few respects – surprising, so it is worth systematising our findings before we move to the examination of social trust. The general findings are enumerated, and a description of evidence on the situation in Poland follows.

(1) As expected, the predictive power of religious factors is mainly limited to religious engagement. Surprisingly, conservatism has a stronger predictive impact than church affiliation, and has a positive influence on formal church-related networks. Moreover, we found a slight negative effect of church attendance on membership in secular networks, which was unexpected. Otherwise, conservatism is negatively related to informal networks, as expected, while churchgoing remains unrelated. In other words, returning to the question addressed in chapter 5, we can say that the "resulting effect" of religion is positive, though limited to religious engagement and that "denomination effects" are stronger than "affiliation effects."

(2) The communist legacy is in general a negative predictor for all kinds of social networks – membership, volunteering and meeting with friends. Surprisingly, a positive effect of post-communism on secular membership was found, which could be a consequence of higher membership in labour unions, which is a characteristic trait of societies with communist experiences.

(3) The consequences of systemic transition are, as expected, detrimental for the building of formal networks. Living in a country with relatively high income inequality decreases an individual's chance of being engaged in formal networks, though it increases the probability of meeting regularly with friends. These findings support the claims of Howard and Rose, that economic hardship decreases associational membership, yet fosters informal contacts among people. Being concerned with the living conditions of one's immediate family is a negative predictor of secular volunteering, while a negative perception of one's subjective well-being slightly depresses the chance of volunteering in formal networks and having friends. These results also underline claims about the negative consequences of disappointment for social participation.

(4) A further unexpected finding is the positive relationship between protest actions and all kinds of networks. In particular, attending demonstrations is positively related to most forms of networks, including informal ones. This means that low social participation cannot be explained by the high protest activity of citizens. So even if Poles have a "rebellious nature" and attend protest actions more frequently than other people, as Ekiert and

Kubik claim, this should foster social networks among the "rebelling" citizens, not discourage them.

(5) **Four** main dissimilarities characterising social network building in Polish society were found. First, in the case of informal networks and membership, the negative impact of post-communism becomes insignificant after the introduction of Poland into the analysis. This evidence shows that the lower stock of social networks (though not volunteering) in post-communist societies can be partly explained by the exceptional situation in Poland. Second, in some cases the impact of religious factors refers especially to the situation in Poland. For instance, the positive impact of church affiliation on membership in church-related groups seems to be a rather Polish characteristic, since this effect becomes insignificant after considering Poland. Likewise, the predictive power of conservatism for weak friendship ties ceases to be significant after the inclusion of Poland. Third, the hampering effect of concern about the family on volunteering appears to be related to the unique situation in Poland. In addition, the Polish context is negative for all kinds of networks examined, which points to a specific Polish feature that is detrimental to social networks. Other countries' contexts have generally significant powers to predict social networks compared to Poland. The only exception is Lithuania, the context of which systematically decreases the probability of formal networks (but not religious volunteering). This indicates that the specific contexts of Poland and Lithuania have a similar decreasing influence on formal networks. The findings could point to the importance of historical legacies, since Poland and Lithuania were one state, the Polish-Lithuanian Commonwealth, from the 16th to the 18th centuries (1569-1795). In sum, the exceptionally low level of social networks in Poland can partly be explained by mechanisms specific to this society (the particular relationship between religious membership and informal networks, and the particular relationship between conservatism and informal networks).

6.4.2 Trust

Are the determinants of social trust different in Poland than in other Catholic countries? Debates over the origins of social trust can be divided into two main streams. While for some scholars trust is generated by personal experiences, for others it is a social feature, mostly stable over the long term (*in extenso*, see chapter 2). Adversaries of this point of view argue that social trust is a cultural resource that is "not based primarily on personal experiences" (Uslaner 2003a, 84). Other authors, however, point to several individual determinants, such as socio-economic status, which are relevant for generating social trust. According to this line of through, in general, the winners in society are more inclined to trust. In our analysis both perspectives are taken into consideration: prior communist experience, countries' GINI coefficient for income inequality and countries' dummy variables refer to macro-level perspectives, while all other independent variables (conservatism, church affiliation, socio-demographic features, subjective well-being, and concern about family) refer to individual factors.

On the one hand, **RRC**, as a reflection of an individual's connection to Catholic religion and teaching, could be positively related to generalised trust, since people internalise good faith in others through religion. On the other hand, one could argue that "religious values may lead people to insulate themselves from strangers – and disbelievers" (Uslaner 2002, 87). The results of the bivariate analysis presented in chapter 5 (see Table 5.18) reveal no relationship between conservatism and social trust at the macro level and a negative correlation in most of the countries at the micro level. In Poland it seems that conservatism and trust remain unrelated. In this respect I expect conservatism to be a negative predictor for trust, and including Poland in the analysis should not change the results. In contrast, the frequency of **church attendance** could be a positive predictor of trust, as demonstrated by the results of the analyses in section 3.5.1.2 (see also Guiso et al. 2003, 227); Poland should not be an exception in this regard.

Scholars who analyse post-communist societies point to several mechanisms of the detrimental impact of communism on generalised trust. First, individuals living under **communist rule** ceased to trust each other due to the oppressiveness of the totalitarian regime (Uslaner 2003b, 177). Second, widespread mistrust of the institutions and civic organisations controlled by the regime led communist citizens to withdraw from the public sphere and concentrate on close clusters of friends and family, and in consequence to restrict trust to a small group of people (Grabowska/Szawiel 2001, 155; Howard 2003, 25). In light of these arguments I expect the communist experience to be a negative predictor of trust. In Poland the mechanisms should be the same as in other countries.

The collapse of communism and subsequent process of systemic transition led to a rise in unemployment and inflation – and in effect to impoverishment and an increase in income inequalities. These circumstances reinforced the anxiousness, uncertainty and mistrust among people across post-communist societies (Sztompka 1995, 269; Paldam/Svendsen 2000, 17; Uslaner 2003b, 177). Therefore I expect all variables related to **systemic transition** – the GINI coefficient for income inequality and concern about family – to be negatively related to trust. And the same mechanisms are expected for Poland, too.

Since the winners across a society are supposed to trust more, education and income should be positive predictors of trust, while age and gender are irrelevant (Kunz 2004, 221). Poland should not be an exception in this regard. I expect a positive relationship between trust and attending protest actions, since trust is usually used as a predictor of protest behaviour (Dekker et al. 1997, 233).

For the exploration of the determinants of social trust, the same research strategy and the same models are applied as in the case of social networks. Table 6.7 presents the results of logistic regression analyses based on the six models described in the previous section.

Table 6.7 Logistic regression analysis of trust (odds ratio Exp (B), R^2 Nagelkerke, and N, unweighted)

Independent variables	Model 1	Model 2	Model 3	Model 4	Model 5	Model 6
	Exp (B)	Exp (B)	Exp (B)	Exp (B)	Exp (B)	Exp (B)
RELIGIOUS FACTORS						
Conservatism (RRCI)	0.255***	0.421***	0.434***	0.475***	0.458***	0.385***
Conservatism (missing values replaced)[a]	0.254***	0.431***	0.455***	0.497***	0.485***	0.399***
Church attendance (1-never; 4-once a week)	1.062**	1.051*	1.054*	1.054*	1.056**	1.010
POST-COMMUNIST LEGACY						
Post-communism (dummy)	0.641***	0.629***	0.658***	0.691***	0.672***	–
SOCIO-DEMOGRAPHIC FEATURES						
Education (1-elementary; 8-university degree)		1.185***	1.184***	1.173***	1.173***	1.184***
Income (1-lowest; 10-highest)		1.081***	1.072***	1.070***	1.071***	1.062***
Age		1.009***	1.009***	1.009***	1.009***	1.010***
Gender (1-male; 2-female)		0.934	0.936	0.957	0.958	0.969
SYSTEMIC TRANSITION						
Income inequality (GINI)			0.995	.995	0.993	–
Happiness (1-happy; 4-not happy)			0.796***	0.794***	0.795***	0.786***
Concerned (1-very; 4-not at all)			1.044*	1.043	1.046*	1.015
PROTEST ACTIONS						
Demonstrations (1-yes; 0-no)				1.307***	1.305***	1.359***
Strikes (1-yes; 0-no)				0.920	0.919	0.938
Occupying buildings (1-yes; 0-no)				0.996	0.990	1.027
COUNTRY DUMMIES						
Poland					1.198	Ref.
Austria						1.695***
Belgium						1.003
France						0.752*
Ireland						2.018***
Italy						1.651***
Portugal						0.598***
Spain						2.017***
Croatia						0.734*
Czech Rep.						0.889
Hungary						1.162
Lithuania						0.959
Slovakia						0.706**
Slovenia						0.888
N	12,853	12,853	12,853	12,853	12,853	12,853
N[a]	*15,224*	*15,224*	*15,224*	*15,224*	*15,224*	*15,224*
Nagelkerke R^2	0.027	0.074	0.080	0.083	0.084	0.109
Nagelkerke R^2[a]	*0.025*	*0.072*	*0.079*	*0.081*	*0.081*	*0.106*

Notes: Significance levels: *p<0.05, **p<0.01, *** p<0.001
[a] results of logistic regression pursued with the same models with a modification concerning the independent variable "conservatism," which is replaced by "conservatism with replaced missing values by countries' means. In this case, the number of cases included in the analysis is higher. Source: WVS 1999.

In all models predicting social trust the levels of explained variances remain low. There are two considerable rises in levels of explained variance when additional variables are stepwise introduced. Nevertheless, variables included in the models explain the differences in the generation of social capital between Poland and other countries, since the odds ratios for the Poland dummy variable are insignificant (Model 5).

Conservatism appears to be a significant predictor of distrust, and its predictive power remains robust in all models, which corroborates expectations. The results remain almost identical when the missing values of conservatism are replaced by the country means. **Church attendance** is a very weak and significant predictor of trust, as expected, though these effects disappear after the introduction of countries' dummies to the analyses.

As expected, prior **communist experience** relates negatively and significantly to social trust. Its predictive power remains relatively stable across the models. Considering the Polish context hardly changes the power of the post-communist experience. This is evidence of a similar impact of the communist experience for Polish respondents when compared to other people from the region.

Socio-demographic variables, excluding gender, are important predictors of trust, as expected. Surprisingly, age is a negative predictor of trust – younger people are less likely to trust others. Similarly, social costs of **systemic transition**, with the exception of income inequality, seem to be important for predicting social trust. Feeling unhappy is a robust, significant predictor for mistrust, as Uslaner (2002) claims, and its power does not change across models. Concern about family is also a negative, weak and significant predictor, though its predictive power is not constant across models. In Models 4 and 6, when attendance of protest actions and countries' dummies are introduced to the analyses, concern about family turns insignificant. These findings are difficult to interpret and mean that concern about family is not a robust and reliable determinant, since its power depends on the inclusion of other variables in the models.

Attending demonstrations is a positive predictor of social trust, which was expected, and its power and significance remains almost unchanged across models. Other forms of protest action, such as strikes or occupying buildings, are unrelated to social trust. The findings indicate that not all kinds of protest activity are relevant for trust: the form of protest matters. Finally, the **Polish context** seems to be unimportant for predicting trust when all factors are considered. This demonstrates that the differences in social trust between Polish and other societies can be explained by the differences in the levels of considered factors, but not by the different mechanisms. Country dummies included in Model 6 show diverse predictive powers of social trust. The context of some countries, for instance France, Portugal, Croatia and Slovakia, decreases social trust. In contrast, the specific country context of Austria, Ireland, Italy and Spain are positive and significant for trust; the contexts of other countries are not significant. It is difficult to find a pattern here.

The main conclusions from these analyses are that generally, patterns of generating trust do not differ between Poland and other Catholic societies. Conservatism, post-communist legacy and unhappiness decrease trust, while social status and attending demonstrations are positive predictors. So we can say that low social trust in Poland can be explained by a relatively high level of two important determinants – conservatism and disappointment. The mechanisms for producing social trust in Poland are similar to those in other countries. Coefficients of countries' specific contexts are mostly significant, and in four countries the context decreases trust when compared to Poland.

6.4.3 Norms and values

The last component of social capital – norms and values – is the main focus of the last section. The question addressed here is whether the acceptance of norms has similar determinants in Poland related to religion, post-communism, systemic transition, attendance of protest actions and socio-demographic characteristics. The operationalisation of norms and values is presented in section 2.4.3. Acceptance of norms is measured by an index for norms of civil behaviour (NCB) and an index for norms of social behaviour (NSB). Both variables are continuous, so the most appropriate model in this case is linear regression.[65] The research strategy remains similar to that of the other components of social capital.

The bivariate analyses presented in section 5.3.1.3 reveal a positive relationship between **church affiliation** and the acceptance of norms of civil and social behaviour in most of the societies, which corroborates the results of other studies. In Poland the relationship between churchgoing and acceptance of norms of civil and social behaviour is also positive (section 5.3.1.3).

As far as **conservatism** is concerned, no relationship to the acceptance of norms is found in bivariate analyses at the individual level. However, we agree that

---

[65] In order to check the reliability of the results of linear models, the same set of models has been examined by using logistic regression. In this case, both indexes have been transformed into a dummy so that the first quartile of respondents supporting norms to the least extent in each country are assigned a value of "0," while the respondents in the last three quartiles, who declare higher support for the norms, are assigned a value of "1." This mode of recoding was enforced by a very uneven distribution of both variables – across most of the societies over 50 percent of the respondents declared acceptance of the norms at the highest level (in several countries the median and maximum have the same value). Although the level of significance of the odds ratios is lower, in a number of cases independent variables turn insignificant, and the models' parameters are much weaker, the results of logistic regression analysis point to the same direction of the relationships between independent and dependent variables. This indicates the robustness of the results of the linear regression applied in this section.

if "religion has a powerful and lasting effect on people's attitudes and behaviours, then religious teachings may contribute to a more civil and caring society" (Cnaan et al. 2003, 29; see also Wuthnow 1991, 51). Furthermore, strong moral attitudes, encompassed in the concept of RRC, should also be positively related to the rejection of free-riding behaviour due to a fear of moral sanctions (see also Roßteutscher 2004, 179). So, two results are plausible: conservatism could be positively related to the acceptance of norms of behaviour in both the civic and public realms, or not related at all.

What predictive power can be expected of the post communist legacies for the acceptance of norms? Sztompka points to the "civilisational incompetence" of **post-communist** citizens (2000) and emphasises a widespread *"homo sovieticus"* mentality, which is the opposite of "civic-mindness" (Sztompka 2004, 14). Several scholars stress that people living under communist rule were socialised in the adversarial social-institutional system.

The results of the empirical analyses of the relationships between norms and post-communism in the literature are not consistent. While several authors provide evidence of the shrinking acceptance of norms in some post-communist states (specifically in Hungary and Eastern Germany) after the collapse of communism (Gabriel et al. 2002, 79-80), others provide evidence of just the opposite – a higher support for law-abidingness in post-communist countries, though a low support for solidarity (Roßteutscher 2004, 184-185). The empirical evidence in my study points to a slightly lower level of acceptance of NCB in post-communist countries compared to Western societies. Similarly, the acceptance of NSB is at a lower level (section 2.4.3). With such contradictory evidence it is difficult to formulate expectations concerning the impact of the communist legacy on norms. It is plausible that the acceptance of NCB rose after liberalisation, because the new system was supported in the society more than the previous one, while approval for NSB remained at the same low level due to the persistence of attitudes despite the systemic change (Howard 2003, 18-20). This is why we might find that the **communist legacy** is negatively related to NSB and positively related to NCB.

Furthermore, **disappointment** with the new post-communist reality could also be related to the acceptance of norms. People disillusioned with post-communist developments might blame the new institutions for the lack of economic performance and for growing income disparities. Political confidence and satisfaction with democratisation is low in Eastern Europe (Badescu 2006, 88; Rose 2009, 164-166), which would indirectly support my hypothesis. People disillusioned by the performance of the system might not be ready to support the laws and rules established by this system (i.e., they might be ready to justify such behaviour as cheating on taxes or abusing state benefits). So I expect a negative relationship between the acceptance of civil norms and factors related to the systemic transition. Besides, the effect of disappointment should diminish the explanatory power of post-communism. In contrast, there should be no correlation between disillusionment and acceptance of social norms.

As far as **socio-demographic** features are concerned, income and education are negatively related to the acceptance of norms, and women tend to accept more norms[66] (Gabriel et al. 2002, 123-127). The relationship to age seems to be curvilinear in this study: middle-aged people support more norms than younger and older cohorts (Gabriel et al. 2002, 123). However, an examination of bivariate correlations between age and NSB and NCB display no relationship at all. Furthermore, it is difficult to formulate expectations about the impact of attendance at protest actions on acceptance of norms, since to my knowledge there is hardly any empirical evidence of the relationships of both. In contrast, **Poland** as a dummy variable could be positively related to the acceptance of norms, since Gabriel and colleagues provide evidence that Poland has one of the highest level of norms acceptance compared to other European countries (Gabriel et al. 2002, 81). Similar evidence was found in my study (section 2.4.3).

Tables 6.8 and 6.9 depict the results of regression analyses with acceptance of NCB as the dependent variable in the first table; the determinants of the acceptance of NSB are explored in the second.

---

[66] These patterns were not found, though, in all societies (Gabriel et al. 2002, 123).

Table 6.8 Linear regression analysis of norms of civil behaviour (unstandardised regression coefficient B, standard error, R^2 and N, unweighted)

Independent variables	Model 1	Model 2	Model 3	Model 4	Model 5	Model 6
RELIGIOUS FACTORS						
Conservatism (RRCI)	-0.017	-0.021	-0.009	-0.010	-0.012	-0.005
Conservatism (missing values replaced)[a]	-0.019	-0.022*	-0.008	-0.008	-0.011	-0.001
Church attendance (1-never; 4-once a week)	0.014***	0.014***	0.013***	0.013***	0.013***	0.014***
POST-COMMUNIST LEGACY						
Post-communism (dummy)	0.023***	0.022***	0.020***	0.019***	0.018***	-
SOCIO-DEMOGRAPHIC FEATURES						
Education (1-elementary; 8-university degree)		0.001	0.001	0.001	0.001	0.001
Income (1-lowest; 10-highest)		-.001	-0.001	-0.001	-0.001	0.000
Age		0.000	0.000	0.000	0.000	0.000
Gender (1-male; 2-female)		0.005	0.005	0.005	0.005	0.004
SYSTEMIC TRANSITION						
Income inequality (GINI)			-0.002***	-0.002***	-0.002***	-
Happiness (1-happy; 4-not happy)			-0.004	-0.004	-0.004	-0.003
Concerned (1-very; 4-not at all)			0.005**	0.005**	0.005**	-0.001
PROTEST ACTIONS						
Demonstrations (1-yes; 0-no)				-0.003	-0.003	-0.004
Strikes (1-yes; 0-no)				0.007	0.007	0.007
Occupying buildings (1-yes; 0-no)				-0.006	-0.007	-0.009
COUNTRY DUMMIES						
Poland					0.010	Ref.
Austria						0.013
Belgium						-0.036***
France						-0.011
Ireland						-0.068***
Italy						0.004
Portugal						-0.023*
Spain						-0.034***
Croatia						0.025*
Czech Rep.						0.039***
Hungary						0.019
Lithuania						-0.003
Slovakia						-0.056***
Slovenia						-0.031**
Constant	0.807***	1.057***	1.061***	1.063***	1.071***	0.984***
N	12,324	12,324	12,324	12,324	12,324	12,324
N[a]	*13,860*	*13,860*	*13,860*	*13,860*	*13,860*	*13,860*
Adjusted R^2	0.009	0.009	0.012	0.011	0.011	0.030
Adjusted R^{2a}	*0.009*	*0.009*	*0.012*	*0.011*	*0.012*	*0.030*

Notes: Significance levels: *p<0.05, **p<0.01,*** p<0.001
[a] results of linear regression pursued with the same models with a modification concerning the independent variable "conservatism," which is replaced by "conservatism with replaced missing values by countries' means. In this case, the number of cases included in the analysis is higher.
Source: WVS 1999.

The level of explained variance is very low, and despite a stepwise growth remains at a very low level (3 percent) in Model 6. Interestingly, after the introduction of the variables related to protest activities the percentage of explained variance declines slightly, then rises again when countries' dummies are considered in the analysis. The introduction of conservatism with replaced missing values has a modest implication for the results, namely the level of explained variances is slightly higher in Model 5.

Only four independent variables are significant for the acceptance of NCB – church attendance, post-communist legacy, income inequality and concern about the immediate family. **Conservatism** remains mostly unrelated to the acceptance of norms, which was one of the possible expected results. In Model 2, when religious variables and socio-demographic features are introduced to the analysis, conservatism (with values replaced by the countries' means) turns significant and negatively related to the acceptance of norms. This effect is quite surprising and means that conservative people are more likely to justify bribes or cheating on taxes. The other religious factor, **church attendance**, is positively related to the acceptance of NCB, as expected, and this effect is robust and significant across all models.

Post-communist legacy is positively related to the acceptance of NCB, showing that despite the adversarial nature of citizen-state relations under communism, the citizenry of post-communist countries supports norms regulating the civic sphere of life and law-abidingness. Turning to the impact of **systemic transition**, the results conform to expectations. Respondents from countries with lower **income inequality** justify free-riding behaviour to a lesser extent, as do people **concerned about family**, though both effects are very weak. In addition, these effects disappear when countries' dummies are introduced to the models. Other variables – **protest actions** and individual **socio-demographic characteristics** – are unrelated to the acceptance of NCB, which corroborates expectations (with the exception of education). The **Polish context** is insignificant for the acceptance of NCB. This finding is also surprising.

Before we turn to the conclusions, let us explore the acceptance of NSB. The results are presented in Table 6.9.

Table 6.9 Linear regression analysis of norms of social behaviour (unstandardised regression coefficient B, standard error, R^2 and N, unweighted)

Independent variables	Model 1	Model 2	Model 3	Model 4	Model 5	Model 6
RELIGIOUS FACTORS						
Conservatism (RRCI)	0.023***	0.027***	0.014*	0.015*	0.011	0.006
Conservatism (missing values replaced)[a]	0.030***	0.033***	0.018*	0.019**	0.015*	0.009
Church attendance (1-never; 4-once a week)	0.005***	0.005***	0.008***	0.008***	0.008***	0.006***
POST-COMMUNIST LEGACY						
Post-communism (dummy)	-0.010***	-0.011***	-0.006**	-0.006*	-0.009***	-
SOCIO-DEMOGRAPHIC FEATURES						
Education (1-elementary; 8-university degree)		0.001	0.001*	0.001	0.001	-0.001
Income (1-lowest; 10-highest)		-0.002***	-0.002**	-0.002**	-0.002**	0.000
Age		0.000*	0.000	0.000	0.000	0.000
Gender (1-male; 2-female)		-0.002	-0.001	0.000	0.000	0.000
SYSTEMIC TRANSITION						
Income inequality (GINI)			0.004***	0.004***	0.004***	-
Happiness (1-happy; 4-not happy)			-0.002	-0.002	-0.002	-0.001
Concerned (1-very; 4-not at all)			0.004***	0.004***	0.004***	0.000
PROTEST ACTIONS						
Demonstrations (1-yes; 0-no)				0.000	0.000	0.001
Strikes (1-yes; 0-no)				0.003	0.003	0.005
Occupying buildings (1-yes; 0-no)				0.008	0.007	0.002
COUNTRY DUMMIES						
Poland					0.018***	Ref.
Austria						-0.036***
Belgium						-0.051***
France						-0.017**
Ireland						-0.009
Italy						0.005
Portugal						-0.032***
Spain						-0.021***
Croatia						-0.001
Czech Rep.						-0.029***
Hungary						0.010
Lithuania						0.016*
Slovakia						-0.131***
Slovenia						-0.051***
Constant	0.899***	0.606***	0.608***	0.606***	0.620***	0.757***
N	13,494	13,494	13,494	13,494	13,494	13,494
N^a	15,189	15,189	15,189	15,189	15,189	15,189
Adjusted R2	0.004	0.006	0.019	0.019	0.020	0.079
Adjusted R^{2a}	*0.005*	*0.006*	*0.019*	*0.019*	*0.020*	*0.079*

Notes: Significance levels: *p<0.05, **p<0.01,*** p<0.001
[a] results of linear regression pursued with the same models with a modification concerning the independent variable "conservatism," which is replaced by "conservatism with replaced missing values by countries' means. In this case, the number of cases included in the analysis is higher.
Source: WVS 1999.

In the case of acceptance of NSB, the level of explained variance is higher compared to civil behaviour, yet nevertheless remains at a low level (8 percent) in Model 6. One important rise in percentage of explained variance appears when the variables related to systemic transformation are added to the model; the second occurs with the consideration of countries' dummies. With the modified variable of conservatism, explained variance remains constant.

To begin with religious determinants, **conservatism** has a positive effect on the acceptance of social norms, which was expected. With the consideration of the Polish context the relevance of conservatism disappears. This finding could indicate a different situation in Poland. However when conservatism with the replaced missing values is analysed, the introduction of the dummy for Poland hardly changes the explanatory power of conservatism – it remains significant also in Model 5. This inconsistency in findings requires a cautious interpretation of the results. It may be that the absence of significance of conservatism in the first case is an artefact resulting from the measurement of RRC. In addition, the effects of conservatism are not robust and decrease when other variables are added to the model.

Quite different findings concern **church attendance** – the effects remain significant and robust even after the inclusion of countries' contextual factors. The positive direction of church affiliation conforms to expectations that churchgoers are more inclined to follow social norms. In other words, both religious factors are positive determinants for acceptance of social norms, whereby the effects of churchgoing are more robust.

The influence of the **post-communist legacy** is, as expected, negative, which supports Roßteustcher's claims concerning low solidarity in post-communist countries (Roßteutscher 2004, 184-185). To put it in another way, individuals living in post-communist countries are more likely to justify behaviour that is harmful to others, but are less likely to accept cheating on state institutions or disobeying laws. It is evidence of the destructive impact of prior communist experience not only on social trust, but also on pro-social attitudes (see also Sztompka 2000, Grabowska, Szawiel 2001, 149).

Furthermore, the effect of **concern about family** is negative and disappears when countries dummies' are included in the analysis. Surprisingly, people from countries with higher **income inequalities** are more likely to follow NSB. We might explain it by a greater need for solidarity in countries with higher income disparities. The subjective state of **happiness** remains unrelated to the acceptance of norms. Attending **protest actions** is insignificant for acceptance of NSB. Among the **socio-demographic** factors, only income seems negative and significant, which corroborates the findings of other studies (Gabriel et al. 2002, 127); age, gender and level of education are insignificant. The effect of the **Polish** context is positive and significant, as expected. The effects of all other countries are negative or insignificant, which means that Poles take a leading position among publics in other Catholic societies in declaring acceptance of NSB.

To sum up the findings concerning the acceptance of norms, most of the expectations were confirmed. Principally, religious factors are positively associated with the acceptance of norms. The only exception is a negative relationship between conservatism and NCB, though it is significant only when the consequences of systemic transformation are not considered. The post-communist legacy is, as expected, positively related to civil norms and negatively related to social norms. Systemic transition seems to have a negative impact on the acceptance of norms, with one exception – the effect of the contextual influence of income inequalities in a country is positive in the case of social norms. Concern about the family has a negative effect on accepting norms. Attending protest actions and most of the socio-demographic characteristics remain unrelated to the norms, except for the negative impact of income.

Poland is characterised by a generally higher level of support for social norms than other societies. Analyses of the determinants of norms show that, principally, they do not differ much between Poland and other countries, with only one exception: NSB. With the inclusion of the Polish context, the positive effect of conservatism disappears, but only when conservatism without the replaced missing values is considered, which suggests the need for caution in interpretation of these findings. In the case of acceptance of NCB, the patterns in Poland are not different from those in other countries, and the Polish context is irrelevant. In general, we can conclude that the higher acceptance of norms in Poland can be explained by higher church attendance and partly by stronger conservatism.

6.5 Different mechanisms of social capital building in Poland: conclusions

The main problem addressed in this chapter was to study the extent to which mechanisms of social capital building in Poland are distinct from those in other countries. Four main factors important for social capital building were considered: (1) religious influence, (2) aspects related to prior communist experiences, (3) consequences of systemic transitions, and (4) protest activity. Additionally, the impacts of socio-demographic characteristics and countries' specific contexts were taken into account.

In general, comparative analyses of determinants of social capital are very complex and, as we saw, distinct components of social capital are influenced by different determinants. This evidence justifies my research strategy concerning the separate analyses of determinants of the single components of social capital. Furthermore, we can see that the patterns of relationships between single determinants and components of social capital are multifaceted. Therefore we cannot say that Poland is exceptional because of one dissimilar factor or because of a decreasing effect concerning one component: in some aspects Poland is an exception, while in others it is not.

A main conclusion is that the mechanisms of social capital building do not differ considerably in Poland from those in other countries with a similar dominant religious tradition or similar prior political system, though there are some exceptions. Table 6.10 outlines an overview of the explored determinants of social capital and the results of the comparative analyses. Cell entries report relationships between single factors and components of social capital, and distinguish between general mechanisms and the mechanisms discovered only in Poland. The positive or negative (+ or -) sign to the left concerns the relations found in Model 6 (Model 5 in the cases of post-communist legacy and income inequalities), when all countries and all variables are included in the models. The +/- sign on the right reports the mechanisms that are characteristic of Poland only (i.e., reports a change in the predictive or explanatory power of a factor when the Polish context is controlled: a change in significance of the variable between Model 4 and Model 5).

As can be seen in Table 6.10, across determinants related to the systemic transitions and attending protest actions, both signs of the cell entries are identical. This means that the consequences of the systemic transition and attending protest actions affected social capital in Poland in a similar way as in other countries. Yet the signs differ in several cell entries concerning religious determinants and the communist legacy. So, principally Catholicism, frequent church attendance and the specific Polish legacy of communism shape social capital in Poland in a different way than other societies. Analysing Table 6.10 in a horizontal direction, social trust is the only component of social capital that seems to depend on similar factors in Polish and other societies. Furthermore, volunteering and acceptance of NCB also display similar patterns in Poland compared to the other societies.

Table 6.10 Comparative overview of the mechanisms of social capital building in Poland and other Catholic societies

		Mechanisms general / Mechanisms in Poland							
Components of social capital		Religious factors		Post-communism and systemic transition				Protest actions		
		Conservatism[a]	Church attendance[a]	Post-communism[b]	Income inequality[b]	Happiness[a]	Concern about family[a]	Demonstrations[a]	Strikes[a]	Occupying buildings[a]
Social networks	Religious membership	+/+	0/+	0/-	-/-	0/0	0/0	+/+	0/0	0/0
	Religious volunteering	+/+	0/0	0/0	-/-	-/-	0/0	+/+	0/0	0/0
	Secular membership	0/-[c]	0/0	+/+	-/-	0/0	+/+	0/0	0/0	0/0
	Secular volunteering	+/+	0/0	0/0	-/-	-/-	-/-	+/+	+/+	+/+
	Informal networks	0/-	0/0	0/-	+/+	-/-	0/0	+/+	0/0	0/0
Trust	Trust	0/0	0/0	-/-	0/0	-/-	0/0	+/+	0/0	0/0
Norms and values	Civil norms	0/0	+/+	+/+	-/-	0/0	0/0	0/0	0/0	0/0
	Social norms	0/+[c]	+/+	-/-	+/+	0/0	0/0	0/0	0/0	0/0

Notes: mechanisms of single factors on single components of social capital found in this study are presented in following way: "+" - positive mechanisms were found; "-" – negative mechanisms were found; "0" – no relationship was found.
[a] Reported general mechanisms concern the results in the full Model 6 / reported mechanisms in Poland concern a change in results found in Model 5, when Poland is introduced as a dummy variable.
[b] Reported mechanisms concern the results from Model 5.
[c] concerns only when conservatism is conceptualised with the missing values replaced by country means.

With the evidence found in this chapter we can give a precise answer to the question: which mechanisms of social capital production differ in Poland? The key differences mostly concern social networks (specifically, informal networks and membership) and norms and values (NSB). The following mechanisms of social capital building are dissimilar in Poland compared to other societies:

(1) Social networks in Poland are weaker because of the negative impact of RRC, which impedes membership in secular organisations and the building of informal networks among people.
(2) Social networks (membership in religious organisations and informal networks) are less developed due to the specific communist legacy in this society.

(3) Church attendance positively influences membership in religious organisations only in Polish society (when controlled for other factors).
(4) The acceptance of social norms is positively influenced by RRC only among Polish people.
(5) For both formal and informal networks, the Polish context is a negative factor, meaning that specific characteristics of the Polish context decrease the propensity to join social networks. Similar decreasing effects on social networks are displayed only in the context of Lithuania. Poland and Lithuania were one state for almost three centuries, which confirms claims about the relevance of historical legacy presented by Putnam (1993) and discussed in chapter 1 of this study.

In a nutshell, social networks are the component of social capital production that differs in Poland to the greatest extent. In general, Polish people are reluctant to join certain types of networks, including informal ones, because of the specific Catholic influence on their value orientations. Other reasons for weak social networks are experiences related to the communist legacy and specific features of the Polish context.

7 Why is Poland an exception among post-communist societies?

7.1 Introduction

In previous chapters I explored the reasons for Poland's exceptionally low social capital endowment. For young democracies social capital is especially important, since it "makes democracy work" (Putnam 1993). The low stock of social capital in Poland is all the more surprising when we recall the vibrant Polish social movement *Solidarność*, which eventually contributed to the collapse of communism. What happened to this enthusiasm and social engagement? Did we find the reasons for Polish social apathy and social fragmentation?

The analyses concentrated on the search for specific cultural and structural traits of Polish society, which distinguish Poland from other countries with similar experiences in the recent past – communist regimes and a similar cultural (Catholic) background. Furthermore, I addressed the question of whether these differences displayed by Polish society could be responsible for the low accumulation of social capital. As similar as they seem, Central Eastern European societies differ in many respects, and their stocks of social capital, though in general lower than in Western Europe, show considerable differences, too. This study demonstrates a whole range of dissimilarities in the conditions and mechanisms of social capital building. The concluding chapter provides an overview of the main findings, seeks to outline possible future developments of social capital in Poland and the consequences for democracy, and contains suggestions for further research.

7.2 Main findings

7.2.1 Crucial factors

The purpose of this study was to find out why Poland is an exception among post-communist societies in regard to its low social capital endowment. First, we needed to closely explore the subject of analysis – the stock of social capital in Polish society. Therefore the following question was addressed: what is the empirical evidence for social capital in Poland? Are all three components of social capital – social networks, trust, and norms and values – indeed low in Polish society? It turns out that Polish social capital is effectively low, though only when referring to two particular components – social trust and social networks (both formal and informal networks). Values and norms, in contrast, appear to be relatively widespread in Polish society compared to other countries.

Second, we focused on exploring the reasons for the exceptionally weak social networks and low social trust in Polish society. This research was conducted in two steps. First, the conditions for social capital building were explored (chapters 3, 4 and 5), and second, the mechanisms of its production were examined (chapter 6). By "conditions" I mean particular factors related to the communist past and Catholicism, which are commonly claimed to hamper the development of social capital. "Mechanisms" refer to the relationships between these factors and components of social capital.

Throughout this study a whole range of causes for Polish exceptionality has been found. The dissimilarities between Poland and other post-communist countries concern both the conditions and mechanisms of social capital production. Relevant factors distinguishing social capital production in Poland are related to (1) particular experiences this society accumulated during communism, (2) several factors resulting from the particularities of the Polish course of systemic transition, and (3) a group of factors with roots in the dominant religious tradition, Catholicism.

Though living under similar communist regimes, societies of Central Eastern Europe somehow accumulated distinctive experiences during this period (chapter 3). Whereas some particularly repressive regimes intimidated their subjects intensively (for instance the Soviet Union), in other societies opposition movements seemed to freeze for many years after a single trial of challenging the system that resulted in a bloodshed reaction of the regime (e.g., Hungary 1956, Czechoslovakia 1968). The situation in Poland was different – protests and strikes erupted every several years, so that the legitimacy of the communist regime was steadily challenged. Therefore Polish citizens won relatively high levels of pluralism and autonomy compared to other communist citizens. One of the manifestations of this pluralism was the relative independence of the Roman Catholic Church. In the 1980s the Church's exceptional position, strengthened by the Polish Pope's first visit in 1979, triggered the mass mobilisation of the *Solidarność* movement and the building of a civil society. The experiences of Polish society are dissimilar from those of other societies in the region – Poles are characterised by a steady and active protest opposition, relative pluralism and eventually a huge social mobilisation against the regime. Why did these experiences not result in *higher* participation in Poland after the collapse of communism compared to other post-communist societies? The reason probably lies in the anti-systemic character of the opposition activities: the experience Polish citizens gained when mobilising **against** the regime became useless when cooperative skills in a friendlier democratic environment were required. In other words, civil society after the system change remained sceptical about the way democracy works and showed non-cooperative attitudes toward state institutions, much the same as scepticism about the legitimacy of the prior communist regime. In my study this claim is confirmed: the examination of the mechanisms of social capital building in Poland indeed shows a negative effect of the post-communist experience on social capital building in this country (see Table 6.10). These negative relationships were found only in Poland for two types of networks (church-related organisations and informal networks). Prior communist experience was negative for social trust and social norms, though these mechanisms were not unique for Poland but concerned all countries from the region. Returning to the research question, I found evidence of a stronger negative impact of prior communist experience on social capital in Poland, which partly explains Poland's exceptionally low participation.

Secondly, post-communist societies differ in their experiences concerning the consequences of systemic transitions (chapter 3). Transition was a dislocating period for the citizenry in the whole region, though I found several differences concerning Poland in particular. These specific dissimilarities imply different conditions for social capital building in this country during the systemic change. Persistent economic hardship during longer transition periods is usually related to growing social disappointment that results in passivity and the resignation of citizens. The main reasons for the disappointment lie in economic turbulences brought about by systemic change (chapter 3). Macroeconomic data confirms (1) higher unemployment rates and (2) higher economic inequalities in Poland compared to other societies undergoing transition. In addition, (3) dissatisfaction among Poles was also at one of the highest levels compared to other countries from the region. Furthermore, we found empirical evidence of a negative relationship between a high level of income inequalities and dissatisfaction on the one side, and social capital on the other side (see Table 6.10). In societies with higher income inequalities, all types of social networks are weaker. In addition, disillusioned individuals are less trustful and less ready to join social networks. Therefore the especially high reluctance to join social networks and to trust others in Poland can be explained by more severe economic hardship and stronger disappointment within society.

In contrast, the higher frequency of protest actions during the 1990s was an insufficient explanation of Poland's low social capital. Contrary to the claims of Kubik and Ekiert (1999), the level of participation in demonstrations is not higher in Poland, though attendance at other forms of protest actions (strikes and occupation of buildings) is slightly higher. Nevertheless, the results of the analyses of mechanisms of social capital building do not show a negative correlation between social capital and attendance at protest actions (chapter 6). This is why higher protest activity in Poland fails to explain its low social capital.

Thirdly, as argued in chapter 5, Poland's exceptionally low social capital endowment can be explained by Catholicism as the dominant religious tradition and the intensity of religious practices. The influence of religion on social capital displays a very complex pattern (see Table 4.1 and Table 4.3). We need to distinguish between structural[67] and cultural[68] religious influences; the impact of each religious aspect on social capital is claimed to point in opposite directions. For one thing scholars postulate there is a general positive effect of church attendance on social capital, especially on social networks. Yet Catholicism negatively affects social capital, mostly networks and trust, because it promotes obedience, passivity, lack of individualism, vertical family bonds, etc. To measure the extent of Catholic influence on people's value orientations in a given society I analysed the levels of conservatism rooted in the Catholic tenets (RRC). Polish society was not only the most religiously devoted – in terms of the percentage of church members and frequency of churchgoing – but also the most conservative in Catholic Europe. This means that the long-term cultural impact of Catholicism in Poland is one of the strongest in Europe – which matters for social capital building.

Turning to Polish social capital: what is the "resulting effect" of religion in Poland? Does the negative influence of Catholicism outweigh the positive impact of church affiliation on social capital? To answer this question, religious impact was analysed empirically in two steps. First, single relationships between both religious factors and social capital were scrutinised (chapter 5). In this way the influence of both religious factors, structural (church attendance) and cultural (RRC) were assessed separately. Second, I compared determinants of social capital across societies, whereby both religious factors were analysed simultaneously to determine the "resulting effect" of religion in Poland (chapter 6).

Let us start with the relationship between **church attendance** and social capital (chapter 5). In general, commonly claimed positive effects of church attendance were empirically confirmed, though primarily at the individual level (see Table 5.16). Churchgoers were found to be more prone to building social capital; however, their social capital is mostly related to church-based groups. Churchgoers in Poland are also more likely to trust others.

Does it matter for social capital that Polish society is devout (i.e., has a high percentage of churchgoers)? Macro-level religious devotion is in general negatively related to social capital endowment. In devout countries the level of social trust is lower, and the same applies to aggregate levels of membership in secular networks

---

[67] I used the term "affiliation effects" in reference to the structural influence of church attendance on social capital.

[68] I used the term "denomination effects" to refer to the cultural influence of religion (Catholicism) on social capital.

(see Table 5.16). In addition, in societies with high levels of church attendance, churchgoers show a relatively lower readiness to join social networks (see Tables 5.8 and 5.9). Moreover, in Poland macro-level religious devotion is not related to informal networks, as is the case in other societies (see Figure 5.28). To summarise, social capital in Poland is weaker because of the high level of religious devotion.

Turning to the second religious factor – **RRC** – does it matter for social capital that Poland is the most conservative society in the sample? In general, RRC is negatively related to social networks (at the macro level), as expected (see Table 5.16). Therefore the low social capital in Poland can be explained by an especially strong Catholic influence on value orientations in society.

The second step of analysis, the determinants of social capital were compared across Catholic societies with and without prior communist experience (chapter 6). This analysis, conducted at the individual level, provided evidence of a **stronger impact of the cultural aspects of religion (RRC) than structural features (church attendance)** (see Table 6.10). In other words, for social capital it matters whether an individual is conservative, but not whether one attends church regularly. Poland displays a clearly *different* pattern of religious influence than other countries. In Poland RRC has an additional negative effect on social capital – conservative individuals are reluctant to join networks,[69] and only in Poland does churchgoing have a positive impact on religious networks.[70] Returning to my research question: why is Polish social capital exceptionally low, and what is the impact of religion? At the macro level, strong religious devotion in Poland partly explains the low levels of social trust, while weak social networks can be explained by the strong impact of Catholicism on value orientations (RRC). Furthermore, the strong conservatism of individual Poles explicates weak informal and partly weak formal ties.

In sum, Poland's low endowment with social capital is a consequence of several factors, which are on the one hand related to the legacies of recent decades, such as Poland's unique collective communist experiences – in particular the heavy social burden of reforms during transformation. On the other hand, cultural traits of Polish society, rooted in strong Catholicism, provide another explanation for the low social capital in this society.

7.2.2   Dissimilar conditions or mechanisms?

Is Poland's social capital endowment especially low because of dissimilar *conditions* of social capital building, dissimilar *mechanisms* of social capital building or both

---

[69] Specifically, conservative individuals in Poland are reluctant to be members in secular organisations and join informal networks.
[70] To be specific, churchgoers in Poland are more likely to be members of church-related groups, but not to volunteer in these kinds of groups.

(chapter 1)? In order to answer this question I systematise the reasons for Polish exceptionality according to both categories. While the first category encompasses different conditions of social capital building in Poland, the second covers dissimilar mechanisms.[71] Table 7.1 presents the results of the study according to both categories.

Table 7.1 Dissimilarities in conditions and mechanisms of social capital building in Poland

DISSIMILAR CONDITIONS of social capital building in Poland, compared to other post-communist countries	DISSIMILAR MECHANISMS of social capital building in Poland, compared to other post-communist countries
- Stronger disillusionment related to systemic transition in Poland negatively affects social networks and social trust; - Higher income inequality in Poland negatively influences social networks; and - Stronger conservatism rooted in Catholicism negatively impacts social networks.	- Relationships between social networks and the collective experience of the communist legacy are negative only in Poland; and - Relationships between social networks and conservatism rooted in Catholicism are negative only in Poland.

Two main conclusions can be drawn from Table 7.1. First, we found both dissimilar conditions for social capital building in Poland and distinct mechanisms. Therefore both **distinct conditions and distinct mechanisms explain the lower social capital in Poland**.

A second observation concerns the mechanisms of social capital building in Poland. In most cases, **dissimilarities in the mechanisms of social capital building concern primarily one dimension – social networks** (with one exception: the positive relationship of conservatism to norms of social behaviour). As for social trust and norms and values, the production mechanisms are principally similar to those of other countries. In other words, the mechanisms of production concerning the cultural dimension of social capital are similar in Poland to those in other countries, whereas the production of the structural component of social capital differs in some respects.

In sum, social capital in Poland cannot be accumulated to the same extent as in other countries in the region, due to a number of unfavourable conditions and different mechanisms, presented above. Some of them – such as income inequality – can be overcome with targeted politics. Some however, such as cultural traits

---

[71] The dissimilarity of the mechanisms of the production of social capital presented here is based on the evidence found in the multivariate models (see Table 6.10), and omits the results of the bivariate analyses (presented in Table 5.16).

related to RRC, will have a durable effect. What can we say about the future development of social capital in Poland, bearing in mind the findings of this study?

7.3 Implications for the future

By the end of this study we know in what respect endowment with social capital is exceptional in Poland, and we know a number of reasons for Polish exceptionality. Finally we address the question of what implications for social capital in Poland flow from this knowledge, especially regarding two issues – further development of social capital and democracy in Poland and further research on social capital.

7.3.1 Future development of social capital in Poland

As far as further development of social capital in Poland is concerned, several implications flow from my findings. Now that we know the reasons *why* Poland is an exception, we can shed some light on the question of whether these particularities are temporary or have an enduring character. Furthermore, we can assess the prospects for democracy in Poland in light of these findings. Principally we deal with three kinds of dissimilarities of social capital building in Poland: the communist experience, the consequences of the systemic transition and factors related to Catholicism. These three aspects are discussed below in reference to further social capital development followed by a discussion on prospects of further consolidation of democracy in Poland.

7.3.1.1 Future developments of social capital in Poland

Starting with experiences related to the communist era, how long can such effects linger in a society? According to socialisation theory, people's attitudes and values are imprinted primarily during their formative years. So, we could expect that the generation socialised after the system changed should not be directly influenced by the communist experience. They will be indirectly influenced by their parents, who were socialised under the communist regime, though this influence should leave weaker imprints. And over the course of time, with new cohorts born and socialised under a democratic system, the percentage of people with memories of the communist experience will diminish. To a certain extent these expectations are confirmed in the empirical findings of my study. Indeed age was significant and negatively correlated with most of the formal social networks and with trust, but not with norms and values (chapter 6). This indicates that younger people are more prone to trust and to join networks. Therefore it is likely that this condition – communist experience – will fade away over time in Poland. We can expect the effect to disappear when the cohorts without communist experience replace the older ones.

A slightly different situation concerns the future impact of the systemic transition in Poland. Three different factors related to this transformation have been disentangled – disappointment, income inequalities and protest actions. While the first two relate to structural problems, and as such depend on the efficiency of policy-makers, the last is probably a cultural trait of Polish society (similar to Italian or French societies, which are characterised by a higher frequency of protest actions compared to other societies). What can we say about the durability of the impact of economic hardship? After a period of sharp rise in unemployment and inflation the situation stabilised, and the long-term indices for economic development across Central Eastern Europe are encouraging. Central European countries are now part of the European Union (EU), which results in external financial support, a rise in direct investment and the benefits of trade in united European markets. On the other hand EU membership provides a basis for political stability in the region. In the long term, the main problem Poland needs to cope with is income inequality, since the GINI coefficient for income inequalities shows an upward trend in Poland (see Figure 3.3). The profits of macroeconomic growth should be more equally and fairly distributed across society. As far as the structural consequences of the transformation are concerned, the short-term effects of economic turbulences could have affected all cohorts in post-communist societies (we probably deal with a "period effect"), though this impact could diminish in the long term, depending on how effective new policies are. On the other hand, long-lasting effects will remain if democratic authorities in Poland fail to deal with the problem of income inequalities. Consequently, high inequalities will not lead to a rise in satisfaction among citizens. In a nutshell, social capital will have a favourable foundation for development when political performance satisfies the needs of citizens.

Turning to protest actions, the findings presented in chapter 6 point to a positive relationship between attending protest actions (mainly demonstrations) and social capital (social networks and trust). It is difficult to say to what extent participation in protest actions in Poland is a kind of "regular" political behaviour in this society, irrespective of economic or political problems. This is why it is also hard to predict the durability of this kind of political behaviour and its future trends. Nevertheless, assuming that attending protest actions is economically or politically conditioned, fewer protest actions would be related to less social capital in Poland. Otherwise no change is expected.

The third factor crucial for social capital endowment in Poland is religion. Of two different aspects of religious influences on social capital – cultural (RRC) and structural (church affiliation) – the former was not found to predict social capital (see Table 6.10). Church attendance, in contrast, positively impacts network building, and specifically one type of network (religious membership). What kind of changes in both religious conditions can be expected, and what are the implications for the future stock of social capital in Poland? Polish people will probably first stop attending mass as frequently and then they may slowly, generation by generation, change their attitudes and values based on religious tenets, too. Generally, the expectation concerning diminishing religious practice in Poland is based on general secularisation trends observed across Europe. I expect the appearance of secularisation trends in Poland too, since the strong position of the Catholic Church in this country, supported by the strong religiosity of the faithful, was partly a societal reaction to the communist reality. Once communism collapsed, the Church lost its "charm," and the level of church attendance will diminish slowly and eventually will be similar to that in other European countries. The newest empirical studies on church attendance in Poland confirm these expectations: clear downward trends in churchgoing are registered in Poland in the 2000s (Kaluza 2010, 6). Poland is not the only devout country slowly converging with general European trends. Similar secularisation tendencies are reported in recent studies on religiosity in Ireland: the weakening political position of the Catholic Church results in shrinking church attendance rates (Coakley 2011, 108). Furthermore, my findings concerning the influence of age on religious engagement seem to also confirm the appearance of secularisation trends. Age is significant and negatively correlated with membership and volunteering in church-based organisations, which points to the decreasing interest of young people in religious participation (see Tables 6.4 and 6.5). In Poland this will mean less religious social capital in the future. Or, if with the convergence of the conditions (church attendance) the mechanisms become similar too, there will be no influence of church attendance on social capital in Poland, since I did not find any relationship between churchgoing and networks in other societies.

Predicting trends in changes of levels of RRC in Poland is more challenging. For one thing we could expect less conservatism with progressing secularisation, as in societies with a higher percentage of frequent churchgoers there are more conservative people (compare Figures 5.4 and 5.11). Yet we have no empirical evidence of downward trends in Polish conservatism, and certainly such changes in attitudes and values will not appear at once. Probably we need one or two generations to be socialised in a more secularised society to display less conservatism rooted in religion. Consequences for social capital will be noticeable with regard to secular membership and informal networks, namely the negative effect of conservatism could disappear, as evidence from other societies shows (see Table 6.12).

In sum, we expect a slow convergence of the stock of social capital in Poland to the levels of other European countries. At least the negative influence of prior communist experience and Catholicism are expected to diminish over time. The negative impact of income inequalities and life satisfaction depends on the general economic and political situation, and will reduce when Poland becomes a "better place to live." This is a challenge for the authorities. It would be interesting to repeat this analysis in about 30 years, when new generations socialised in the new free Poland (the Fourth Republic) will come into adulthood. We could see then whether Poland remains an exception among post-communist societies, or indeed is converging with the rest of Europe.

7.3.1.2 Future development of democracy in Poland

Social capital has attracted so much scholarly attention in recent years because it matters for democracy (Putnam 1993). So, what are the implications for democracy in Poland? Until now democracy has consolidated in Poland despite its low social capital endowment, and Poland is not an exception in this regard. Empirical findings show a lack of short-term relationships between progress in democratic consolidation and social capital across several countries in Central Eastern Europe. In contrast, the long-term positive effects of social capital on democratisation have been empirically confirmed. Therefore in the long term there are positive prospects for social capital development in Poland – certain negative factors will diminish, as argued above – which will make further increases in the quality of democratic government possible. Social capital can become an effective societal resource supporting better government in Poland in the long term.

Moreover, recent studies show that the structure of civil society affects the quality of democracy – Paxton claims that not all types of organisations have a positive impact on democracy (2002, 272). According to Paxton, three types of associations (sport organisations, church-based groups and trade unions), which she labels *isolated associations*, "had a strong negative influence on democracy" (Paxton 2002, 272) because they produce bonding, not bridging, social capital. In Poland the most popular type of organisations are trade unions, followed by church-related organisations and sport associations (see Figure 5.26). If with the progress of secularisation church-related organisations weaken in Poland (in chapter 6 we saw a positive relationship between churchgoing and religious membership in Poland), this will not be negative for democracy. Less religion-based social capital will be a better condition for the further development of democracy. On the other hand, the level of membership in all three types of *isolated associations* is lower in Poland than in other societies, which implies that the negative effect of *isolated associations* in Poland should not be stronger than in other countries in the region.

On the other hand, Paxton claims that the relationship between social capital and democracy is reciprocal (2002, 272). Enduring democracy is a positive determinant for social capital development. As my findings show, failures in governance, such as neglecting the increase of income inequalities, suffocate the development of social cohesion (chapter 6). More effective governance in Poland would make citizens more interested in joining networks, and engaged citizens are more satisfied and supportive of democracy in the long term.

To summarise, the prospects for democracy in Poland look positive, assuming that levels of social capital increase, especially based on secular engagement, as presented in this study.

7.3.2   Implications for further research

This research found a number of explanations for Polish exceptionality, yet it also raised new questions. At least four aspects of the specific Polish situation could be explored in future studies.

First, I found dissimilar effects of prior communist experience in Poland (chapter 6), and we know that the experience of the communist past was different in Poland (chapter 3). A plausible explanation why this effect of the communist experience is different in Poland may lie in the anti-systemic character of political engagement under communism in Poland. However this claim could only by indirectly confirmed in my study, since the dataset does not contain questions referring to this specific situation in Poland. Therefore this question should be examined in more depth. The best way would be to interview people who were involved in the anti-regime movement before 1989 in Poland in order to find out whether they are reluctant to participate nowadays, and learn about their reasons for this reluctance. Furthermore, we could examine their level of support for democracy and the current authorities. If they are indeed less ready to be engaged and less supportive of the current system and authorities, then the claim of the persistence of anti-state socialisation patterns would be confirmed. Only then could we be sure that the negative effect of the communist legacy (found in chapter 6) indeed has its roots in the anti-systemic character of oppositional activity under the communist regime.

Second, negative effects of income inequalities were found only at the macro level. The measures of the effects of the systemic transition such as deprivation or disappointment at the micro level were only proximal, since there are neither direct questions concerning disappointment with the systemic transition, nor questions concerning the material situation after the systemic change. Measures applied in my study, such as "concern about the material situation of the immediate family" did not refer directly to the effects of the systemic transition, and across post-communist respondents the level of concern was not systematically higher compared to Western societies. Similarly, the level of life satisfaction only approximately measures disappointment with systemic changes. More precise empirical explorations of the effects of disappointment and income inequalities at the micro level are required. Indirectly, my study confirms that material status matters for engagement and trust, since a higher socio-economic status (measured by income and education levels) has a positive effect on engagement and trust (chapter 6). With new data we could examine whether those who perceive themselves as deprived and disappointed after the transition (to be sure that this effect is directly related to the systemic transition) are indeed less connected and less trusting.

Third, we discovered different mechanisms of social capital production in Poland, especially the impact of RRC on secular networks and informal ties. Only in Poland were conservatives reluctant to meet friends and to join secular organisations (chapter 6). The reasons for these specific Polish behavioural patterns must be explored more deeply, for instance in open interviews, comparing conservative and non-conservative groups. We could ask them directly about why they are reluctant to join networks.

Fourth, informal networks in Poland are especially weak (chapter 2). In addition, they are the type of networks that show the strongest dissimilarity of production mechanisms (see Table 6.12). Unfortunately data on informal networks are very scarce in the WVS, especially with regard to Polish society; therefore the examination concerned only friendship networks. Therefore an in-depth exploration of different forms of informal networks – for example those produced through the workplace, church or neighbourhood, as well as friendship and family ties – is needed in order to find out whether other kinds of informal networks are also weak, and to understand why these kinds of ties are so weak in Poland.

These supplementary studies would certainly deepen our understanding of the specifics of social capital in Poland. New findings, though, are unlikely to change my predictions that in the course of time Poland will probably get "tediously normal," as Michael Moran predicts.

References

Adloff, Frank. 2010. „Dichotomizing Religion and Civil Society? Catholicism in Germany and the USA Before the Second Vatican Council." *Journal of Civil Society* 6 (3): 193-203.
Alber, Jens/Florian Fliegner/Johannes Hemker. 2010. "Ungleichheit differenziert gemessen. Armut und materielle Not in der Europäischen Union." *WBZ Mitteilungen* 128. Berlin: Wissenschaftszentrum Berlin für Sozialforschung
Alesina, Alberto F./Paola Giuliano. 2009. "Family Ties and Political Participation." *NBER Working Paper Series* 15415. Cambridge: National Bureau of Economic Research
Almond, Gabriel A./Sidney Verba. 1963. *The Civic Culture: Political Attitudes and Democracy in Five Nations*. Princeton: Princeton University Press.
Badescu, Gabriel. 2006. „Historical and cultural borderlines in eastern Europe." In: Hans-Dieter Klingemann/Dieter Fuchs/Jan Zielonka (ed.). *Democracy and Political Culture in Eastern Europe*. London: Routledge: 85-98.
Badescu, Gabriel 2003. „Social trust and democratization in the post-communist societies." In: Gabriel Badescu/Eric M. Uslaner (ed.). *Social Capital and the Transition to Democracy*. London: Routledge: 120-139.
Bahlcke, Joachim. 1997. „Calvinism and estate libaration movements in Bohemia and Hungary (1570-1620)." In: Karin Maag (ed.). *The Reformation in Eastern and Central Europe*. Hants: Scholar Press: 72-91.
Banfield, Edward C. 1958. *The moral Basis of a Backward Society*. Glencoe/Ill.: Free Press.
Barnes, Samuel H. 1998. „The mobilization of political identity in new democracies." In: Samuel H. Barnes/János Simon (ed.). *The Postcommunist Citizen*. Budapest: Erasmus Foundation, Budapest and Institute for Political Science of the Hungarian Academy of Sciences: 117-137.
Bartkowski, Jerzy. 2003. *Tradycja i polityka. Wpływ tradycji kulturowych polskich regionów na współczesne zachowania społeczne i polityczne*. Warsaw: Wydawnictwo ŻAK.
Batt, Judy (ed.). 1994. *The international dimension of democratization in Czechoslovakia and Hungary*. London: Leicester University Press.
Becker, Penny Edgell/Pawan H. Dhingra. 2001. „Religious Involvement and volunteering: Implication for civil society." *Sociology of Religion* 62 (3): 315-335.
Berend, Ivan, T. 2007. „Social shock in transforming Central and Eastern Europe." *Communist and Post-Communist Studies* 40 (3): 269-280.
Berggren, Niclas/Christian Bjørnskov. 2009. "Does Religiosity Promote or Discourage Social Trust? Evidence form Cross-Country and Cross-State Comparisons." The Ratio Institute. *The Ratio Institute Working Papers* http://pure.au.dk/portal-asb/files/9154/wp_09-142
Bernhard, Michael. 1993. „Civil Society and Democratic Transition in East Central Europe." *Political Science Quarterly* 108 (2): 307-326.
Borowik, Irena. 2002. „The Roman Catholic Church in the process of democratic transformation: The case of Poland." *Social Compass* 49 (2): 239-252.
Borowik, Irena 2000. *Odbudowywanie pamięci. Przemiany religijne w Środkowo-Wschodniej Europie po upadku komunizmu*. Kraków: Zakład Wydawniczy Nomos.
Bozóki, András. 1994. „From Soft Communism to Post-Communism. Authoritarian Legacy and Democratic Transition in Hungary." In: János Mátyás Kovács (ed.). *Transition to Capitalism? The Communist Legacy in Eastern Europe*. New Brunswick, London: Transaction Publishers.

Bruszt, László. 1994. „Transformative Politics: Social Costs and Social Peace in East Central Europe." In: János Mátyás Kovács (ed.). *Transition to Capitalism? The Communist Legacy in Eastern Europe.* New Brunswick, London: Transaction Publishers: 103-120.
Cameron, Euan. 1991. *The European Reformation.* Oxford: Clarendon Pres.
Campbell, David E./Steven J. Yonish. 2003. „Religion and Volunteering in America." In: Corwin Smidt (ed.). *Religion as Social Capital. Producing the Common Good.* Waco/Tex.: Baylor University Press: 87 - 106.
Castle, Marjorie. 1996. „The Final Crisis." In: Jane L. Curry/Luba Fajter (ed.). *Poland's Permanent Revolution. People vs. Elites, 1956-1990.* Washington: The American University Press: 211-223.
Cnaan, Ram A./Stephanie C. Boddie/Gaynor I. Yancey. 2003. In: Corwin Smidt (ed.). *Religion as Social Capital. Producing the Common Good.* Waco/Tex.: Baylor University Press: 19 - 32.
Coakley, John. 2011. „The Religious Roots of Irish Nationalism." *Social Compass* 58 (1): 95-114.
Coleman, James S. 1988. „Social Capital in the Creation of Human Capital." *American Journal of Sociology* 94: 95-120.
Coleman, John A. 2003. „Religious Social Capital." In: Corwin Smidt (ed.). *Religion as Social Capital. Producing the Common Good.* Waco/Tex.: Baylor University Press: 33-48.
Curry, Jane L. 1996. „Introduction." In: Jane L. Curry/Luba Fajter (ed.). *Poland's Permanent Revolution. People vs. Elites, 1956-1990.* Washington: The American University Press.
Curtis, James E./Douglas E. Baer/Edward G. Grabb. 2001. „Nations of Joiners: Explaining Voluntary Association Membership in Democratic Societies." *American Sociological Review* 66: 783-805.
Dalton, Russell J. /Hans-Dieter Klingemann. 2007. „Citizens and Political Behavior." In: J. Russell Dalton, Klingemann, Hans-Dieter (ed.). *The Oxford Handbook of Political Behavior.* Oxford: Oxford University Press: 3-27.
de Hart, Joep/Paul Dekker. 2005. „Churches as Voluntary Associations: their contribution to democracy as a public voice and a source of social and political involvement." In: Sigrid Roßteutscher (ed.). *Democracy and the Role of Associations: Political, Organizational and Social Contexts.* London: Routledge: 168-196.
Dekker, Paul/Ruud Koopmans/Andries van den Broek. 1997. „Voluntary associations, social movements and individual political behaviour in Western Europe." In: Jan W. van Deth (ed.). *Private groups and public life. Social participation, voluntary associations and political involvement in representative democracies.* London: Routledge.
Diamond, Larry. 2008. *The Spirit of Democracy. The Struggle to Build Free Societies Throughout the World.* New York/N.Y.: Times Books. Henry Holt and Company.
Djilas, Milovan. 1983. „The Disintegration of Leninist Totalitarianism." In: Irving Howe (ed.). *1984 revisited. Totalitarianism in our century.* New York/N.Y.: Harper & Row, Publishers. Inc.
Ekiert, Grzegorz/Jan Kubik. 1999. *Rebellious Civil Society. Popular Protest and Democratic Consolidation in Poland, 1989-1993.* Ann Arbor/Mich.: The University of Michigan Press.
Emeliantseva, Ekaterina/Arié Malz/Daniel Ursprung. 2008. *Einführung in die Osteuropäische Geschichte.* Zürich: Orell Füssli Verlag.
Esser, Hartmut. 2007. „The two meanings of social capital." In: Dario Castiglione/Jan W. van Deth/Guglielmo Wolleb (ed.). *The Handbook of Social Capital.* Oxford: Oxford University Press: 22-49.
Eysymontt, Jerzy. 1989. „Reform in the Polish Economy." In: Roger Clarke (ed.). *Poland: The Economy in the 1980s. Perspectives on Eastern Europe.* Chicago/Ill.: St. James Press.
Fidrmuc, Jan/Klarita Gërxhani. 2007. "Mind the Gap! Social Capital, East and West " *Working Paper, Centre for Economic Development & Institution* 07-10. London: Brunel University West London.
Fioramonti, Lorenzo/Finn V. Heinrich. 2007. *How Civil Society Influences Policy: A Comparative Analysis of the CIVICUS Civil Society Index in Post-Communist Europe.* Research and Policy in Development, Overseas Development Institute.
Fukuyama, Francis. 1995. *Trust. The Social Virtues and the Creation of Prosperity.* New York/N.Y.: Simon & Schuster Free Paperbooks Press.

Fukuyama, Francis. 1999. *Social Capital and Civil Society*. IMF Conference on Second Generation Reforms. George Mason University.
Gabriel, Oskar W./Volker Kunz/Sigrid Roßteutscher/Jan W. van Deth (ed.). 2002. *Sozialkapital und Demokratie. Zivilgesellschaftliche Ressourcen im Vergleich*. Wien: WUV-Universitätsverlag.
Giza-Poleszczuk, Anna. 2007. „Rodzina i system społeczny." In: Mirosława Marody (ed.). *Wymiary życia społecznego. Polska na przełomie XX i XXI wieku*. Warsaw: Wydawnictwo Naukowe Scholar.
Giza-Poleszczuk, Anna/Jan Poleszczuk. 2004. „Partnership, Marriage, and Children - Cultural Differentiation of Attitudes." In: Aleksandra Jasińska-Kania/Mirosława Marody (ed.). *Poles among Europeans*. Warsaw: Wydawnictwo Naukowe Scholar: 199-228.
Grabowska, Mirosława. 2001. „Partie i elektoraty." In: Mirosława Grabowska/Tadeusz Szawiel (ed.). *Budowanie demokracji. Podziały społeczne, partie polityczne i społeczeństwo obywatelskie w postkomunistycznej Polsce*. Warsaw: Wydawnictwo Naukowe PWN: 35-71.
Grabowska, Mirosława/Tadeusz Szawiel (ed.). 2001. *Budowanie demokracji. Podziały społeczne, partie polityczne i społeczeństwo obywatelskie w postkomunistycznej Polsce*. Warsaw: Wydawnictwo Naukowe PWN.
Grant, Jordan/William Maloney/Emma Clarence. 2007. *Democracy and Interest Groups. Enhancing Participation?* Hampshire, NY: Palgrave Macmillan.
Greeley, Andrew. 1997. „Coleman revisited: Religious structures as a source of social capital." *American Behavioral Scientist* 40 (5): 587-594.
Guiso, Luigi/Sapienza Paola/Luigi Zingales. 2003. „People's opium? Religion and economic attitudes." *Journal of Monetary Economics* 50: 225-282.
Halpern, David. 2005. *Social Capital*. Cambridge: Polity Press.
Harris, Fredrick 2003. „Ties That Bind and Flourish." In: Corwin Smidt (ed.). *Religion as Social Capital. Producing the Common Good*. Waco/Tex.: Baylor University Press: 121-138.
Howard, Marc Morje. 2003. *The Weakness of Civil Society in Post-Communist Europe*. Cambridge: Cambridge University Press.
Huntington, Samuel. 1991. *The Third Wave. Democratization in the Late Twentieth Century*. Norman/Okla.: University of Oklahoma Pres.
Inglehart, Ronald. 1997. *Modernization and postmodernization: cultural, economic, and political change in 43 societies*. Princeton/N.J.: Princeton University Press.
Inglehart, Ronald. 1999. „Trust, well-being and democracy." In: Mark E. Warren (ed.). *Democracy and trust*. Cambridge: Cambridge University Press: 88-120.
Inglehart, Ronald/Wayne E. Baker. 2000. „Modernization, Cultural Change, and the Persistence of Traditional Values." *American Sociological Review* 65: 19-51.
Inglehart, Ronald/Gabriela Catterberg. 2002. „Trends in Political Action: The Developmental Trend and the Post-Honeymoon Decline." *International Journal of Comparative Sociology* 43: 300-316.
Inglehart, Ronald/Christian Welzel. 2005. *Modernization, Cultural Change, and Democracy*. Cambridge: Cambridge University Press.
Jagodzinski, Wolfgang/Karel Dobbelaere. 1995a. „Secularization and Church Religiosity." In: Jan W. van Deth/Elinor Scarbrough (ed.). *The Impact of the Values*. Oxford: Oxford University Press: 76-119.
Jagodzinski, Wolfgang/Karel Dobbelaere. 1995b. „Religious and Ethical Pluralism." In: Jan W. van Deth/Elinor Scarbrough (ed.). *The Impact of the Values*. Oxford: Oxford University Press: 218-249.
Johnston Gordon, Rona. 1997. „Patronage and parish: the nobility and the recatholicization of Lower Austria." In: Karin Maag (ed.). *The Reformation in Eastern and Central Europe*. Hants: Scholar Press: 211-228.
Kaluza, Andrzej. 2010. "Die katholische Kirche in der Defensive - auch in Polen." Deutsches Polen Institut. *Polen-Analysen* 79/10: http://www.laender-analysen.de/polen/pdf/PolenAnalysen79.pdf

Kamiński, Tadeusz. 2008. „Kościół i trzeci sektor w Polsce." *Trzeci Sektor. Instytut Spraw Publicznych* 15: 7-22.
Klingemann, Hans-Dieter/Dieter Fuchs/Susanne Fuchs/Jan Zielonka. 2006. „Introduction. Support for democracy and autocracy in central and eastern Europe." In: Hans-Dieter Klingemann/Dieter Fuchs/Jan Zielonka (ed.). *Democracy and Political Culture in Eastern Europe.* London: Routledge: 1 - 21.
Kolankiewicz, George. 1996. „Social capital and social change." *British Journal of Sociology* 47 (3): 427-440.
Koralewicz, Jadwiga/Marek Ziółkowski. 2007. „Zmiany systemu wartości w Polsce." In: Bogdan W. Mach/Edmund Wnuk-Lipiński (ed.). *O życiu publicznym, kulturze i innych sprawach.* Warsaw: Collegium Civitas, Instytut Studiów Publicznych PAN: 199-228.
Koralewicz, Jadwiga/Marek Ziółkowski. 2006. „Changing Value System." In: Teresa Rakowska-Harmstone/Piotr Dutkiewicz (ed.). *New Europe. The impact of the first decade Vol.I. Trends and Prospects.* Warsaw: Institute of Political Studies, Polish Academy of Sciences, Collegium Civitas Press: 177 - 206.
Kozarzewski, Piotr. 2007. „Społeczeństwo i elity o transformacji." In: Maria Jarosz (ed.). *Transformacja Elity Społeczeństwo.* Warsaw: Instytut Studiów Politycznych PAN: 23-64.
Kramer, Mark. 2002. „Collective protests and democratization in Poland 1989-1993: was rebellious civil society really "rebellious"?" *Communist and Post-Communist Studies* 35 (3): 213-221.
Krizek, Petr. 2003. „Tschechische Republik." In: Manfred Spieker (ed.). *Katholische Kirche und Zivilgesellschaft in Osteuropa. Postkommunistische Transformationsprozesse in Polen, Tschechien, der Slowakei und Litauen.* Paderborn: Schöningh: 145-241.
Kunz, Volker. 2004. „Soziales Vertrauen." In: Jan W. Van Deth (ed.). *Deutschland in Europa. Ergebnisse des European Social Survey 2002-2003.* Wiesbaden: VS Verlag für Sozialwissenschaften.
Kurczewska, Joanna. 2005. „National Identities Vis-à-vis Democracy and Catholicism (The Polish Case After 1989), ." *Polish Sociological Review*: 329-347.
Kuznets, Simon. 1955. „Economic Growth and Income Inequality." *American Economic Review* 65: 1-28.
La Porta, Rafael/Florencio Lopez-de-Silanes/Andrei Shleifer/Robert W. Vishny. 1997. „Trust in Large Organizations." *The American Economic Review* 87 (2): 333-338.
Lam, Pui-yan. 2002. „As the Flocks gather: How Religion Affects Voluntary Association Participation." *Journal for Scientific Study of Religion* 41 (3): 405-422.
Lasinska, Katarzyna. 2009. *Religiously rooted conservatism: an international comparative study of the social networks.* ECPR Joint Session. Lisbon.
Lenschen, Dirk. 2003. „Kirche und Zivilgesellschaft in Polen." In: Manfred Spieker (ed.). *Katholische Kirche und Zivilgesellschaft in Osteuropa. Postkommunistische Transformationsprozesse in Polen, Tschechien, der Slowakei und Litauen.* Paderborn: Schöningh: 420-442.
Letki, Natalia. 2003. *Explaining Political Participation in East-Central Europe: Social Capital, Democracy and the Communist Past.* Paper presented at the Annual Meeting of American Political Science Association.
Letki, Natalia/Geoffrey Evans. 2005. „Endogenizing Social Trust: Democratization in East-Central Europe." *British Journal of Political Sociology* 35: 515-529.
Linde, Jonas. 2009. „Why Feed the Hand that Bites You? Quality of Government and System Support in the Post-Communist EU Member States." *QoG Working Paper Series* 2009 (20): 1-20.
Linz, Juan J./Alfred Stepan. 1996. *Problems of democratic Transition and Consolidation: Southern Europe, South America and Post-Communist Europe.* Baltimore: The John Hopkins University Press.
Lipset, Seymour Martin 1994. „The Social Requisites of Democracy Revisited." *American Sociological Review* 59: 1-22.
Lubiński, Marek. 2000. *Poland. International Economic Report 1999-2000.* Warsaw: World Economy Research Institute. Warsaw School of Economics.
Luers, William H. 1990. „Czechoslovakia: Road to Revolution." *Foreign Affairs* 69 (2): 77-98.
Luks, Leonid. 1993. *Katholizismus und politische Macht in kommunistischen Polen 1945-1989. Die Anatomie einer Befreiung.* Köln: Böhlau Verlag.

References

Madeley, John T. S. 2003. "A Framework for the Comparative Analysis of Church-State Relations in Europe." In: John T. S. Madeley/Zsolt Enyedi (ed.). *Church and State in Contemporary Europe: The Chimera of Neutrality.* London: Frank Cass Publishers: 23-50.
Marody, Mirosława. 1987. "Antynomie zbiorowej świadomości." *Studia Socjologiczne* (2): 4-9.
Marody, Mirosława/Sławomir Mandes. 2007. "Religijność a tożsamość narodowa Polaków." In: Mirosława Marody (ed.). *Wymiary życia społecznego. Polska na przełomie XX i XXI wieku.* Warsaw: Wydawnictwo Naukowe Scholar: 401-418.
Michelat, Guy/Michel Simon. 1997. "Religion, Class and Politics." *Comparative Politics* 10: 159-186.
Michta, Andrew A. 1997. "*Democratic consolidation in Poland after 1989.*" In: Karen Dawisha/Bruce Parrott (ed.). *The consolidation of democracy in East-Central Europe.* Cambridge: Cambridge University Press: 66 - 108.
2009. *Polska 2030. Wyzwania rozwojowe.* Kancelaria Prezesa Rady Ministrów.
Mishler, Wiliam/Richard Rose. 1997. "Trust, Distrust and Skepticism: Popular Evaluations of Civil and Political Institutions in Post-Communist Societies." *The Journal of Politics* 59 (2): 418-451.
Mohr, Philip 2005. "Economic policy and performance and the consolidation of democracy." In: Ursula J. van Beek (ed.). *Democracy under construction: Patterns from four continents.* Bloomfield Hills & Opladen: Barbara Budrich Publishers: 165 - 242.
Murphy, Michael. 2008. "Variations in Kinship Networks Across Geographic and Social Space." *Population and Development Review* 34 (1): 19-49.
Myant, Martin. 1989. "Poland - The Permanent Crisis?." In: Roger Clarke (ed.). *Poland: The Economy in the 1980s. Perspectives on Eastern Europe.* Chicago/Ill.: St. James Press.
Neller, Katja. 2004. "Politik und Lebenszufriedenheit." In: Jan W. van Deth (ed.). *Deutschland in Europa. Ergebnisse des European Social Survey 2002-2003.* Wiesbaden: VS Verlag für Sozialwissenschaften: 27 - 54.
Newton, Kenneth 1999. "Social and Political Trust in Established Democracies." In: Pippa Norris (ed.). *Critical Citizens. Global Support for Democratic Government.* Oxford: Oxford University Press: 169 - 187.
Norris, Pippa/Ronald Inglehart. 2005. *Sacred and Secular. Religion and Politics Worldwide.* Cambridge: Cambridge University Press.
Nowak, Stefan. 1979. "System wartości społeczeństwa polskiego." *Studia Socjologiczne* 75 (4): 155-174.
OECD Publications. 2001. *The Well-being of Nations. The Role of Human and Social Capital.*
Offe, Claus/Susanne Fuchs (ed.). 2002. *A Decline of Social Capital?* Oxford: Oxford University Press.
Paldam, Martin/Gert Tinnggaard Svendsen. 2000. *Missing social capital and the transition in Eastern Europe.* IMAD conference Portorož (Slovenia).
Parrott, Bruce (ed.). 1997. *Perspectives on postcommunist democratization.* Cambridge: Cambridge University Press.
Paxton, Pamela. 2002. "Social Capital and Democracy: An interdependent Relationship." *American Sociological Review* 67 (2): 254-277.
Pichler, Florian/Claire Wallace. 2007. "Patterns of Formal and Informal Social Capital in Europe." *European Sociological Review* 23 (4): 423-435.
Pomian, Krzysztof. 1985. *Wymiary polskiego konfliktu.* London: Aneks.
Przeworski, Adam/Adam Teune. 1970. *The Logic of Comparative Social Inquiry.* New York, London: Wiley-Interscience.
Putnam, Robert D. 1993. *Making Democracy Work: Civil traditions in modern Italy.* Princeton/N.J.: Princeton University Press.
Putnam, Robert D. 2000. *Bowling Alone. The Collapse and Revival of American Community.* New York: Simon & Schuster.
Putnam, Robert D./Kristin A. Goss. 2002. "Introduction." In: Robert D. Putnam (ed.). *Democracies in flux. The evolution of social capital in contemporary society.* Oxford [u.a.]: Oxford Univ. Press: 3-20.
Rose, Richard. 1998. *Getting things done in an anti-modern society: social capital networks in Russia.* Glasgow: Centre for the Study of Public Policy University of Strathclyde.

Rose, Richard. 2009. *Understanding Post-Communism Transformation. A Bottom Up Approach.* London/New York: Routledge.
Roßteutscher, Sigrid. 2004. „Die Rückkehr der Tugend?" In: Jan W. van Deth (ed.). *Deutschland in Europa. Ergebnisse des European Social Survey 2002 - 2003.* Wiesbaden: VS Verlag für Sozialwissenschaften: 175 - 200.
Roßteutscher, Sigrid. 2007. „Social Capital and Civic Engagement: A Comparative Perspective." In: Dario Castiglione/Jan W. van Deth/Guglielmo Wolleb (ed.). *The Handbook of Social Capital.* Oxford: Oxford University Press: 208-240.
Roßteutscher, Sigrid. 2009. *Religion, Zivilgesellschaft, Demokratie. Eine international vergleichende Studie zur Natur religiöser Märkte und der demokratischen Rolle religiöser Zivilgesellschaften.* Baden-Baden: Nomos.
Roßteutscher, Sigrid. 2010. „Social Capital Worldwide: Potential for Democratization or Stabilizer of Authoritarian Rule?" *American Behavioral Scientist* 53 (5): 737-757.
Ruiter, Stijn/Nan Dirk De Graaf. 2006. „National Context, Religiosity and Volunteering: Results from 53 countries." *American Sociological Review* 71 (2): 191-210.
Salamon, Lester M./Wojciech S. Sokolowski/Regina List. 2003. *Global Civil Society. An Overview.* Baltimore/Md.: The John Hopkins University, Institute for Policy Studies, Center for Civil Society Studies.
Sanford, George (ed.). 1994. *Communism's weakest link - democratic capitalism's greatest challenge: Poland.* London: Leicester University Press.
Schmidt, Christoph. 2000. *Auf Felsen gesät. Die Reformation in Polen und Livland.* Göttingen: Vandenhoeck & Ruprecht.
Schöpflin, George. 1994. „Conservatism in Central and Eastern Europe." In: János Mátyás Kovács (ed.). *Transition to Capitalism? The Communist Legacy in Eastern Europe.* New Brunswick/London: Transaction Publishers: 187-204.
Siemienska, Renata. 2006. „Poland. Citizens and democratic politics." In: Hans-Dieter Klingemann/Dieter Fuchs/Jan Zielonka (ed.). *Democracy and Political Culture in Eastern Europe.* London: Routledge: 203-235.
Słodkowska, Inka. 2006. *Społeczeństwo obywatelskie na tle historycznego przełomu. Polska 1980-1989.* Warszawa: Instytut Studiów Politycznych Polskiej Akademii Nauk.
Smidt, Corwin (ed.). 2003. *Religion as Social Capital. Producing the Common Good.* Waco/Tex.: Baylor University Press.
Socha, Mieczysław W. 1989. „Wages and Incentives Problems." In: Roger Clarke (ed.). *Poland: The Economy in the 1980s. Perspectives on Eastern Europe.* Chicago: St. James Press: 45-60.
Staniszkis, Jadwiga. 1995. „In Search of a Paradigm of Transformation." In: Edmund Wnuk-Lipiński (ed.). *After Comunism. A multidisciplinary Approach to Radical Social Change.* Warsaw: Polish Academy of Science, Institute of Political Studies: 19-56.
Stolle, Dietlind. 2003. „The Sources of Social Capital." In: Marc Hooghe/Dietlind Stolle (ed.). *Generating Social Capital. Civil Society and Institutions in Comparative Perspective.* New York: Palgrave Macmillan: 19-42.
Sztompka, Piotr. 1991. „The Intagibles and Imponderables of the Transition to Democracy." *Studies in Comparative Communism* 24 (3): 295-311.
Sztompka, Piotr. 1995. „Vertrauen: Die fehlende Ressource in der Postkommunistischen Gesellschaft." In: Brigitta Nedelmann (ed.). *Politische Institutionen im Wandel.* Kölner Zeitschrift für Soziologie und Sozialpsychologie Westdeutscher Verlag: 254-276.
Sztompka, Piotr. 2000. "*Civilisational Competence: A Prerequisite of Post-Communist Transition.*" *Centre for European Studies.* www.ces.uj.edu.pl/competence.htm
<http://www.ces.uj.edu.pl/competence.htm>
Sztompka, Piotr. 2004. *From East Europeans to Europeans: Shifting Identities and Boundaries in the New Europe.* Netherlands Institute for Advanced Study in the Humanities and Social Sciences. Antwerpen.
Sztompka, Piotr. 2007. *Zaufanie. Fundament społeczeństwa.* Kraków: Wydawnictwo Znak.
Tomka, Miklós. 2002. „Introduction." *Social Compass* 49 (4): 483-495.

Tworzecki, Hubert. 2008. „A disaffected new democracy? Identities, institutions and civic engagement in post-communist Poland." *Communist and Post-Communist Studies* 41 (1): 47-62.
Uslaner, Eric M. 2002. *The Moral Foundations of Trust*. Cambridge: Cambridge University Press.
Uslaner, Eric M. 2003a. „Trust and civic engagement in East and West." In: Gabriel Badescu/Eric M. Uslaner (ed.). *Social Capital and the Transition to Democracy*. London: Routledge: 81-94.
Uslaner, Eric M. 2003b. „Trust, Democracy and Governance: Can Government Policies Infuence Generalized Trust?" In: Marc Hooghe/Dietlind Stolle (ed.). *Generating Social Capital. Civil Society and Institutions in Comparative Perspective*. New York/London: Palgrave MacMillan: 171 - 190.
Uslaner, Eric M. 2007. „Trust as a moral value." In: Dario Castiglione/Jan W. van Deth/Wolleb Guglielmo (ed.). *The Handbook of Social Capital*. Oxford: Oxford University Press: 101-121.
Uslaner, Eric M./Gabriel Badescu. 2003. „Legacies and conflicts. The challenges to social capital in democratic transition." In: Gabriel Badescu/Eric M. Uslaner (ed.). *Social Capital and the Transition to Democracy*. London: Routledge: 219 - 232.
Valkov, Nikolay. 2009. „Membership in voluntary organizations and democratic performance: European post-Communist countries in comparative perspective." *Communist and Post-Communist Studies* 42 (1): 1-21.
van der Meer, Thomas. 2009. *States of Freely Associating Citizens. Cross- National Studies into the Impact of State Institutions on Social, Civic, and Political Participation*. Dissertation University of Nijmegen.
van Deth, Jan W. 1997. „Introduction: social involvement and democratic politics." In: Jan W. van Deth (ed.). *Private groups and public life. Social participation, voluntary associations and political involvement in representative democracies*. London: Routledge.
van Deth, Jan W. 2003. „Measuring social capital: orthodoxies and continuing controversies." *International Journal of Social Research* 6 (1): 79-92.
van Deth, Jan W. 2004. „Soziale Partizipation." In: Jan W. van Deth (ed.). *Deutschland in Europa. Ergebnisse des European Social Survey 2002 - 2003*. Wiesbaden: VS Verlag für Sozialwissenschaften: 295 - 315.
van Deth, Jan W. 2007. „Measuring social capital." In: Dario Castiglione/Jan W. van Deth/Guglielmo Wolleb (ed.). *The Handbook of Social Capital*. Oxford: Oxford University Press: 150-176.
van Deth, Jan W./Elinor Scarbrough. 1995. *The Impact of the Values*. Oxford: Oxford University Press.
Verba, Sidney /Lehman K. Scholzman/Henry E. Brady. 1995. *Voice and Equality: Civic Volunteerism in American Politics*. Cambridge/Mass: Harvard University Press.
Wallace, Claire. 1995. „Young people and families in Poland: Changing Times, Changing Dependencies?" *Journal of European Social Policy* 5 (2): 97-109.
Warren, R. Mark. 2003. „Faith and Leadership in the Inner City." In: Corwin Smidt (ed.). *Religion as Social Capital. Producing the Common Good*. Waco, Texas: Baylor University Press.
Wasilewski, Jacek. 1995. „The Crystallization of the Post-Communist and Post-Solidarity Political Elite." In: Edmund Wnuk-Lipiński (ed.). *After Comunism. A multidisciplinary Approach to Radical Social Change*. Warsaw: Polish Academy of Science, Institute of Political Studies: 117-134.
Welch, Michael R./David Sikkink/Eric Sartain/Carolyn Bond. 2004. „Trust in God and Trust in Man: The Ambivalent Role of Religion in Shaping Dimensions of Social Trust." *Journal for Scientific Study of Religion 43* (3): 317 - 343.
Wilson, John/Thomas Janoski. 1995. „The contribution of religion to volunteer work." *Sociology of Religion* 56 (1): 137-152.
Wnuk-Lipiński, Edmund. 2007. „Vicissitudes of Ethical Civil Society in Central and Eastern Europe." *Studies of Christian Ethics* 20 (1): 30-43.
Wnuk-Lipiński, Edmund/Susanne Fuchs. 2005. „Theoretical framework and methodology." In: Ursula J. van Beek (ed.). *Democracy under construction: Patterns from four continents*. Bloomfield Hills & Opladen: Barbara Budrich Publishers: 39-62.
Wuthnow, Robert. 1991. *Acts of compassion: Caring for others and helping ourselves*. Princeton/N.J.: Princeton University Press.

Wuthnow, Robert. 1996. *Christianity and civil society: The contemporary debate*. Valley Forge/Pensylvania: Trinity Press International.
Wuthnow, Robert. 2002. „Religious Involvement and Status-Bridging Social Capital." *Journal for the Scientific Study of Religion* 41 (4): 669 - 684.
Žaloudková, Luba. 2003. „Slowakei." In: Manfred Spieker (ed.). *Katholische Kirche und Zivilgesellschaft in Osteuropa. Postkommunistische Transformationsprozesse in Polen, Tschechien, der Slowakei und Litauen*. Paderborn: Schöningh.
Zarycki, Tomasz. 2007. „History and regional development. A controversy over the 'right' interpretation of the role of history in the development of the Polish regions." *Geoforum* 38 (3): 485 - 493.
Ziółkowski, Marek. 1998. „With or against the Tide? Changes in the Inerest and Value Orientations of the Polish Society in the Systematic Transformation." In: Edmund Wnuk-Lipiński (ed.). *Values and Radical Social Change Comparing Polish and South-African Experience*. Warsaw: Institute for Political Studies, Polish Academy of Sciences: 25-40.
Zmerli, Sonja/Ken Newton. 2008. „Social Trust and Attitudes Toward Democracy." *Public Opinion Quarterly* 72 (4): 706-724.